GARDENING WITH CLEMATIS

GARDENING WITH CLEMATIS

DESIGN & CULTIVATION

LINDA BEUTLER

TIMBER PRESS
PORTLAND • CAMBRIDGE

Frontispiece: *Clematis* 'Madame Baron-Veillard'

Published in 2004 by
Timber Press, Inc.   Timber Press
The Haseltine Building   2 Station Road
133 S.W. Second Avenue, Suite 450   Swavesey
Portland, Oregon 97204-3527, U.S.A.   Cambridge CB4 5QJ, U.K.

www.timberpress.com

Printed in China

Library of Congress Cataloging-in-Publication Data

Beutler, Linda.
    Gardening with clematis : design and cultivation / Linda Beutler.
        p. cm.
    Includes bibliographical references (p.   ).
    ISBN 0-88192-644-2 (hardback)
    1. Clematis. I. Title.
SB413.C6B48 2004
635.9'3334—dc22   2003022000

A catalog record for this book is also available from the British Library.

For Brewster Rogerson, who is a mentor, friend, and critic.
After thirty-five years of clematis collecting, he remains,
more than ever, filled with wonder.

Clematis 'Duchess of Waverly' in the Rogerson Clematis
Collection, October 2002.

CONTENTS

PREFACE

It was a random encounter with a misnamed plant that started me seriously collecting clematis. In the late 1980s my experience of clematis was limited and uninspired. My husband and I were renting an apartment adjoining one of Portland's best urban gardens (owned by Lucy and Fred Hardiman), where only a few clematis were in the ground. The large-flowered hybrids were new to me and had yet to exert their mysterious allure, and *Clematis montana* var. *rubens* made a nice show for a mere three weeks every spring.

Like most gardeners, I run a trapline of nurseries during the growing season; some are visited weekly or monthly, others less frequently. At one of my regular haunts in 1988, I was stopped by a funny little plant clearly mislabeled *Clematis montana*. The flowers of this specimen were four-sepalled, bell-shaped, and very definitely blue. I may not have known much about clematis then, but I did know that *C. montana* is white and makes a huge plant. This fey creature was blooming away at about 15 in. tall and showed no upward ambition whatsoever. Certain I had purchased a strange campanula, I brought the little plant home.

It took me a year to discover that what I had purchased was *Clematis integrifolia*. In the meantime, I had become totally smitten and fascinated. And this leads us, in part, to why I collect clematis and why this book needed to be written. How can one ever say or write or learn enough about a genus as diverse as clematis? It contains vines and herbaceous plants that can be anywhere from 6 in. (*C. marmoraria*) to 40 ft. tall (*C. ligusticifolia*). The flowers can be tiny as thimbles (*C. rehderiana*) or as wide and flat as a salad plate (*C.* 'Peveril Pearl'). A few forms are fragrant. The species come in all colors—the large-flowered hybrids are everything except truly yellow or orange. For a gardener with an overactive collecting chromosome, there is no better genus with which to become obsessed.

Since I have over 250 taxa in my personal collection, you will find yourself reading about cultivars and species I have grown or am familiar with from seeing them repeatedly in certain gardens over a period of years. When I lecture I am asked how I remember them all—they are my children, that's how.

So I stand before you as something of a cheerleader. Or a stage mother: "Smile, Louise!"

The other reason for writing this book is to discuss what to actually do with the eclectic members of this clan. It can be overwhelming for a gardener to peruse the clematis lists in current plant catalogs. Although there are plenty of new and comprehensive books about the species, the most widely available cultivars, and the basics of clematis care, there is still more to say: Now that you've got your desired plant, where are you going to put it, and with whom?

Before clematis came into my life, there were old garden roses. Notes about them formed copious lists that were my reference when I started working in a garden of my own. In Europe these roses are often combined with clematis, although in the major English public gardens we tend to see the same clematis combined with the same roses over and over. In America there is no model for growing anything with roses, so tight is the stranglehold of Hybrid Teas on the public consciousness. Hybrid Tea roses are like lovely but fussy children. Bring them plant friends to comfort them and they respond with a churlish shrug, stubbornly dropping a few more black-spotted leaves. Old garden roses are used to being jostled and like nothing so much as a mixed border, but to be growing old garden roses in America at all nowadays is going out on a limb. They are not what Americans are used to. At your local garden center you will likely be told that clematis and roses should never be grown together, that neither plant will survive. If you live in the United States, the only way to see clematis and roses growing together is to do it yourself. Or go to England. Or come to my house.

Then there is the issue of a garden's evolution. We often read about gardeners progressing from the junior flower junky stage to the effete foliage fanatic phase, but I believe this isn't so much a change in the refinement of a gardener's tastes as a pragmatic approach to dealing with reality. We obtain a garden, we begin planting the plants we are passionate about, and they grow. The benefits of beginner's luck cannot be overstated. (I believe in beginner's luck and wish I still had it.) Plants gain maturity and begin making shade. Lots of plants that flower madly need lots of sun, and therein lies the evolution of both the garden and the gardener. I am removing roses now, not because they aren't good plants or I have ceased to love them, but because the small trees and shrubs that I planted are now shading them.

But the clematis go on growing to find the sun. They sense little constraint in having their roots in the soil in a given place; the top growth just wanders to where it can give of its best. These plants have a genius for their own placement. You might think you have put it near a worthy associate, but the vine will find its superlative place independently. Clematis revel in companionship—with their own kind, with roses, and with most any shrub or tree. Even the short, herbaceous perennial clematis are delighted to dress the legs of roses and shrubs and to consort with other perennials. There is no limit to how this versatile genus of plants can be grown.

All shrubs and trees were put on the planet to support and enhance clematis.

Having set our parameters sufficiently wide, let us consider garden design using clematis. I hope you will be amazed, as I am, at the scope for creativity this genus brings to our gardens. No matter what color combination you want to explore, no matter what cultural niche needs filling, no matter what plant in your garden looks as if it could use a friend, there is a clematis waiting for you. Probably more than one.

CHAPTER 1

CLEMATIS AS COMPANION PLANTS

*I*t is easy for even beginning gardeners to be inventive when using clematis in plant marriages. As you are filling up your garden's layers, you will find clematis to scramble on the ground, embrace your shrubs, and swing from the treetops by their tails. Flower shapes are varied, as is their color, so you can opt for a refined, painterly vignette of monochromes or go for maximum contrast, fashioning color combinations that wake up the neighborhood.

As you wander your garden searching for the right place for a clematis, try to keep several criteria in mind: Besides size and shape, another factor to consider is the color of the clematis flower that will best embellish a companion. Everyone sees color differently and, rather than adhering slavishly to the dictates of the color wheel, it will satisfy you more to put together colors you like and will be happy to see each time you venture into your garden.

Just as colors can contrast or blend, so can textures. Garden designers tell us that textures (spikes, towers, spheres, daisies, lace, froth, and the like) should be combined for contrast and that each good composition should have several textural components. However, there is a lot to be said for a buxom old garden rose flowering in luxurious excess with a plump, large-flowered hybrid clematis. Globes *can* reinforce globes. The fringe of an early *Clematis macropetala* blossom can improve the flowers of a winter hazel (*Corylopsis* spp.) by repeating their shaggy texture

Clematis 'Roko-Kolla' forms a vivid color and textural blend with *Rosa* 'Roger Lambelin' and Spanish lavender, *Lavandula stoechas.* In the author's garden.

Clematis 'Huldine' looks round and plump with an old garden rose, the repeat-flowering *Rosa* 'Jacques Cartier'. In the author's garden.

in a larger form and varied color. Slight variations within one texture grouping can emphasize your preferences.

If you are not going to vary textures, do vary colors. Monochromatic garden designs, such as an all-white garden, rely on multiple textures to keep the whole view from looking blobby. If you do opt for all one texture, such as the romantic look of globes and curves, then contrasting the colors will allow the eye some respite from too much sameness. Repeating a texture or a color gives a garden rhythm. It doesn't even matter at what level of your garden's layers (ground, midsize shrub, or up in the sky) you make your repetition—our eyes are wide-angle lenses that pick up patterns easily wherever they can be found in our field of vision.

Clematis 'Anita' makes a monochromatic texture trio with *Asphodelus* 'Albus' and *Rosa* 'Ghisline de Féligonde'. In the author's garden.

What height should the clematis be when it blooms for you? Where will you see it to get the best effect? Answering these two questions will initially influence what clematis you buy and later may control how you choose to prune it. The street trees you may have in your parking strip are a case in point. My house sits atop a retaining wall, and the tops of my golden chain trees (*Laburnum* spp.) are at eye level from my front porch. Like me, you must ask yourself at what level will I be when looking at my clematis? From a second-story balcony you will be able to see the faces of upturned large-flowered hybrids. A *Clematis montana* form will decorate your balcony and be at the perfect height for whatever grooming it might need, with no ladders involved. The perfume will be right where your nose is. You may set your heart on a cultivar that makes only a small amount of growth a year, so viewing it at eye level from your balcony will mean hardly ever pruning it.

During which season do you want the clematis to be at its most prolific? Some gardeners, like me, are at their best in spring and want their gardens to be so too. However, I know many, many gardeners, perhaps even a majority, who love the autumn, with its crisp days and last bursts of color. These are the gardeners who will select clematis hybrids from the species *Clematis tangutica,* with their yellow or gold bells produced in quantity in August and September. This group has evocative seed heads—where one person sees spun silver, another will see a cartoon character. Many of the showiest large-flowered hybrids are at their best only in May and June. If you are an autumn person, you can search for the likes of *C.* 'Lady Betty Balfour' (dark purple or blue) and *C.* 'Madame Baron-Veillard' (pink or mauve), which require a summer's worth of sunny weather to produce their August and September performance.

Do you want your clematis to bloom with its companion, or do you want it to fill a green space with color when the partner is resting? The summer garden can be awash in an unbroken sea of green. Broad-leafed evergreen (rhododendrons, some viburnums, some ceanothus) and deciduous shrubs (weigelas, lilacs, antique roses) just sit there in July and August, taking up space. They may be rehearsing a production of berries for the fall season, but in the summer they are boring. This can be remedied by a liberal application of clematis, jazzing up the summer

The spun-silver seed heads of clematis add more design options to the garden. *Clematis tangutica* 'Golden Harvest'. In the author's garden.

doldrums. The *Clematis viticella* hybrids are particularly effective at fulfilling this function, especially since their old vines should be removed in late fall, leaving the now-welcome leaves of evergreens open to the winter sun. If you have a large, mature shrub, there is no reason not to have your cake and eat it too by sending two clematis into the plant. You can select one companion to increase the floral volume by blooming with the shrub (or small tree) in the spring and another to bloom in the summer when everyone else is quiet. Your only concern will be to select clematis that won't get too large for their woody host.

SELECTING YOUR NEW PLANTS

Once you have decided on the function you want your clematis to serve, as well as their color and texture, you can begin the search for the species and cultivars that will meet your needs. If you are new to clematis, it is best to start with those vines recommended as being easiest to grow. You will see several cultivars and species repeated on more than one of the lists throughout this book, including a list of my ten favorites for beginners at the end of this chapter. These are your guides to which varieties are most accommodating and rewarding. If the clematis that strikes your fancy sounds like a challenge, however, do not underestimate the power of beginner's luck!

For now, let's start with the basics: selecting your new plant. When visiting your local garden center or specialty nursery, the choice of clematis will be overwhelming, and it's easy to have your head turned by a pretty face. It is best for your peace of mind to go forth armed with a list. If you find a plant you've been wanting, carefully examine the specimens offered for sale. Select a plant in the largest size pot you can afford, and try to avoid plants in small pots or on sale bare-rooted in boxes. If the plant you pick up does not show new roots through the drainage holes, or shows other signs of being recently repotted, pass it by.

Examine all the plants of the variety you're shopping for to see how many stems are emerging from the soil—the more, the merrier. If I have the choice of two plants—one about to bloom atop a frail stem and one with several stems and lush growth but no bloom—experience has taught me to opt for the multistemmed plant. This is the vine that will reap the greatest rewards in the long run. When it comes to clematis, the instant gratification of ready blooms can distract from the fact that you may have selected a fragile plant with a less than robust root system, a plant that may be easily damaged during transport and transplanting, a plant that may be more vulnerable to pests and disease and is less able to make a quick recovery.

Sometimes you must select a plant with just one shoot holding up the top growth, this being the only choice to get the cultivar you want. Plan to prune it rather hard when you get it home, even if you cannot plant it right away. At garden centers and nurseries, clematis are usually grown in pots with a 3-ft.-tall hardwood or bamboo stake affixed inside. Remove any growth stretching or drooping beyond the stake. This may mean cutting off blooms and buds. If you have reason to believe the plant is misnamed, as unfortunately happens from time to time, let it bloom before pruning it. Assure yourself of the plant's identity, then cut it back, leaving three to four nodes on the stem before planting. (Nodes are the joints or junctions where the leaves emerge from the main stem.) When you've bought a plant with extremely lush top growth, feel confident about pruning it down to only 2 ft. tall. Stimulating root growth and new shoots forming from the crown is crucial to the ultimate good health of your plant, whether it is a species or a hybrid. Luxuriant top growth is actually detrimental to a young plant that has an inadequate root system and, vicious as this early pruning seems, your plant will amply reward you later. Clematis teach us patience.

Growing clematis well *does* require patience, and there's no sense buying a small plant that will either die immediately when planted in the ground or will limp along in a pot taking years to form a decent root system and strong top growth. The obvious exception is if you find yourself turning into a clematis collector and you stumble upon a form that you can't get any other way than by bare-root through the mail. My plant of *Clematis texensis* came home with me from a visit to England. It had to be severely pruned and all its soil removed to make its journey in my carry-on bag. It bloomed—quite magnificently I might add—four years later.

If you do find that you must buy a small or bare-rooted plant to get the form you want (or if the price is simply too good), transplant it into a one-gallon-size pot before transferring it into the garden. Let the clematis stay in this pot as long as it takes to get it into "fighting trim." A clematis should have a large root mass and strong new shoots before venturing into the ground. Small plants put to earth too soon will simply dissolve away, never to be heard from again. Strong plants will grow boldly once they are placed in your soil and given proper support.

A healthy clematis can be planted or transplanted anytime with the following exceptions: Avoid hot weather, especially if your soil is dry; avoid planting into soil that is waterlogged (even if this is a temporary condition), especially during cold weather; avoid planting into heavy clay soil without adding organic material or heavy grit (not fine sand) to improve soil workability (both for you and the clematis' roots). *Clematis texensis* and its hybrids (such as *C.* 'Gravetye Beauty', *C.* 'Duchess of Albany', and *C.* 'Étoile Rose') are especially happy in gravelly soil.

HORIZONTAL OR VERTICAL?

A great part of the fascination of the genus *Clematis* is that it contains such a seemingly disparate selection of species (however, if you dissect their flowers, they are all essentially alike). Some of my favorite clematis are not vines at all, but are, rather, herbaceous perennials (see chapter six). A few of the most charming of these are North American species native to the Midwest and are not appropriate for the mayhem of the average mixed border. They can, however, be grown well in containers where their soil environment is carefully controlled, and we will visit them again in the container chapter.

The European native *Clematis integrifolia* is a superb herbaceous perennial, thriving in a wide range of habitats, and it has been used to create numerous hybrids that do not grab hold of things with their leaf stems (petioles) as the vining clematis do but, instead, wander through host plants and low structures, popping their flowers into the sun as their whimsy strikes them. These can drape over retaining walls with graceful languor. Of all the clematis, the integrifolias are the ones that seem best able to think for themselves, making pictures with other plants to surprise and impress their gardener.

Full sun and sharp drainage are preferred by the texensis hybrids such as *Clematis* 'Étoile Rose', shown here with *Geranium* 'Ann Folkard' at Northwest Garden Nursery in Eugene, Oregon.

These plants give us the opportunity to grow clematis in both the vertical and horizontal planes, with plants that will spread their arms wide instead of growing strictly up. Of course, some gardeners like to be strict and use the herbaceous clematis to indulge in plant bondage. They tie the 4- to 8-ft. lengths of these various cultivars up tree trunks or nonliving upright supports, creating columns. Herbaceous clematis can look corseted this way, but there is a great deal that is "unnatural" about gardening, and we ought not judge. But we do. I don't practice this style of clematis culture, but you might try it and see what you think.

Using clematis as ground cover is an option not often exercised, and it isn't limited to the herbaceous varieties. Many large-flowered hybrids have up-facing flowers that are not seen to their best advantage if the plant bolts to the top of a tree. Clematis flowers are pretty when viewed from their reverse, but this can hardly be said to be their best side. Cultivars such as *Clematis* 'Marie Boisselot' (syn. *C.* 'Madame le Coltré', which was Marie's married name) in white, *C.* 'Dawn' in pale pink, or *C.* 'Will Goodwin' in pale blue, to name but a few, will run along the earth, covering such traditional ground covers as ajuga and vinca quite well in partial sun situations or romping over sedums in a brighter exposure, lightening the lowest layer of the garden as long as no woody companion plant offers to hoist them aloft.

Up is not the only direction.

CLEMATIS BY THE POUND

As you wander this book, your garden, and garden centers looking for good clematis to grow, think about the ultimate mature weight of the whole vine. This is difficult information to glean directly, but over time as you become familiar with the different groups within the genus, certain clues will tell you how to predict how heavy the vine will be. To a certain extent this will help you decide which vine or sprawling herbaceous form is appropriate for the companion plant or structure you are planning to use for support.

Examples of poorly paired clematis are, unfortunately, numerous. The mistake of using a vine that is too heavy is an easy one to make, especially for gardeners who are timid with the clippers. There are many

Pyrus calleryana (callery pears) grown along the boulevards in my neighborhood. In the spirit of "when in Rome, do as the Romans do," my husband and I planted *P. calleryana* 'Aristocrat' the first spring after we bought our house. Soon, I was able to find one of my favorite purple clematis, *Clematis* 'Gipsy Queen' (sometimes spelled 'Gypsy Queen'). The young tree was 5 ft. tall. *Clematis* 'Gipsy Queen' will reach 12–15 ft. tall in a summer before getting hard-pruned in the winter. This vine produces many fairly thick new shoots from the base each year. Soon the young pear was thoroughly overwhelmed. The solution was to put temporary yet decorative supports on either side of the tree so it was bearing only a third of the vine's weight. Now the pear is 20 ft. tall and *C.* 'Gipsy Queen' no longer reaches the top. In fact, I do believe the tree is now stout enough to host an additional clematis!

Each of the commonly encountered groups of clematis within the larger genus contains a few thugs. These are not bad plants, they just get big, and we need to know that before letting the plant loose in the garden. This sounds a bit like dog training—perhaps no bad clematis, only bad gardeners? Here is a list of species and cultivars that can be very heavy even though they may not get particularly tall. Plan accordingly.

HEAVIES

Selected *Clematis alpina* and *C. macropetala* cultivars (if left unpruned) such as *C. alpina* 'Odorata', *C. alpina* 'Willy', *C.* 'Helsingborg', *C. macropetala* 'Maidwell Hall', *C. macropetala* 'Markham's Pink'

All *Clematis armandii* cultivars

Large-flowered hybrids such as *Clematis* 'Comtesse de Bouchaud', *C.* 'Edomurasaki', *C.* 'Gipsy Queen', *C.* 'Jackmanii', *C.* 'Jackmanii Superba', *C.* 'Madame Edouard André', *C.* 'Marie Boisselot', *C.* 'Perle d'Azur', *C.* 'Peveril Pearl', *C.* 'Silver Moon', and *C.* 'W. E. Gladstone'

All *Clematis montana* cultivars except 'Jenny Keay'

HEAVIES (continued)

Most *Clematis tangutica* forms, with the notable exception of the petite 'Helios'

Clematis texensis 'Étoile Rose' and 'Duchess of Albany'

All *Clematis viticella* cultivars, especially 'Huldine', 'Étoile Violette', 'Purpurea Plena Elegans', and 'Alba Luxurians'

Experience will reveal more clematis that get hefty as they grow. In most parts of North America where clematis grow well, you can be assured that any of the vines will get a bit (or a lot) bigger than the plant tags or written advice suggests. I have read in English sources that *Clematis* 'Comtesse de Bouchaud' should get only 8 ft. tall, but I have not seen one in bloom in North America at less than 12 ft. tall. Of course, clematis can't read and do not know when to stop growing!

Length does not imply weight by itself. A combination of characteristics can add up to a portly plant that needs extra support. In addition to length, consider leaf size and abundance, diameter of the main stems, and the number of branches and new shoots produced in a year. It bears repeating that just because a particular clematis is hard-pruned every year it doesn't mean the plant can't become massive in one growing season.

A WORD ABOUT STRUCTURES

Not every plant you want to combine with a clematis is going to be able to hold the vine over its head. You may want to hoist your large-flowered hybrids above your herbaceous perennials to create a band of color on a higher level, but without planting shrubs behind the shorter plants. You may not want to plant small trees to house your clematis, since these may eventually create more shade than you want your garden to have. In these situations freestanding structures are the answer, and the options are limitless.

When contemplating such items, do not forget to consider the architecture of your house or any other outbuildings (sheds, garages, gazebos) within sight of the mixed border you are creating. As Gertrude Jekyll put it, "The garden should curtsy to the house." And this is still

Clematis montana var. *rubens* blooms in swags of pink frosting across the porch at Lonesomeville, the personal Eden of Danny Hills and Wayne Hughes in Portland, Oregon.

true. It will never look quite right to put modern ornaments around a Victorian cottage without completely refacing the building. Modern homes with industrial finishes will not be happily accented by obelisks, arbors, and pergolas with curlicues and lathe-turned spindles.

If you have garden rooms that are somewhat removed from major buildings, walled by hedges and fences, then you can create garden spaces that pay homage to other eras or use contrasting materials. Often what we like to live with inside our home is different from the public face we want our garden to show. You may like a lean minimalist style within your personal space, but want a blowzy country garden scene when you look outside. That's fine, as long as your country garden looks good with the outside of your home.

In Europe angular wooden tuteurs are often used for roses, and smaller versions are available. Kits and patterns abound. The shape is classic and transcends many architectural styles. Tuteurs are usually made of wood and may be painted or left with the bare wood aging to a gray patina. Cedar is a good choice of wood for the tuteur, since it contains natural water-resistant oils.

Rusted metal objets d'art have become popular in country gardens, using found objects for function as well as ornament. Modern garden artists cut shapes of all kinds from sheet metal and weld these to the tops of rebar (reinforcement bars used in building construction) to make fantastical finials ready to be further adorned by clematis.

Rebar itself has become the first choice for structure by many gardeners. Bending devices are for sale and classes are given on how to use this versatile material. Bends and twists can be interlocked to create amazing shapes that still function as sturdy plant supports.

More and more garden structures are being created with high-density, recycled plastic, often with various types of metal reinforcement within to provide more longevity for the plastic, which can become brittle with extended exposure to the sun. The applications of recycled plastics in the garden have only begun to be explored.

Arches are the most common structures used to support vines, and these are made from many materials. Treated lumber, impregnated with rot-resistant chemicals, has lengthened the life span of wooden configurations that are set in the ground (anchored in concrete or not). These can be wrapped with chicken wire or fence cloth to give clematis a boost to their mature height.

Speaking of chicken wire, it is important to remember that clematis like to wrap their petioles (a petiole is the little stem that attaches a leaf to its main branch) around other stems or structures of ½-in.-diameter or less. If you are building with 2 × 4 or 4 × 4 posts, the only way the clematis can climb is to reach around and grab itself. Over time, your vine will get big enough to do this, but when the plant is young, it will

Cedar tuteurs make excellent clematis supports. This one was made by Carla Beutler and was quickly covered by *Clematis* 'Warszawska Nike'. In the author's garden.

Curls and squiggles of rebar, created by Carla Beutler for the author, are used in a trio to support *Clematis* 'Gravetye Beauty'.

need some help from you, such as a wire wrap or vine nails or a pre-existing plant that shares the same nonliving support.

Vine nails are particularly useful in holding up young vines because the metal flange on the head of the nail is bendable and will accommodate growing canes. The nails can be placed wherever you want them to direct new growth and can be removed later when your clematis has reached the height you want and is well affixed to the top of its host plant or support.

As for nonvining clematis, I often like to let them sort things out with their nearest neighbors, but I do use a 12- to 18-in.-tall, and as wide, metal ring on legs to define the root space for these plants. On the soil surface within these rings, no intruders are allowed. Thick and thuggish ground covers such as violets and ajugas, lysimachias and mints, are not permitted to wander in and smother the spring shoots of emerging herbaceous clematis. The ring reminds me where the dormant clematis are in the winter and where to weed, fertilize, and prune.

Providing structure for clematis can certainly be a source of frivolity in the garden. Uprights that are both silly and nostalgic are well within reason as long as these items are functional. Vintage grocery carts (trolleys, in England) fall into this category, wacky yet extremely utilitarian. Clematis can be planted underneath them to venture up and spill out, or a generously sized pot can sit in the basket (and one in the baby seat) to make the most of the space. Why not do both? Shopping carts look best in the vegetable garden where they emphasize the "grocery store" function of that part of the garden. I would not hesitate to place one as the focal point of an old-fashioned four-square pottager, but then, consider who's talking.

Clematis are by nature rowdy, comical, and surprising, as well as lovely. Structures for them can be likewise.

TEN BEST CLEMATIS FOR BEGINNERS

Clematis alpina 'Willy': 'Willy' has a pale pink flower with darker pink on the reverse concentrated at the flower-stem junction.

Clematis 'Comtesse de Bouchaud': This is a grand old gal, blooming late-season, a large-flowered hybrid with pink flowers.

Clematis ×*durandii*: This herbaceous perennial clematis is more dark blue than purple, wholly deserving of the many praises heaped upon it.

Clematis 'Fujimusume': This is a large-flowered hybrid of a particularly plant-lust-inducing clear, uniform blue.

TEN BEST CLEMATIS FOR BEGINNERS (continued)

Clematis 'Helios': This shorter *C. tangutica* hybrid has down-facing, open yellow flowers; a plant blooming with enthusiasm.

Clematis 'Huldine': The flowers have a white face with mauve-reversed sepals; sometimes grouped with *C. viticella* forms.

Clematis montana var. *rubens* 'Tetrarose': This cultivar makes a large vine with fragrant pink flowers and bronze new growth.

Clematis 'Niobe': A large-flowered hybrid, burgundy-red, this cultivar would be in the clematis Hall of Fame, if there were one.

Clematis 'Silver Moon': Another large-flowered hybrid, pale silver-lavender, it blooms freely in partial shade.

Clematis 'Viola': A popular large-flowered hybrid with royal purple blooms, this is a reliable vine.

A family of shopping carts in the author's vegetable garden support *Clematis* 'Ruby Glow' and *C.* 'Minuet'.

CHAPTER 2

GROOMED TO PERFECTION: PRUNING, TIDYING, GROOMING, AND MANIPULATING BLOOM TIME

Because the genus *Clematis* is so varied, it has been broken down into large groups based on flower form and, to a lesser extent, geography and habitat. Appendix 2 is a list of which common cultivars and species are from which larger clematis groups (Atragene, Montana, Viticella, Viorna, and the like).

A DIGRESSION INTO NOMENCLATURE

Large-flowered hybrids are always called simply by their cultivar names in single quotation marks. Their genetics are so complex that the records of their origin species are often lost in the mists of time. If you observe the large-flowered species closely (although *Clematis patens* is the only one of these regularly seen in collections), you can make some guesses about cultivar origin, but they are, at this moment, only that—a guess.

With the advent of plant licensing, large-flowered hybrids may have both a commercial name (trade designation) and a cultivar name, and it is hard for the average gardener to know which one to use. An example is the plant most gardeners call "Josephine." This plant's actual cultivar name is 'Evijohill', which incorporates part of the introducer's name, Raymond Evison, with that of the plant's discoverer, Josephine Hill. The trade name of this plant is JOSEPHINE™, commonly and incorrectly written 'Josephine'. Most home gardeners, like myself, refer to these plants by their trade names; I've included the true cultivar names of such "trademarked" plants in the index.

Clematis JOSEPHINE™ has the unpleasant true name *C.* 'Evijohill'. Regardless, it is a fun plant to grow. In the author's garden.

This reminds me a great deal of the standard practice in dog-showing circles of officially registering purebred dogs under convoluted titles incorporating kennel, breeder, and parent names, while the nickname the dog responds to—its call name—is something else quite different and more normal. I once met an Irish setter named Lucky Red's Sir Joshua Strider of Isle. By the time you spit that out the dog has lost interest. His call name was "Big Red." Were I a clematis, I would respond to "Josephine" much more readily than "Evijohill." Of course, neither "Evijohill" nor "Josephine" tell us anything about the plant's color (pink), style (double), or habit (spring bloomer with good repeat), but that is another matter entirely.

To the best of my ability, I will refer to the names of large-flowered hybrids by the commonest name found most often in the trade and actually used by gardeners. Thus 'Evijohill' shall be JOSEPHINE™. I will also endeavor to call plants by the name they were given by their breeder or discoverer, in the appropriate language. We regularly see names anglicized or Americanized, as if we regular Joes shopping at garden centers will be put off by anything foreign. If a plant is sufficiently beautiful and gardenworthy, gardeners will seek it under its proper name.

Thus the large-flowered hybrid 'Pink Champagne' shall be known properly herein as 'Kakio', so named by the late Kazushige Ozawa, who bred it. I have a more than passing acquaintance with the beverage pink champagne, and this flower looks nothing like it. In any case, the fact is the plant was named 'Kakio' by its Japanese breeder, and so it should be called by all of us.

Clematis cultivar names that formerly included the dominant parent species name—*Clematis viticella* 'Venosa Violacea', for instance—will be written in the new, recommended manner in this book—now *C.* 'Venosa Violacea'. I still think too much information is lost when the species name is removed. The standard nomenclature is that only true species seedling selections will include the species and a cultivar name. Hybrids, however close to one or the other parent they may be, will have only a cultivar name.

As if all this isn't confounding enough, I have the disturbing habit of assigning nicknames to familiar and beloved cultivars. These will appear in double quotes—"GQ" for 'Gipsy Queen', for instance—after they are first mentioned by their normal cultivar name written in the conventional way. Under no circumstances should you approach a clematis grower requesting a clematis by a nickname. They will treat you as if you are nuts. At least that's how they treat me!

THE TRADITIONAL ADVICE ABOUT PRUNING

The pruning of clematis is often misrepresented, made to seem so complex as to render the plants intimidating. Many new gardeners back away from their natural curiosity after reading a convoluted explanation of which clematis should be pruned when. Even some eminent clematis growers have reduced any discussion of the genus to a series of letters or numbers representing pruning methods: A, B, and C (sometimes 1, 2, and 3). Some folks would have you select your plants based on when they are pruned rather than for the merits of their flowers. In point of fact, your plants will let you know when they need to be pruned. If your vines have become unsightly, they are sending you a message: Prune me this very minute.

Before we visit the niceties of freestyle clematis pruning, let's familiarize ourselves with the pruning groups. The first grouping, A, is made of those clematis thought to not need pruning at all except to take out deadwood. We can call this grooming. This would include the two major atragene species (atragene is a collective term for a group of mainly early-flowering species who used to have their own genus), *Clematis alpina* and *C. macropetala* plus their hybrids. Group A also embraces the Montanae (who are themselves quite embracing).

The second group I call the "Killer B's" because they comprise those unfathomable large-flowered hybrids that will defy you at every opportunity. Contrary in nature, these plants bloom early, sporting their largest blooms mid-May to mid-June. Some can be mildly pruned in winter and will nonetheless bloom early. Others, if pruned too late or too hard in winter, will wait to give you small blooms later in the summer. It is a sweeping generalization to say that the vines of this group bloom best on their old wood. While this *can* be true, the blooms that come later on new wood are more generously produced, if smaller in diameter (as typical of *Clematis* 'Allanah' or *C.* 'The President'). It all depends on your definition of "best." Is your preference size or volume? Some in group B will bloom at the same time, and with blossoms of the same size, no matter when you prune them. *Clematis* 'Niobe' behaves in just this manner for me.

The double large-flowered hybrids are included in group B, and they, at least, are reasonably standard in their behavior. Most double blossoms do come from the big buds produced on lower, more mature stems. These should be tidied as necessary right after their flush of spring bloom has faded. After this light pruning (think of it as aggressive deadheading), some doubles will produce new growth and single flowers in late summer. The true doubles, producing thick pom-poms at every opportunity, like *Clematis* 'Duchess of Edinburgh' (who is white) and *C.* 'Kiri Te Kanawa' (who is dark blue) may have a late wave of equally double blooms after a light pruning, but both are just as likely to flower again generously if they are left to their own devices. For their benefit I take off only the spent flowers, leaving as much woody stem as possible.

Clematis 'Louise Rowe' can bloom single, semi-double, and fully double, all at the same time. In the author's garden.

There's an exception in every group and, in the group B doubles, the ringers are *Clematis* 'Louise Rowe' and *C.* 'Proteus'. These vines will often have double, semi-double, and single flowers every time they bloom. The blooms of *C.* 'Louise Rowe' are pale silvery lavender (toward pink or toward blue at times), similar in color to *C.* 'Belle of Woking'. *Clematis* 'Louise Rowe' is a reliable bloomer but not overly vigorous, making it an excellent container plant. *Clematis* 'Proteus' is mauve, or what I define mauve to be, with blowzy flowers bigger and less crisp than *C.* 'Louise Rowe'. *Clematis* 'Proteus' can become a very large plant.

Clematis 'Romantika' is hard-pruned each winter and recovers quickly. In the author's garden.

The easiest group to handle in the garden is group C, which includes the late large-flowered hybrids that need a lot of heat to perform well (such as *Clematis* 'Lady Betty Balfour'), the viticellas, the texensis hybrids, and the tangutica clan. This entire pruning group is supposed to be cut nearly to the ground just above the lowest nodes (reminder: a node is a point on the clematis stem where the two opposite leaves emerge and where new buds wait for their call to arms) in the fall or winter and all the top growth removed. This is what is meant by "hard pruning" because you are leaving only 1–3 ft. of old wood where you once had a 10- to 15-ft. plant. These clematis bloom on their new growth and will create tall, heavy snarls if not harshly dealt with. If you are a timid pruner, you will need to harden your heart to grow the group C clematis well.

PRUNING IN THE REAL WORLD

There are clematis in my garden that the prevailing wisdom says must be hard-pruned every year (group C) that I prune only once in every three to five years. Getting a big plant such as *Clematis* 'Ernest Markham' or *C.* 'Jackmanii' up into its host high enough to create the show I want is a process that can take two or three years. Therefore, I am loathe to cut them back with any kind of regularity. To do so would mean that the plant combination I want to showcase (or the blank space I want to fill) will look right in the garden only once every few growing seasons instead of every year. My alternative is to give certain clematis their heads (as the horse racers say) and leave them to it. So just as *Rosa* 'Zepherine Drouhin' blooms from the ground up into the sky, her companion *C.* 'Ernest Markham' will too if left unbothered.

This treatment works just as well for *Clematis* 'Jackmanii', that venerable but common antique clematis. This is such a good plant that it can be found anywhere clematis are sold. Even though it is not rare, there is much about it to cherish. If you hard-prune it (and most of its named siblings and offspring) every winter, it will rebloom in July (in USDA Zone 7) at about 12 ft. tall. However, this need not be a binding rule. I have chosen *C.* 'Jackmanii' to grow into the street trees in front of our house and the reasons are twofold. It is a common vine, and I can easily replace the two plants should they meet with foul play. Secondly,

I can enjoy the flowers earlier in the season from our elevated front porch and view them easily. The host laburnums (golden chain trees) bloom from late April into early May, followed by climbing roses (*Rosa* CHIANTI™ in the western tree and *R.* 'John Cabot' in the eastern tree), which are then followed by the clematis, extending the season of interest. As the laburnums grow taller, the clematis grow taller with them. If I pruned *C.* 'Jackmanii' as I am told I should, the vine would bloom at too short a height to be noticeable.

Another large-flowered clematis that responds well to infrequent pruning is the deliciously red *Clematis* 'Madame Edouard André'. It is a color disparagingly termed "beetroot red," but I happen to like beets enormously. This clematis is exactly the same shade as the old rambling rose *Rosa* 'Bleu Magenta'. If I hard-pruned the clematis, it would start blooming too late to be a companion to the rose. I clean up only the dead and wind-broken stems, leaving as much burgeoning growth as possible. This is done sometime during the early spring when the development of new buds on clematis is quite obvious.

Clematis 'Madame Edouard André' has the additional charming habit of laying some of its branches on the horizontal plane rather than growing insistently up. This makes for a vine easily combined with shrubs and herbaceous perennials. All in all, a very useful plant— "Madame Ed" often blooms at random intervals clear into the fall, stopped only by the first serious frost.

There is really nothing to be said about large-flowered clematis as winter interest plants. Most of them look wretched. Some are reliably deciduous, so at least we are spared the glum spectacle of hundreds of limp brown and black former leaves hanging inconsolably from the tenacious vines. If you are fearful of losing early spring bloom on those large-flowered hybrids that bloom in May, wait until later in the winter or very early spring when the buds are swelling to take off the longest unsightly layer of spent vines.

The Viticella Group, a uniformly virtuous tribe of clematis offering great success to beginners, can all be hard-pruned to the ground or nearly so in late fall. Such huge plants as *Clematis* 'Huldine' and *C.* 'Purpurea Plena Elegans' are literally rolled off their supporting shrubs like a blanket off a bed. Once the many brittle vines are crushed and compacted, each pile barely takes up half a yard debris bag. This seemingly severe method of shaving a plant serves two purposes. First, as I've said before, this forces a vigorous amount of growth from the crown, just what you want from a clematis that blooms on the new wood. Secondly, the viticellas get 10–15 ft. tall in a single season (or larger when in happy circumstances), racing to their mature height and then blooming at the ends of the canes. If they go unclipped, they just get longer and heavier, making an unholy mess that detracts from the blooming display. The ultimate disaster happens when unpruned viticellas get so heavy they collapse the tree or structure under them or the wind lifts the plant like a sail and deposits the tangle unceremoniously where it is most unwanted.

There is no harm in pinching out the new soft growth on the viticellas (two nodes worth or so, whatever you can easily sever with a fingernail) in March and April to encourage a bushier plant. This delays flowering only slightly. Most of the viticellas can be taken back by about one-third their length shortly after blooming, assuring some rebloom in areas with long growing seasons. A viticella that blooms in July will give a modest rebloom in September or October if pruned and fed when the first flowers are finished.

Incidentally, the texensis cultivars (hybrids who had *Clematis texensis* as a parent) should be treated the same way. *Clematis texensis* forms such as *C.* 'Duchess of Albany', *C.* 'Gravetye Beauty', and *C.* 'Étoile Rose' can all become very large plants, blooming on new wood, and should be hard-pruned to 3 ft. tall or less. I do this in late autumn. They can also be coaxed into some rebloom if modestly pruned and fertilized right after they flower in the summer.

The one exception to the hard pruning of viticellas is the combination of *Clematis* 'Étoile Violette' leaping up into a 75-ft.-tall Douglas fir. Ernie and Marietta O'Byrne in Eugene, Oregon, have left *C.* 'Étoile Violette' unshorn and it has reached 25 ft. The vine does bloom earlier than it would if hard-pruned and for the O'Byrnes there is no repeat bloom such as gardeners who groom their plants after flowering can expect.

Clematis 'Étoile Violette' bounds into a Douglas fir at Northwest Garden Nursery in Eugene, Oregon.

It just doesn't seem wise to lump clematis together on the basis of when they should be pruned. Pruning is a human endeavor, not something the clematis do for themselves, nor does pruning happen in any regular way to species in the wild. For them, pruning is left to the vagaries of fate. What the plants do is bloom—at certain times preset in their genes—and bloom time is a better guide to telling us gardeners when to intervene with our opposable thumbs and tools. Although these plants will seem quite smart and even obedient once you have grown them for a while, they actually are operating according to their genetic setting and, to a lesser extent, the weather. After observing a plant's habits for a season or two, let the manipulations begin!

WOULD YOU REPEAT THAT?

The large-flowered hybrids that bloom early in the year, which for me is in May (for instance *Clematis* 'Guernsey Cream', *C.* 'Duchess of Edinburgh', *C.* 'Daniel Deronda', *C.* 'Niobe', *C.* 'Dawn', and *C.* 'Kimiidera'), do not ever need to be hard-pruned unless you are trying to build up the crown of canes of a new plant. I'll get to the exceptions to this rule after a word or two. With clematis there are always exceptions.

These early-blooming plants, and we'll include all the May to mid-June large-flowering cultivars and species (notably *Clematis patens*) in this discussion, can be trimmed to tidy them for receiving visitors, but most will get only 8–10 ft. tall. These plants won't get heavy, but they can get unsightly because many don't lose their winter leaves or they lose them slowly. Typically, the early large forms will not rebloom on last year's late-flowering stems, although some books say they will. These stems are the dead lengths of vine that have branched into three twigs, each probably having a seed cluster or its remains at the end. This entire length of branch should be cut back to a nice fat bud emerging from a leaf axil (the upper corner of the leaf where the petiole attaches to the main stem) or, failing that, cut back to the main stem. It is best to groom these plants carefully in late winter when the buds are expanding and the viable buds are easily differentiated from those that are likely to wither. If this sounds as if you need to be a bit of a plant mind reader, yes, you do.

When you are pruning in late winter and early spring, expanding buds reveal which axils have viable buds and which do not. In the author's garden.

One of many exceptions to the no hard pruning rule of group B clematis is *Clematis* 'W. E. Gladstone'. My plant occupies a stout metal upright and wanders into the nearby Carolina silverbell (*Halesia carolina*), clothing the tree shortly after it flowers. When the clematis is through, I hard-prune it (the time will be late June or early July) to 18 in. tall and feed it. *Clematis* 'W. E. Gladstone' will be back in bloom by September and the flowers will be as large as they were in the spring. This same treatment can be used with *C.* VINO™, *C.* 'Sunset', *C.* 'The President', *C.* 'Lasurstern', *C.* 'Fujimusume', *C.* 'Peveril Pearl', *C.* 'Silver Moon', and *C.* 'Corona'. And these are just the ones I tried this style of pruning with. It would not surprise me to find any number of other group B large-flowered hybrids that flourish with such treatment. Keep in mind that all these plants will rebloom anyway, but often to a lesser extent, and the flowers will be small. By definition, these plants are *supposed* to bloom best on older stems, but when there is only new wood, which has ripened during the height of the growing season, miracles become regularly occurring events.

HAVING IT BOTH WAYS

Many gardeners have discovered, by accident or observation, that it is sometimes possible to hard-prune half your plant and leave the rest merely groomed. If your plant has made a grand snarl of itself, drastic action cannot be avoided. However, if your vine has grown with a spreading habit and the routes of several main stems clearly diverge, then some stems can be cut back hard in the winter, while others are left longer with just the old flower stems and deadwood removed.

The result of this half-and-half approach is that the longer stems will bloom sooner than those that were heavily cut back, but those, too, will bloom in time. The overall effect is usually a prolonged period of bloom, which the plant would not achieve if pruned in the manner of the prevailing wisdom. The stems left long bloom first, then the new growth, stimulated by your pruning, flowers to carry the show forward and, in some cases, the plant will give you a blooming-from-the-ground-up display. Observing the structure of your plant (does it fan out, grow straight up, or bloom when short no matter when it is pruned?) will guide you should you choose to experiment with partial pruning.

This method can work well with all the large-flowered hybrids. Either early- or late-blooming cultivars can be treated this way, blurring further the line between groups B and C, a line the clematis don't see, anyway. The viticellas can also benefit from partial hard pruning. If errant stems can be left long—assuming they have sufficient support— it is possible to achieve something like having almost any clematis bloom from the ground up over a period of many weeks.

Pruning doesn't have to be all or nothing.

TO DEADHEAD OR NOT TO DEADHEAD?

Here is a list of the group B clematis that I find benefit from being dead-headed (only spent flowers removed) when the first seed clusters start to look shaggy, usually about mid-June. These plants are large-flowered hybrids offering seed heads that look like spun gold until they are thoroughly dry, when the seeds turn to plumes and the collective shatters.

CLEMATIS THAT BENEFIT FROM DEADHEADING

Clematis 'Allanah' (red)
Clematis 'Barbara Dibley' (screaming pink with variable bar)
Clematis 'Barbara Jackman' (lavender with dark pink partial bar)
Clematis 'Beth Currie' (dark pink-to-burgundy with variable darker bar)
Clematis 'Burma Star' (dark purple)
Clematis 'Daniel Deronda' (blue with occasional lighter bar)
Clematis 'Dawn' (palest pink)
Clematis 'Fujimusume' (Wedgwood blue)
Clematis 'Guernsey Cream' (cream)
Clematis 'H. F. Young' (light blue)
Clematis 'King Edward VII' (pink stippled with lavender)
Clematis 'Lady Northcliffe' (Wedgwood blue)
Clematis 'Marie Boisselot' (white)
Clematis 'Maureen' (plum-red)

CLEMATIS THAT BENEFIT FROM DEADHEADING (continued)

Clematis 'Miss Bateman' (white with dark stamens)
Clematis 'Mrs. George Jackman' (white, often gives extra sepals)
Clematis 'Mrs. N. Thompson' (purple with red bar)
Clematis 'Nadezhda' (mauve with darker pink stripe, floppy)
Clematis 'Niobe' (burgundy)
Clematis 'Peveril Pearl' (opalescent pale lavender)
Clematis 'Pink Fantasy' (pale pink or peach with variable pink bar)
Clematis 'Roko-Kolla' (white)
Clematis 'Sally Cadge' (soft lavender or blue, barred in cold weather)
Clematis 'Sano-no-murasaki' (dark purple)
Clematis 'Silver Moon' (pale lavender-blue)
Clematis VINO™ (wine fading quickly to pink)
Clematis 'Warszawska Nike' (plum)
Clematis 'Westerplatte' (rich velvet red)

The relative merits of leaving the seed heads on the plants can be debated. It pleases me that the seeds are decorative, but the flowers please me more, and so I deadhead to get the plants back into whatever additional bloom as is likely to come, as quickly as possible. This may have to do with plant combinations I anticipate creating later in the growing season. Getting the clematis to bloom again just in time to coincide with a companion is a good motivator for removing spent blooms and keeping the garden tidy. If admiring seed heads is not your reason for living, remove the spent flowers as soon as the sepals fall.

Florists, especially those who enjoy working with dried fruit and flowers, covet clematis seed heads and will not deadhead so quickly. As they dry, the seed tails become plumes and it is not always possible to preserve seed heads in the "spun gold" stage. Sealing them with a floral setting agent, sometimes called "spray porcelain," or using inexpensive, lacquer-type hair spray, will preserve enough moisture in the seeds to keep them from taking flight.

Some of the cultivars discussed here will show sunscald on their leaves if they are in full sun and are not protected by a companion's tougher foliage. Even though we keep our plants well watered, temperatures over 90°F will produce brown crispy patches on the foliage. This damage should be removed, what I call "deleafing." You may have to take all the foliage off a plant in July or August. The new leaves will be produced rapidly and may well be better able to meet the season's demands. This situation is all the more reason to grow clematis through other plants who will obligingly shade clematis foliage with their own.

Sometimes the decorative seed heads of large-flowered hybrid clematis must be sacrificed to bring the plant back into bloom more quickly. In the author's garden.

You may well ask how to detect the difference between leaf scald and wilt disease. Wilt disease is indicated when the flower buds and leaves wilt, usually in the spring when the plant is about to bloom. It does not seem to be related to the weather. Heartbreaking as this is, wilt disease will not kill the vine. On the other hand, foliage with sunburned patches does not droop but, rather, becomes crispy. The cooked patches eventually spread to the leaf edges, indicating that the entire leaf has died. If squeezed, the leaf will crackle and crumble. This happens within a day or two of hot weather later in the season. (For a more thorough description of wilt disease, see appendix 1.)

Some roses won't rebloom as vigorously, or at all, if their hips are left to develop. This is true of some of the clematis species and their near hybrids as well. *Clematis* 'Brunette' is a willing bloomer, producing almost continual bloom throughout the entire growing season *if kept deadheaded.*

All these techniques—hard pruning, grooming, tidying, deleafing, deadheading—can be used by you, the gardener, to adjust the bloom time of your clematis and keep the vines looking healthy, even when they are dormant.

Some gardeners decry the bare legs of certain large-growing hybrids and species clematis, but they don't complain about tree trunks, do they? If your clematis have naked legs that have become like trunks rather than vines and you are offended, cover them with shorter clematis, herbaceous perennials, or annual vines.

A smooth, bark-covered stem looks healthier to me than one left with untidy leaves. Keep in mind that once their dead foliage is gone, the dark woody vines of many clematis will mirror the angles and curves of their host structures and plants, perhaps adding a certain architectural interest to the winter garden. You can find beauty even in this, if you are willing.

No matter what pruning method works for you and your vine, remember to give your clematis a half-strength dose of your preferred fertilizer after each pruning manipulation. Clematis are heavy feeders, and it is necessary to combine appropriate pruning with a fertilizing regimen to get your climber back into bloom as quickly as possible.

Clematis 'Brunette' is a willing bloomer that responds well to deadheading. In the author's garden.

VOICES OF EXPERIENCE

Let's visit some of the ways gardeners keep clematis looking fluffed and buffed that might not be obvious if we stick to the standard rules of thumb about pruning. This is what I call "freestyle" pruning and it is best attempted once you have gotten to know your particular plants and have seen what they are capable of (or not).

Clematis nurseryman Maurice Horn is a firm believer in hard pruning the *Clematis alpina* and *C. macropetala* forms right after they bloom, in late May. These vines can get tangled and heavy over time, and they do not shed their dead leaves. Both these species are native to areas with cruel climates, and it is clematis collector Brewster Rogerson's theory that the dead leaves protect the next season's buds from cold, drying winds. But most of us don't garden in Siberia. This means that after a few years of unclipped growth, you could have a real bird's nest of vine that detracts from the many charming blossoms produced at the height of their special season in April. They do bloom on their old wood, but are willing growers and will rebuild for the coming spring if taken down by two-thirds of their length in late May (when blooming is through). Keep these plants well fed and well watered. It is not uncommon for vines so treated to give a little bit of a show in late summer, by way of thanking you.

If you have inherited such a plant by moving into a new home with a neglected garden, there is hope. Use Maurice's method at half strength. If you find yourself faced with a small-flowered, spring-blooming clematis that is unsightly and out of control, cut half the canes coming out of the ground at about 3 ft. tall. Then work up from each cane you've cut, removing the disconnected top growth in small sections. Next year, take off the other older half of the plant.

Even the ambitious montana clan can be revitalized in this way. This group will form woody trunks as big around as your arm. If pruned in late spring, even these monsters will push out new vines from old stems. Garden designer Lucy Hardiman had her venerable *Clematis montana* var. *rubens,* with its several 3-in.-diameter trunks, unceremoniously cut by an ignorant neighbor. Assuming this had killed her plant, Lucy and

Clematis montana var. *rubens* has resurrected itself after a cruel twist of fate in the Hardiman garden, Portland, Oregon.

her husband, Fred, designed a new trellis to screen out the antagonizing oaf. Two years later, *C. montana* var. *rubens* was back, sending canes toward the new trellis, well out of harm's way. Best of all, her offending neighbor has been retrained and is now more garden savvy.

I've already mentioned the amazing recovery and rebloom of such large-flowered hybrids as *Clematis* 'W. E. Gladstone' in my own garden after hard pruning in July. Most group B large-flowered hybrids will respond with a variable quantity of smaller flowers in August and September rather than flowers of normal spring size (typically *C.* 'Allanah', *C.* 'Rhapsody', *C.* 'Warszawska Nike'). The first time I saw Brewster Rogerson's splendid clematis collection was one September, with over ninety species and cultivars in bloom. The careful combination of grooming, deadheading, and hard pruning had produced the bountiful display.

MY BEST ADVICE ABOUT PRUNING?

With the surrounding companions in mind, try to select a clematis that will bloom at the best time for maximum effect. Most vines are sold with their standard pruning code listed on the care tag. Be guided by this information, but not burdened by it. Whatever else you do, don't pass up a beautiful flower on a healthy vine simply because you are flummoxed by the conservative pruning manifesto. Watch your plant carefully to see that it does what you want it to do. If it doesn't, or if it shows an inclination to do something even more stupendous than you had envisioned, start experimenting with the various degrees of pruning. See if you and your vine can't come to some meeting of the minds, repeating the same glorious effects year after year.

If you want a generalization that will carry you right through the entire genus, here it is: When all other logic fails, the best time to prune any clematis—to whatever degree you wish—is right after it has finished its first flowering of the growing season. You won't have to worry about disrupting the flower timing, and there will be more growing season remaining for the plant's recovery. Carry this pearl of wisdom with you always.

TEN CLEMATIS NOT RECOMMENDED FOR BEGINNERS

Clematis alpina 'Jacqueline du Pré': This atragene has lovely, dark pink flowers edged in lighter pink, but this particular form is slow to establish. It makes pretty flowers, but it is not for those gardeners needing immediate gratification. The bigger the plant you can buy of this form, the better.

Clematis ARCTIC QUEEN™ ('Evitwo'): Although the double white flowers are large, this plant is slow growing and liable to die back at inopportune moments.

Clematis florida var. *sieboldiana*: Also known as *C. florida* 'Bicolor', this large-flowered double is a natural sport of the rare and fussy *C. florida*. Although *Clematis florida* var. *sieboldiana* has showy flowers (white with a profuse crown of purple staminode petals), it is slow to establish and seems somewhat tender. The best plants of this that I have seen are container grown indoors and rolled outside when the plant blooms.

Clematis 'H. F. Young': Some consider this a fussy plant, although it has always been simply great for me. It can fall prey to juvenile wilt disease, so don't say you weren't warned.

Clematis ranunculoides: This late-flowering Chinese species is quite variable. The plants available are seed grown, and a truly winter-hardy, reliably blooming selection has yet to be identified. The flowers are rosy lavender chubby bells, heavily ridged. If my plant blooms before November 1st, I know we've had a warm autumn. It needs full sun and rich soil with sharp drainage.

Clematis 'Snow Queen': White with burgundy anthers, this is another large-flowered cultivar that is slow to get started, dislikes being moved, and may be short-lived.

Clematis 'Sunset': Although this cultivar was bred in North America, it is not long-lived. It behaves rather the opposite of *C.* 'Will Goodwin' for me. It blooms quite well and seems healthy as a juvenile plant, but in my own garden and in the gardens of friends, I have noticed *C.* 'Sunset' start to fail as it matures. This problem manifests itself when the plant is about to bloom and half of it collapses.

Clematis tangutica 'Radar Love': This should be a bright yellow, small-flowered summer bloomer with delicate foliage. Unfortunately, it is often propagated by seed and the seedlings are pale and wan compared to the true form.

Clematis 'Will Barron': Ditto what is said below about *C.* 'Will Goodwin', although early pruning will create a bushier plant, more resistant to life's ups and downs.

Clematis 'Will Goodwin': This plant is slow to establish and susceptible to wilt disease until it is three to five years old. I was ready to dig up poor "Will" until I saw a splendid picture on a magazine cover that dared me to persevere.

Chapter 3

CLEMATIS WITH EACH OTHER

For true lovers of the genus *Clematis,* there is no greater plant combination than to pair these vines with each other. Some partnerships, such as *C.* 'Étoile Violette' with *C. tangutica* 'Bill MacKenzie' have become standard in public gardens. This can happen only because these are such good plants, reliable comrades we can count on to provide a bright show at the right time. As Groucho Marx said when speaking of comedy, "Timing is everything." This is certainly true when putting clematis together.

We are again faced with the question, "When?" Do we want our chosen clematis to bloom in riotous partnership, or do we want to layer their flowers over the growing season chronologically? How can we get the best effects to repeat themselves later in the season? Do we want other plant companions to join in the glee of two (or more!) well-chosen vines?

THE HIGHEST GOAL TO WHICH A GARDENER CAN ASPIRE

Be ever vigilant for the happy accident. In my own garden I watch the wanderings of my clematis into plant medleys that I had not thought possible or practical. These vines find their own way into beautiful compositions, and it is then up to me, the gardener, to figure out how to make the same harmony replay. Quite often the haphazard placing of new plants into their staging area on my back deck—a mishmash of plants sitting in flats just as they came from a nursery buying spree—will

Yellow *Clematis tangutica* 'Bill MacKenzie' and purple *C.* 'Étoile Violette': a classic combination in a classic garden, Sissinghurst Castle in Kent, England.

reveal associations that I would not have seen but for random chance. This is, in fact, how I came to place *Clematis* 'Iubeleinyi-70' (a large-flowered hybrid with soft purple flowers produced over a long season, with the Americanized name tag reading 'Jubilee 70') with *C. pitcherii* (with its small silver-purple bells lined inside with dark purple velvet). I call this "deck designing." Some of my favorite planting schemes have come to me in this way, and I don't say it isn't a possible conspiracy among the plants themselves.

PRUNING PARTNERSHIPS

The single most important component to consider when pairing clematis together is the blooming habit of each and how you may have to modify this to achieve the picture you have in your mind. The easiest thing to do is combine like with like. All the clematis that flower at the same season (in the temperate zone anywhere from March through November) can be planted together and then are groomed together. What could be simpler?

This doesn't mean that you have only small-flowered cultivars to choose from in the later seasons. Such large-flowered hybrids as *Clematis* 'Gipsy Queen', *C.* 'Lady Betty Balfour', *C.* 'Viola', *C.* 'Victoria', *C.* 'Madame Baron-Veillard' (pronounced "vay-yard"), and *C.* 'Comtesse de Bouchaud' (pronounced "boo-show") are late bloomers. You can make them later still by waiting until early spring to prune them, thus setting them back and ensuring August or September bloom instead of July. The shoots of the plants will be well along, and you will have lived with last year's tired vines throughout the winter. Avoid this by hard-pruning in late fall, then pinching the new growing tips in April. This is essentially double-pruning, but it does get these large-flowered hybrids on the right schedule. Both "Comtesse" and *C.* 'Gipsy Queen' (or "GQ," as we call her at home) form quite a thicket of stem growth over the years, and it would certainly be possible to tip-prune only part of each plant and see if that doesn't give you a longer overall period of flower.

Clematis 'Gipsy Queen' is quite likely to send out a few shorter horizontal stems if treated this way, in addition to rocketing to the top of her tree and then cascading down as usual (use a tall stately tree, such as

Clematis 'Gipsy Queen', the gappy flower on the right, pops over to visit *C*. 'The President'. In the author's garden.

Pyrus calleryana, the callery pear). One year she surprised me by popping into the middle of the much shorter clematis *C.* 'The President', which is not quite the dark purple of "GQ" and not gappy. I did the requisite double take, thinking that *C.* 'The President' had lost his mind. Careful inspection revealed he had taken up with a gypsy.

Here in Portland the viticella tribe all seem to want to bloom in late June and early July and, because of their mass, I usually combine them with other big vines—like the honeysuckles and climbing roses. If you have a vision of beauty and loveliness involving a viticella and a large-flowered hybrid, make sure they are planted so the large-flowered hybrid can wander over into the viticella. Putting them into the same planting hole will eventually spell death for the less vigorous plant (which one *that* turns out to be may surprise you). Also, you will have a devil of a time hard-pruning the viticella while not taking away too much of the large-flowered hybrid. If you chose a late-flowering large-flowered hybrid, your problem is solved, and everyone is cut at the same time.

The texensis hybrids tend to be less thuglike than the viticellas, with the possible exception of *Clematis* 'Duchess of Albany'. It can take several years for these cultivars to establish sufficient root balls to support masses of top growth. Once they are mature, however, *C.* 'Gravetye Beauty' and *C.* 'Étoile Rose' can summon a proud quantity of stem and leaf with a solid sheet of flowers. Be sure that any other clematis you pair with these has its own root space.

FAIR-WEATHER FRIENDS

A tour through the growing season will highlight which clematis groups can overlap without a lot of fancy pruning. Our trip will also reveal which rebloomers will blend with later-flowering species and cultivars. We can take notes of which clematis might need special attention (deadheading, grooming). For the sake of this discussion, I am putting in the species parent in the name, rebel that I am.

In my garden the earliest clematis to bloom outside are the Atragene Group (cultivars from *Clematis alpina, C. macropetala, C. siberica, C. fauriei*). First comes *C. macropetala* 'Jan Lindmark', followed quickly by *C. alpina* 'Constance'. Both are plummy or mauve in color. The first blue

The relatively new (1984) texensis cultivar *Clematis* 'Princess Diana' makes a colorful partnership with a royal antique, *C.* 'Victoria' (1870). In the Rodal garden, Sauvie Island, Oregon.

form to flower is *C. macropetala* itself, then the paler blue *C. alpina* 'Odorata' and *C.* 'Floralia'. The best early white for me is *C. macropetala* 'White Lady', but others prefer *C. siberica.* The darkest colors come from *C. macropetala* 'Maidwell Hall' and *C.* 'Helsingborg', who wear navy blue. *Clematis fauriei* 'Campanulina Plena' (as it is called in America) and *C.* 'Pruinina' are smoky purple. These are similar in size of flower and texture and are rarely grown together, although they certainly could be. All the early atragenes do, however, make excellent companions for woody shrubs and early herbaceous perennials. More on that later.

The latest-flowering cultivars from this group will sometimes overlap with the early montanas or the large-flowered hybrids. Hanging on the longest is *Clematis alpina* 'Pamela Jackman' (blue or lavender with cream underskirt), whose delicacy of flower delights me by persisting in open bloom for several weeks with her little sepals thrown back to welcome the mild spring sun, almost like a cyclamen. Other late starters are *C. alpina* 'Willy' in pale pink and *C. macropetala* 'Pink Flamingo' in darker pink. Any of these will look best with an early white montana, especially *C. montana* itself. Because *C. montana* gets quite tall, any *C. macropetala* or *C. alpina* partner must be allowed to grow to its full height as well. On the plus side, montanas and the spring-blooming atragenes can be pruned immediately after flowering, so everyone gets tidied or groomed by several feet, as needed, at the same time.

I'll insert a word here about the evergreen *Clematis armandii.* *Clematis armandii* is hardy only to USDA Zone 8, and Zone 7 is really pushing the cold edge of its range. The montanas can be successfully grown in colder areas because they are deciduous. Gardeners are attracted to *C. armandii* because it *is* evergreen and its frothy clusters of creamy flowers smell like heaven. However, there are drawbacks to this plant that make it a poor companion for other clematis. *Clematis armandii* needs careful placement in the garden, especially at the edge of its temperature range. It is evergreen, but if planted in a location exposed to drying winter winds, this plant is ever black—the dried leaves blacken but do not drop. This species blooms in March in the Pacific Northwest, a month when late frosts can ruin the year's bloom and there is little chance of rebloom. The other thing to remember is that this is an exceptionally vigorous vine and needs constant maintenance to keep it in bounds. It is a big, heavy plant. In the vine's defense, I have seen *C. armandii* and its few cultivars looking handsome in mild coastal areas with soil that is not overly sandy. I'm all for impulse clematis buying, but you should really have a clear idea of siting and the amount of maintenance involved before attempting *C. armandii*.

As the montanas hit their stride, the first of the large-flowered hybrids start their show, and these can combine in more intriguing ways than the last group. Although the montanas are limited to white, cream, and various pale-to-midpink shades, there are both double and single forms and all can look elegant with their larger and more colorful cousins. The montanas have the advantage of being fragrant, the pink forms most notably so. There is little fragrance in the double-flowered montana cultivars.

Everyone wants an evergreen vine for their front porch. Be careful what you want, for you may get it! The flowers of *Clematis armandii,* and its fragrance, are worth the risk of having an overgrown plant.

We find ourselves in May (in USDA Zone 7 anyway) when the whole garden seems to explode. The double montanas lead the fireworks. *Clematis montana* var. *rubens* 'Marjorie' is a particular favorite of mine. This vine finds a way to look good with as many partners as it can by virtue of its spread. Spanning 20+ ft., *C. montana* var. *rubens* 'Marjorie' (whom we call "large Marj" at home) will mingle with honeysuckles (*Lonicera*), rambling roses, and other clematis all at the same time. Mix her soft pink, shaggy flowers with other soft colors if you like, but I prefer more contrast with a brilliant red like *C.* 'Allanah'. This large-flowered hybrid is also capable of flinging itself about with festive abandon, spreading its arms wide for several feet with swags of big, gappy blooms at the branch tips. *Clematis* 'Allanah' will want pruning by one-third at the end of her first period of bloom, which would be a good time to remove excessive growth from *C. montana* var. *rubens* 'Marjorie'.

Not all the *Clematis montana* tribe get to be huge vines. There are a few reasonably petite forms that work well in urban gardens or other

Clematis 'Allanah' and *C. montana* var. *rubens* 'Marjorie' make a bold color statement with maximum textural contrast. In the author's garden.

tight quarters. My favorite of these is *C. montana* 'Jenny Keay', named for the wife of Alistair Keay, the clematis authority from New Zealand. He has introduced several fine clematis, including the just-mentioned *C.* 'Allanah'. *Clematis montana* 'Jenny Keay' matures to 12–15 ft. tall, about half the height of your typical montana. This cultivar is double and the individual flowers are quite long-lasting. The color is variable, but a good general description is cream to pale pink. The newest blooms can look yellowish green, and if the flowers develop in partial shade they will be totally cream, without a hint of pink. (*Clematis montana* var. *rubens* 'Marjorie' does this too.)

Clematis montana 'Jenny Keay' is quite pretty when combined with the early, double, large-flowered hybrids, such as *C.* 'Proteus' and *C.* 'Vyvyan Pennell'. Both have enough pink tint in their mauve coloring to make the difference in texture with *C. montana* 'Jenny Keay' more notable. These big, curvaceous doubles are brought to life by the multi-pointed stars of this refined montana cultivar.

The short *Clematis montana* cultivar 'Jenny Keay' is useful because of its long period of bloom and its ability to combine with other clematis without overwhelming anyone. In the author's garden.

Another relative of *Clematis montana* is an excellent choice for small gardens, if you can find the legitimate plant. I'm speaking of *C. chrysocoma,* a Chinese species often encountered in the wild by modern plant explorers. In its native habitat this plant, which has single white montana-like flowers (rarely pink), is not seen growing more than a modest 6–8 ft. This species does not climb. It prefers to scramble over lower shrubs rather than set height records in tall trees. If you think you have a *C. chrysocoma* that gets 20 ft. tall, you may actually have *C. spoonerii,* another montana cousin.

Clematis chrysocoma has an engaging ripple at the edge of its sepals, giving the flowers more individual personality than is usually seen among the other Montanae. I particularly like to use this plant to dress the lower regions of such dark large-flowered hybrids as *C.* 'Serenata' and *C.* 'Mrs. N. Thompson'.

LIVING LARGE

The early large-flowered hybrids, those that bloom in May and June, look marvelous together and can, of course, be pruned together. Although some of the "pajama-striped" pinks might seem daunting, they can always be toned down with white. You will find that the intensity of striping on any clematis varies with the weather and the season. Clematis thought not to have bars will show a shadow of a bar, if not an actual gaudy stripe, if the buds mature during unusual weather (too hot, too cold, and sudden drastic changes from one to the other).

The large-flowered hybrid *Clematis* 'Pink Fantasy' can give the impression of quite a strong stripe that is not normally characteristic of this cultivar. *Clematis* 'Pink Fantasy' should be a soft true pink, occasionally showing a peach cast or a soft bar like a faint brush stroke that doesn't reach the point of the sepal. The environmentally induced alteration of what is normal is impossible to predict. This type of color variation can sometimes have us thinking we have purchased a misnamed plant. Fortunately in my case, *C.* 'Pink Fantasy' had been in its place several years, blooming as expected, before showing this aberrant spring coloration. The later summer flowers during the same year were right as rain again. Many large-flowered hybrids may look out of whack when their colors develop during unusually cool spring weather.

Another variation to consider when combining clematis is the tendency of most large-flowered hybrid doubles to produce single flowers when they rebloom in mid- to late summer. Certain cultivars, such as *Clematis* 'Proteus' and *C.* 'Louise Rowe' may have double, semi-double, and single flowers all at once. In my garden there is no break in service for *C.* 'Vyvyan Pennell', who will go from a long period of producing double flowers directly into an equally long period of producing single flowers before taking a midsummer rest. *Clematis* 'Proteus', on the other hand, will take a break after the double flowers have gone, reappearing in time to mingle with that most vigorous viticella form, *C.* 'Huldine'. The mauve bar on the reverse of the sepals of *C.* 'Huldine' makes it a particularly good choice with the single flowers of *C.* 'Proteus', which tend to be a softer color than its double flowers are.

Many of the large-flowered hybrids said to be blue are not really blue by anyone's definition of the color. We can discuss their relative blueness, if everyone agrees that what we are talking about are shades of lavender that tend toward blue. The human eye is easily deceived into seeing blue, but camera film is not, which adds further to our confusion. Observing a display of lots of large-flowered hybrids at a flower show is the best way to decide for yourself which blue is blue. My money is on *Clematis* 'Fujimusume'. Others might prefer *C.* 'H. F. Young', *C.* 'Will Goodwin', or *C.* 'Lady Northcliffe'.

The best way to get a blue large-flowered hybrid clematis to look its bluest is to combine it carefully with another clematis that is purple or white. Most of the reds have a touch of blue in them, making any nearby blues seem all the more lilac. The clean whites, such as *Clematis* 'Mrs. George Jackman' and *C.* 'Marie Boisselot', give a crisp background that brings blue tones to the fore. Yellow would be the best companion to bring on the blues, but alas, there are as yet no vividly yellow large-flowered clematis. *Clematis* 'Guernsey Cream', *C.* 'Moonlight', and *C.* 'Wada's Primrose' are near yellow and so help reveal the best in blue clematis.

Clematis 'Huldine' is well into its long summer-blooming period when *C.* 'Proteus' produces a second wave of bloom with single, mauve-pink flowers. In the author's garden.

Clematis 'H. F. Young' intermingles with *C.* 'The President'. In the author's garden.

Because the overall texture of most of the early large-flowered hybrids is the same, we look to contrasts in both sepal and stamen color to make a pretty picture. Penny Vogel, of Estacada, Oregon, is particularly adept at this sort of combination. Her garden, Kinzy Faire, is co-owned by Millie Kiggins, and together they have devised many ways of growing clematis and getting the flowers together.

Penny combines the size and poise of clematis flowers, while supplying contrast with color. (By poise I mean how the flower is held on its stem, how it faces us.) Dark purples might be met with dark reds and, as the summer continues, dark burgundy is contrasted with paler blues and lavenders. No structure is ever installed with just one clematis. The pavilion built by Millie in the midst of the original farmyard garden is home to dozens of clematis, with each new vine carefully matched by color to its nearest neighbors.

Tall, dark, and handsome: *Clematis* 'Niobe' and *C*. 'Edomurasaki' make a rich color harmony at the garden of Kinzy Faire in Estacada, Oregon.

The light and the dark of it: *Clematis* 'Royal Velours' with the pale *C.* 'Blekitny Aniol' (*C.* Blue Angel™) at Kinzy Faire in Estacada, Oregon.

At Kinzy Faire we can see the progression from the early large-flowered hybrids in their heyday to the vines of high summer. The Viticella Group carries the garden into the hot weather and mingles with the late large-flowered hybrids and other summer species. Penny has combined her viticellas for color contrasts and hopes they will continue blooming long enough to pick up some of the rebloom of earlier-flowering cultivars. Arched arbors explode into flower around the garden, each luring us on as we visit, like bees, from one to the next, glimpsed just ahead.

One great clematis duo leads to another. The pair here (dark *Clematis* 'Romantika' with light blue *C.* 'Prince Charles') is hard-pruned in late fall to reduce the weight on the arches. Kinzy Faire, Estacada, Oregon.

The juxtaposition of very large- and very small-flowered clematis has a charm of its own and always brings a smile, like seeing a big dog play with a puppy. Summer-blooming North American natives such as *Clematis crispa, C. viorna,* and *C. versicolor* have long periods of bloom in a cultivated setting—through July and August—and will flower readily with large-flowered hybrids that rebloom in midsummer or start their bloom at that time. If you do choose to make this type of partnership, try to match the colors of the species with the larger cultivar you use. If you want color contrast, make sure that the smaller-flowered vine has

The very large and the very small, but the color remains the same. *Clematis* 'Peveril Pearl' with *C. crispa* in the author's garden.

the brighter hue. This is suggested because matching a gaudy large-flowered hybrid with a small subtle species will completely negate the smaller blooms; the eye will simply ignore the faint color in favor of the bolder, eye-commanding expanse of color on larger sepals.

In the picture of *Clematis* 'Peveril Pearl' with *C. crispa,* the crowns of these two plants are about 6 ft. apart, yet the top growth and flowers manage to find each other. *Clematis crispa* is hard-pruned each winter down to a mound of 6-in. stems, and *C.* 'Peveril Pearl' is pruned by one-third its height at the same time. *Clematis* 'Peveril Pearl' first blooms in mid-May, but if kept deadheaded and fertilized, it extends its first flush of bloom well into high summer, making its floral assignation with its diminutive familiar. Their textures couldn't be more different.

SUMMER'S SMALL WONDERS

Also making their appearance in midsummer are the fine hybrids of *Clematis texensis,* itself a plant of rare beauty and influence (and an American native). These, along with other fine species from North America and a few from Asia, are all lumped into a clematis section named for *C. viorna.* The Viorna Group is characterized by the unique, bonnet-shaped flower—although some vary to a bell shape—that constricts before flaring to pointed or curled lips at the sepal ends. *Clematis texensis* passes its brilliant red color (in the breeding-worthy forms of the species) on to its offspring, and it is the progenitor (from breeding programs in France in the 1800s) of all the red large-flowered hybrids. But for *C. texensis,* there would be no *C.* 'Niobe', no *C.* 'Ville de Lyon', no *C.* 'Westerplatte'. Horrors!

The direct hybrids of *Clematis texensis* are a distinctive bunch of plants, all having flowers the shape of lily-flowered tulips. These are mainly of intense pink (*C.* 'Duchess of Albany'), dark pink (*C.* 'Princess Diana'), and red (*C.* 'Gravetye Beauty'). With the possible exception of "The Duchess," the texensis hybrids take a bit of time in the ground to get their roots established and they like a gritty, free-draining soil. *Clematis texensis* is found in its native habitat (Texas) scrambling along stream banks in gravelly soil. Sharp drainage and plenty of water is their preference.

Clematis 'Star of India': A *C.* 'Jackmanii' offspring, rich purple and showing a faint red bar especially when backlit, enhances its neighbors.

Clematis tangutica 'Bill MacKenzie': These small, bright yellow bells are particularly fine with any purple summer-blooming clematis.

CHAPTER 4

CLEMATIS WITH ROSES

There is an undeniable lure to placing clematis with old garden roses. Modern rose experts notwithstanding, this is one of the most sensuous and evocative textural combinations a gardener can produce (without being arrested). The dense, full blossoms of antique roses look even more decadent when blooming while swathed in the plump sepals of double large-flowered hybrid clematis. Who can deny spring its excesses?

Although I sincerely think that growing clematis together well is the highest form of garden artistry, I have to admit that it is the flagrant affair of roses with clematis that gets the most notice by those newly acquainted with the genus *Clematis.* It is hard not to look.

Placing clematis into climbing roses is an obvious choice. Most modern roses—that is to say the Hybrid Teas and Floribundas—do not want the close companionship of *any* other plants, let alone something that is going to climb over the top of them. Many of the newest rose introductions of the last fifty years need excellent air circulation to prevent disease, an impossibly high standard to meet in most gardens unless spring and summer are dry with low humidity and the plants are watered with a drip system. The southwestern United States has such weather as this, where we see little foliage disease on roses. (A gardener with deep pockets to afford loads of fungicide spray is helpful too.)

Clematis 'Guiding Star' and the old garden rose *Rosa* 'Louise Odier' typify the best characteristics of roses and clematis together—sumptuous colors and full, rounded textures combining for a romantic composition. In the author's garden.

For the rest of us mere mortals who garden where the springs are wet or the summers have high humidity, the selection of roses is trickier. This is what sends me back to the old garden roses, those antiques that are winter hardy, more disease resistant, and tremblingly fragrant. Often old roses mature to become large upright shrubs, easily capable of raising a moderately sized clematis vine to eye level. Since large-flowered clematis are not—generally speaking—fragrant (an exception is *Clematis* 'Fair Rosamond'), we can pretend they are by combining them with roses.

ONCE-BLOOMING ROSES

All roses are once-blooming by my charitable definition; it is just that for some roses "once" lasts for four months and for others it only lasts four weeks. If I like the look of a blossom and its fragrance, if the plant forms hips and it has clean habits—meaning little foliage disease—I don't quibble about the length of its flowering season. We all tolerate the other "once-blooming" shrubs in our gardens, rhododendrons, *Philadelphus* (mock orange), *Syringa* (lilacs), and a host of others. We simply figure out a way to liven them up later in the summer when they are not blooming. Lo and behold! We can usually use clematis to do this. Why should roses be treated any differently?

Roses have as many attractions as any other ornamental shrubs in our gardens. Many beautiful species and cultivars have flaming fall color (*Rosa* 'Morletti' and *R. moyesii,* for instance), and many more form hips (seed pods) of various colors and shapes. A few will even continue to flower as they form hips—the single-flowered *R. rugosa* and its cultivars; PINK MEIDILAND™ and LYDA ROSE™—relieving us of deadheading completely.

For some reason, the shape of the unopened bud and the garish colors of Hybrid Tea roses have become the modern standard of floral beauty. This escapes me completely. Roses should be at their best when fully open or nearly so, exposing the most petal surface to our eyes and nostrils. Colors should not shout at you from across the yard and be impossible to blend. (Of course, Hybrid Teas that are loud are not meant to be grown with other plants, hence breeders don't worry about anything but developing the next new color.) Many gardeners have small urban spaces to beautify and haven't the room to create rose ghettos where no other plant invades a rose's personal space and the soil surface is a sea of naked bark dust.

There are hundreds of old garden roses (for the sake of argument, those introduced before 1900), and some good mid-twentieth-century modern groups (Hybrid Musks, early Floribundas, English Roses) that won't quarrel with you about where they are placed or with whom as long as they have enough sun. How often they bloom is a negligible point as long as you love the flowers and appreciate them while they last.

TALLER THAN ADVERTISED

On travels to gardens far from and near my home in the Pacific Northwest, I have noticed that roses in North America tend to grow larger than they do in England. Many excellent reference books on roses are from British authors who speak from their firsthand knowledge. The introduction of the English Roses by David Austin, and now their followers from other British rose breeders and the Romantica series from France, first made me aware that there is a great discrepancy between the British and European experience of these plants and what we can expect on our side of the Atlantic. Instantly smitten when Mr. Austin's roses arrived in Oregon, I began growing them. So did many of my gardening friends. The literature about them always underestimated what these plants could accomplish here. *Rosa* 'Leander' should be grown as a climber of 10–12 ft., not as an upright shrub of 8 ft. *Rosa* MARY ROSE™ always reaches 7–8 ft., not the advertised height of 5 ft. Of course, we gardeners have the pruners, and therefore the control.

My rule of thumb when reading about roses in British and European books is that in American gardens the shrub roses will get 1–3 ft. taller than the author specifies. Ramblers and climbers will get *much* taller. The term "shrub roses" has been revived and enlarged to accommodate modern roses that do not otherwise fit into a preexisting category as recognized by the American Rose Society.

Also keep in mind that clematis tend to get taller here too.

FINDING THE RIGHT PARTNERS

Using once-blooming roses in our gardens gives us at least two options for using clematis with them. We can select vines that will bloom with the rose, and we can choose forms that will bloom later, clothing the green bush with color in midsummer or after.

It is quite dramatic to have the rose and clematis bloom together, but it may take a bit of experimentation to see that the vine and rose cooperate with you. My vision of loveliness involving the early-blooming large-flowered hybrid *Clematis* 'Kakio' and the old Gallica rose *Rosa* 'Charles de Mills' has not yet materialized. If the once-blooming "Charles" is pruned in the winter to force the plant to flower later, the rose will not flower at all because the latent flower buds have been removed. *Clematis* 'Kakio' always wants to bloom weeks earlier than the

Clematis 'Viola', if allowed to flower early, will bloom with the Bourbon climbing rose *Rosa* 'Great Western'. In the author's garden.

rose, and no manipulation of its timing is successful either. Hard pruning in late winter can get this clematis to produce smaller than its typical flowers later in the season *after* the rose has bloomed.

The final blow to this fantasy combination came when the rose simply wandered away. Like many other Gallica roses, *Rosa* 'Charles de Mills' tends to send up suckers from its roots. (These new baby plants can be controlled by shovel pruning: Take your shovel and plunge it to its full depth at a 15-in. radius around the rose. This detaches the current suckers, which can then easily be pulled away. But more will be produced; the task must be repeated about twice a year.) In the case of my plant, one intrepid shoot ran from the original shrub to a walkway, went under it, and came up unseen at the top of a retaining wall. Meanwhile, the original plant began to run out of gas, as if the wood were wearing out, no matter what I did to boost its morale. I discovered the sucker when it had matured enough to come into bloom and I decided to leave it and send the mother plant back to the goddess Flora. The new rose in its place is the white English Rose *R.* 'Glamis Castle', which will start flowering earlier and perhaps be a better, though theoretically less sensational, partner for *Clematis* 'Kakio'.

As for the remaining *Rosa* 'Charles de Mills', it now partially drapes down a retaining wall, while a section of this "new" rose plant is more upright. The two clematis *R.* 'Charles de Mills' has joined are the purple *Clematis* 'Guiding Star', which blooms spring and fall, and the summer-blooming integrifolia cultivar *C. integrifolia* 'Pangbourne Pink', both of which were already in place.

But for every minor failure like the one just described, there are hundreds (yes, *hundreds*) of possible successes. The robust red *Clematis* 'Madame Edouard André' blooms right in step with the rambler *Rosa* 'Bleu Magenta'. The double white clematis *C.* 'Duchess of Edinburgh' will bloom with the old Bourbon rose *R.* 'Variegata di Bologna', which has vivid red stripes on a white ground. The above-mentioned *C.* 'Guiding Star', a charming clematis because of the flippant twist at the tip of its sepals, blooms abundantly with the pink rambler *R.* 'Thelma' and her partner *R.* 'Louise Odier'.

Clematis 'Kakio' and the Gallica rose *Rosa* 'Charles de Mills' can be shown together on a printed page, but they would not bloom at the same time in the author's garden.

One of my favorite marriages is the old damask rose *Rosa* 'Hebe's Lip' with *Clematis* 'Maureen'. The rose has profuse red buds that surprise me by opening to reveal a white single flower with each petal tipped in red lipstick. *Clematis* 'Maureen' has a difficult color to define, certainly not purple, but then not red either. Some folks call this color plum, but I think it is a shade or two lighter than that. *Clematis* 'Maureen' must be allowed to become established in one place before giving of its best. This is not a vine you can change your mind about a number of times. Placing *C.* 'Maureen', who only wants a bit of grooming at the time when the shriveled hips come off the rose in mid-February, with a rose that requires little care has meant that this clematis could develop a strong root system and an understory of pro-

The color of large-flowered *Clematis* 'Maureen' draws attention to the pink buds and rouged petal tips of *Rosa* 'Hebe's Lip'. In the author's garden.

ductive old wood in relative peace and quiet. The two bloom together on cue in late May, with a repeat performance by *C.* 'Maureen' in the fall (especially if deadheaded) when the rose has reddened its hips. What a team!

In using clematis with old garden roses, especially those with a shrubby habit such as the Gallica, Alba, Damask, and Centifolia Groups, it is important to note the mature size of the rose and whether or not it tends to have lax growth. Those that are lax—meaning that the stems, rather than stiff and upright, are slender and inclined to drape— will need a shorter clematis and one that does not produce masses of heavy old woody vine. We can look at the example of *Rosa* 'Hebe's Lip' with *Clematis* 'Maureen' again. *Rosa* 'Hebe's Lip' is a sturdy-stemmed plant, reaching only 4 ft. high, but well branched with thick canes nonetheless. Although *C.* 'Maureen' has produced a lot of heavy old vine, the clematis has wound around the rose's interior (with only a little

Another old-fashioned spring combination is *Clematis montana* var. *rubens* 'Marjorie' and the Alba rose *Rosa* 'Madame Legras de Saint Germain'. In the author's garden.

guidance from me), and the stout stems of the rose have no trouble holding the clematis in place.

The Gallica and Centifolia Groups are often horizontal, with twiggy growth that scampers along the ground, layering, suckering, and generally forming thickets wherever such opportunity is allowed. This is especially true if the cultivars in question are not getting enough sun. They cannot support the added weight of an entire clematis vine. For these roses it is best if the mass of the clematis is borne by something else (such as another plant or a structure) or if the clematis is a nonvining type of smaller proportion.

The antique Alba rose *Rosa* 'Madame Legras de St. Germain' throws tall stiff canes into the air. These canes are immediately clothed with many twiggy shoots that like to flow downward and will quickly pull the tall canes down. This rose should be grown with support and then a clematis can be grown into it. This works especially well if the clematis is placed in the ground some distance away so the rose need bear only a couple of feet of flowering clematis stem rather than the entire vine.

Some of the more modern shrub roses, from the 1950s, are also once-blooming, but they have the advantage of modern breeding for more varied colors. *Rosa* 'Alchymist' surely must have been named for its ability to change its open flower color with the prevailing weather. It opens from apricot to gold (some say egg-yolk yellow) and becomes quite strawberry blonde in warming weather. It has a long period of spring bloom on a plant that really should be grown as a small climber. Its stiff canes are best trained while they are young and supple. This rose looks quite smart with any shade of blue or purple clematis.

Also tall and handsome (and exceptionally thorny) is *Rosa* 'Cerise Bouquet'. This rose is aptly named, featuring clusters of cerise flowers, and each stem is indeed a perfect nosegay of bloom. The shocking pink of this rose blends well with blue clematis having strong hues, such as *Clematis* 'Fujimusume' and *C.* 'Perle d'Azur'. In the case of both *R.* 'Alchymist' and *R.* 'Cerise Bouquet', you want to use a clematis that will get big and give enough show to hold its own with its rose. Delicate clematis need not apply.

COMING UP

Garden vignettes can be painted on the largest scale using the very biggest plants. Sometimes we want a mural rather than a miniature. This is why dramatic combinations of climbing roses and clematis are so appealing. Although we have discussed spring-blooming rambling roses, we don't want to leave the repeat-flowering climbing roses behind. Blending them with a clematis that has a long or repeated period of bloom, or mixing several clematis of moderate size and variable timing into a big mature climber, gives sustained climax to the upper layer of the summer garden.

You may well ask the difference between a rambling rose and a climber. Rambling roses are older cultivars or naturally occurring hybrids. Not many ramblers are bred these days. Rambling roses tend to be spring blooming and there are few exceptions to this, although one is the lovely apricot and yellow *Rosa* 'Phyllis Bide'. Rambling roses have very pliable canes. This makes them more versatile for training onto intriguing supports. Rambling roses usually get taller than our modern climbers, with canes averaging 20 ft. in length, while a few can reach 60 ft. (*R.* 'Kiftsgate' leaps to mind). Modern climbers usually reach 12–15 ft. Rambling roses tend to be cluster-flowered, holding myriad smaller blossoms in ready-made bouquets at the end of each year-old branch or sideshoot. Rambling roses have a somewhat limited color palette. Most of the antique ramblers still available to us were bred before the introduction of modern rose colors, such as orange, peach, and vivid stripes and outlines. Rambling roses tend to be hybrids bred (by humans or nature) from species roses with rambling habits, such as *R. wichuriana,* and these species tend to be spring flowering.

Rambling roses need a bit more maintenance than modern climbers to this extent: Ramblers flower best on wood that is one to two years old. Older canes become woody and tired, making them shy to flower. The remedy for this is to remove the current year's blooming canes right after flowering and to encourage the new canes with regular fertilizer and training. Normally, the new canes of rambling roses are emerging and clearly visible when the plant is in bloom. At times the new foliage can even obscure the flowers. Ramblers are so vigorous you can easily take off any of the new shoots that are obscuring your enjoyment of the current season's roses, knowing there will be plenty of new stems left to create the next year's plant once the old wood has been pruned.

Many of the roses we grow as climbers—as opposed to ramblers—are sports from Hybrid Tea and Floribunda cultivars, which have complex and unstable genetics. These plants are created when an astute grower notices that a short rose of shrubby habit is suddenly throwing up long canes in a stock field or display garden. That new longer cane will produce flowers just like the parent plant, but always on long stiff stems. If the long cane is chopped into cuttings to make new plants or has its axillary buds grafted onto an understock, each piece will produce a climbing version of the original shrubby parent. This is how we have come to have *Rosa* 'Climbing Peace', *R.* 'Climbing Playgirl', and *R.* CLIMBING FRAGRANT CLOUD™. The other way to create a modern climber is to cross two climbing roses with each other, creating a new rose flower on a long-caned plant. When named, these climbers will not have the word "climbing" or the abbreviation "Cl." before or after the given name. Examples of created climbers (instead of sported climbers) are *R.* 'Guinée', *R.* 'Lady Waterlow', and *R.* 'Paul's Lemon Pillar'.

Climbing roses are stiff caned and want to grow straight for the stratosphere. These shoots can be trained only while they are young. Attempting to entwine old stems onto a structure results in breakage. Climbing roses that are sports from Hybrid Teas will tend to produce fewer flowers per cane, but these flowers will have the elegant shape and larger head size of a Hybrid Tea rose. Climbing sports from Floribundas will be cluster flowered. Both types will repeat bloom over the entire growing season, either with sparse continuous bloom after a spring crescendo or in waves of bloom produced between brief rests.

It is best to mention now that climbing and rambling roses are not true climbers in the sense of ivy (which has anchoring structures), wisteria (which twines), or clematis (which have wrapping leaf stems). Apart from thorns, long-caned roses have no mechanism to hoist themselves upward. Thorns are easily broken and don't grasp effectively into walls, milled lumber, and tough tree bark. Several popular climbing roses are nearly thornless (*Rosa* 'Zepherine Drouhin', for one). How do

The luminous lavender-blue *Clematis* 'Blue Ravine' tumbles over a pathway with the English Rose *Rosa* 'Leander'. In the author's garden.

they get up? Their habitat (they happen to germinate under a low-branched tree) or the weather (a tall cane is blown over to lean into a nearby tree) or a human helps them (we tie them up).

Climbing and rambling roses are excellent clematis supporters. The roses have lots of twiggy growth for the clematis to grasp. We only need to remember that clematis reach their mature size well before roses do. If your garden plan calls for a climbing rose to be the main support of a clematis, it is wise to plant the rose first and let it gain some ground before planting its partner vine. If both rose and clematis will be held aloft by a stout structure, such as a pergola or an existing large tree, then both the rose and the clematis can be planted into the same hole. Roses need a 2-ft.-by-2-ft. hole to start properly. This seems excessively large, but it is best for the rose over the long length of its life. Clematis like an 18-in.-by-18-in. hole, so a new clematis can easily share a hole with a young rose. The rose will tend to produce deeper roots, and since both rose and clematis like regular water and heavy feeding, there will be no adverse root competition. All the roses in my garden grow in close soil proximity to clematis (it is a small garden and there are lots of each), and I have yet to have a rose complain about cramped roots. Roses are far more likely to complain about loss of sunlight from overhead due to the encroachment of neighboring trees. Sunlight is the best rose fertilizer.

Often climbing roses that have attained a certain age will develop bare legs, that is, an inability to maintain or produce leaves on the lower reaches of their canes. I don't mind this so much, since I like the look of maturity rose trunks give a garden, but some folks do mind. (Probably the same folks who put crushed Styrofoam in vases of flowers to hide the stems—as if no one knew what's holding the flowers above the vase and the stems were somehow indecent.) Clematis easily solve this problem. A large unpruned clematis growing into a tall, naked-from-the-waist-down rose will also develop the same trait, so coverage is best provided by a shorter clematis. Japanese hybridizers have made a point of creating shorter-growing large-flowered hybrids, perfect for this application. Of the several available, 8 ft. or less, I recommend any of these (all are large-flowered hybrids):

LARGE-FLOWERED CLEMATIS, 8 FT. OR LESS

Clematis 'Asao': Bright, mauvy pink flowers, with sepals often having a paler center, even white; early initial bloom in spring. Japan.

Clematis 'Burma Star': Similar in every way to *C.* 'Sano-no-murasaki'. England.

Clematis 'Kakio': Similar to *C.* 'Asao' with larger flowers and brighter color. Japan. Sometimes incorrectly called "Pink Champagne."

Clematis 'Kimiidera': Pale lavender with a darker outline and dark stamens. Japan.

Clematis 'Niobe': A cherished older variety with burgundy-red flowers; likes to bloom at about 5 ft. tall. England.

Clematis 'Red Pearl': Deliciously red. Japan.

Clematis 'Sano-no-murasaki': Dark purple and quite short. Japan.

Clematis 'Toki': A plump-looking flower, in pristine white. Japan.

Clematis 'Tsuzuki': Clean white flowers, more star-shaped than *C.* 'Toki'. Japan.

Clematis 'Yukikomachi': Pale lavender often touched with green, as if not quite ripe. Japan.

It bears repeating that many large-flowered clematis hybrids reaching taller than 5–6 ft. will work as long as you are vigilant with the clippers to keep them blooming at the height you want. Some cultivars will argue with you and may not cooperate.

Certainly many small-flowered hybrids will also be happy to cover rose trunks. Any of the following are good about hanging onto their lower foliage as long as they are kept well watered and protected from sunburn:

SMALL-FLOWERED CLEMATIS THAT KEEP THEIR LOWER FOLIAGE

Clematis 'Étoile Rose': Bright pink with lighter bar. France.

Clematis 'Gravetye Beauty': Brilliant red. England.

Clematis montana 'Jenny Keay': Pale pink double flower, creamier in partial shade. New Zealand.

Some viticellas get too large for this purpose, but good drapers among that group are:

Clematis 'Alba Luxurians': White, with early flowers tipped in green. England.

Clematis 'Emilia Plater': Soft periwinkle blue. Poland.

Clematis 'Margot Koster': A subdued red individually, lovely en masse. England.

Clematis 'Minuet': Charming white flowers outlined and veined in dark pink. France.

SPECIFICALLY SPEAKING

Many species clematis make useful color and texture compositions with roses. I speak here of the roses that came as standard features of our planet as we humans began to garden. They are not plants created by the hand of man to serve some particular function or aesthetic ideal. These are just the roses that were here, in the Northern Hemisphere, from the beginning.

Wild roses tend to show up anywhere, in any habitat. *Rosa rugosa* (called the sea tomato for its giant hips) grows in salt spray and sand along the beaches of Japan and Korea as well as in Mongolia. In the eastern United States is *R. palustris,* with its roots in boggy soil (aptly known as the swamp rose). On the shores of Scotland, *R. spinosissima* (the Scotch briar rose) makes thickets that control erosion. To the east is *R. phoenicia,* a short, twiggy plant of the dry steppes of the Middle East. In China *R. gigantea* covers rocky faces along sub-Himalayan streams, and, yes, it makes a very big, if cold-tender, plant. It is small wonder that these many species combined to make a contorted family tree. Early wandering humans took roses (or at least the seeds) with them as they spread around the globe. We know this because Georgia's state flower, the Cherokee rose (*R. laevigata*), is actually from China, brought to the New World by pioneers who settled in coastal Georgia.

Native roses, and their near hybrids (those hybrids created by simple crosses), make excellent garden plants and have many applications, not the least of which is combining with clematis. In North America alone we have roses in a fine variety of sizes and blooming times from which to choose. We tend to think of wild roses as being early blooming, appearing in their delicate simplicity just a few weeks after the last frost. In fact, by careful selection we can have wild roses in our gardens from April through August, and then we have their hips for autumn interest.

Two of my favorite species are from the American Midwest, *Rosa foliolosa* and *R. setigera.* Although the former is a short, lax shrub and the later is a thumping great rambler, both start blooming on or just before the Fourth of July, making them All-American species indeed!

Rosa setigera, known as the prairie rose, was already in place to welcome settlers as they crossed the plains. Blooming throughout the month of July, the prairie rose has bright pink, single flowers produced in big clusters, followed by trusses of small and brilliantly colored red hips. It has long sinuous canes that meander into trees or lean languorously over a tall fence. In my garden I have combined this rose with the species *Clematis viticella* (the last syllables are pronounced "sella," not "chella," this being a Latin word, not Italian). This clematis is amazingly hardy, considering it comes from the Mediterranean region, and has produced a whole fleet of well-loved cultivars. The species itself is bluish purple, with four sepals in the shape of a nodding pagoda roof. This clematis is in its flowering peak at the same time as *R. setigera. Clematis viticella* forms a broad but lightweight mass of vines and blooms on the newest growth, so hard pruning in the late winter is a must. It is a charming clematis species, and it is no surprise that early hybridizers couldn't resist it.

It took me a bit of research to find a commercial source for *Rosa foliolosa* after seeing it in flower at the Denver Botanic Garden (and thanks to Bill Hoffman of Oregon City, Oregon, for the hot tip!). This Midwest native has large, bright, single flowers of an unusually well-saturated shade of pink. This rose has few thorns and a ferny, fine-textured foliage that complements the relaxed habit of the 4-ft.-by-4-ft. shrub. Because I had seen it growing in a display garden, I knew it would need a peony cage around it to hold the draping canes above the ground, and the cage is completely covered by the summer foliage. This rose blooms throughout July and August, followed by handsome burnished red hips and golden autumn foliage color. Towering over this rose's head is the classic antique purple *Clematis* 'Gipsy Queen'. This large-flowered hybrid can be hard-pruned in the winter so its cascades of grape-jelly-colored flowers can tumble out of its host tree, an ornamental pear. The swags and lateral branches of clematis bloom intensify the pink of the rose as they bloom together.

WORLD TOUR OF SPECIES ROSES

We often forget that prior to around 1790 truly red and bright yellow roses were not available in Europe, existing only in traveler's tales. Until they came west along silk and spice trading routes, species roses of these colors were not obtainable by European and American gardeners and rosarians. Nonetheless, these roses thrived in central Asia and China, and the Chinese had a well-established heritage of rose growing long before the western world understood rose breeding. Many of the species roses still available to gardeners today come from distant locales where they have their own place in myth and legend.

The truly, deeply red *Rosa moyesii* is one of the chief rose treasures to come to us from China. This rose makes a big, vase-shaped shrub of stiff canes, with the plant reaching 10 ft. tall and the canopy expanding as wide. The May and June flowers are single with cheery yellow stamens, and the bees love them. A happy *R. moyesii* will require annual thinning unless you want it to create dense shade. The shape of this rose's orange hips is unusual; they are elongated and pendulous. A red flower with this much self-confidence can be hard to work with, so I have taken the cheater's way out and selected clematis partners for it that bloom before and after the red flowers hold serve. In early spring (March), the cold-hardy *Clematis alpina* 'Odorata', with rich, blue, bell-shaped flowers, is nearly the first clematis to bloom and is just finished when the rose blossoms start to open. I don't notice much "ordorata," but others with more sensitive noses find a light, spicy scent. When *R. moyesii* is through, the viticella form *C.* 'Mrs. T. Lundell' begins her season of lavender flowers with darker purple reverses. This clematis looks not too far removed from *C. viticella* itself and that species could fill the rose just as well.

The rose known as Persian Yellow, *Rosa foetida* 'Persiana', and its single form, *R. foetida,* were instrumental in the creation of modern yellow roses when ancient Crusaders carried them back from the Middle East to Europe. These roses are bright yellow, with a shrubby habit and thorns and stems of dark brown. They prefer dry climates and are fairly cold tolerant. In the Pacific Northwest these roses of historic value tend to get fungal diseases because of our warm and rainy spring and early summer. Disease on these roses should not be a problem in the Southwest or in areas with generally dry weather. Blue or purple clematis look terrific with these spring-blooming roses, especially early-flowering large-flowered hybrids such as *Clematis* 'Daniel Deronda', *C.* 'General Sikorski' (now sometimes called *C.* 'Jadwiga Teresa', incorrectly), and the Wedgwood blue *C.* 'Lady Northcliffe'.

From Europe come the two very fine species, *Rosa eglanteria* (with such synonyms as *R. rubiginosa* and Shakespeare's Eglantine), known as the sweet briar rose, and *R. glauca* (syn. *R. rubrifolia*). Both these roses have their botanical names messed with by the taxonomists and other such pundits with regular frequency. We gardeners seem to be sticking by the names I've shown here.

Rosa eglanteria and several of its offspring have foliage heavily scented with green apple, chief among its many charms. This characteristic is most notable when the new leaves unfurl in the spring, especially on moist mornings. The rest of the season the leaves must be bruised to catch the scent, and the rose's mighty thorns will nip you if you are careless. The single flowers of this wildling have a fine, rich shade of pink and a plump outline. I grow it with *Clematis* 'Victoria', which I only partially prune so there is some overlap between the rose's late flowers and *C.* 'Victoria's' early lavender ones.

Snobby plantsmen grow *Rosa glauca,* even if they shun most other roses. In partial shade the foliage of this rose is steel blue, and this color is highlighted with a red tint in full sun. The small, starry flowers appear in May, and the orange hips swell in August and September. The foliage is eminently blendable with other burgundy-leafed plants. For years I felt there must be a written rule in England that *R. glauca* could be grown only with purple cotinus (smoke bush), such as *Cotinus coggygria* 'Royal Purple'. *Clematis viticella* and any of its cultivars strike a happy balance with this rose, although the rose will need help holding up the big plants like *C.* 'Étoile Violette' and *C.* 'Purpurea Plena Elegans'. The striped large-flowered hybrids can be hard to situate in the garden, but the unusual foliage of this rose seems to mollify harsh contrasts such as might occur with the striped clematis *C.* 'Doctor Ruppel' and *C.* 'Bees' Jubilee'.

Two especially fine species roses from China perform well in a wide range of climates. The first is the showy *Rosa chinensis* 'Mutabilis', which could be an early Chinese garden hybrid rather than a species, but its origins are lost in the mists of time. It was brought out of China in 1932, but it is centuries older than that. This shrub can get 8 ft. tall in warm climates, but will be more dwarfed where hard winters prevail. What is mutable about this rose are its remarkable flowers that open into a single row of petals from apricot-colored buds. This color deepens to pink, then on to salmon, and the petals are deep cerise just before they fall. *Rosa chinensis* 'Mutabilis' is often seen jazzing up hot color borders, and its continuous bloom production means you have a constant array of color. The darkest hue of the old blooms is the color I like best, and I add such rich clematis as *Clematis* 'Kardynal Wyszynski' (you can get away with saying "war-SHIN-ski") or *C.* 'Ernest Markham' with this shade. These clematis will be found in the lists as red, but they are actually dark pink.

The second notable species from China is *Rosa sericea* f. *pteracantha* (also known as *R. omeiensis* f. *pteracantha*—oh my!), another victim of taxonomic indecision. This plant is not grown for the simple, single, white flowers or the delicate foliage that turns yellow in the fall. This rose is grown for its frighteningly large red thorns, which are most pronounced on new growth. I have seen many clematis run into this rose, but my favorite display is found in the Portland, Oregon, garden of Jill

The multicolored *Rosa chinensis* 'Mutabilis' is a perfect host for the Polish large-flowered hybrid *Clematis* 'Kardynal Wyszynski'. They always bloom together energetically. In the author's garden.

Schatz, who has quite brilliantly grown *Clematis* 'Niobe' into her *R. sericea* f. *pteracantha.* This is another plantsmen's rose, and since the thorns are most resplendent on new growth, the tallest canes are typically coppiced in the winter to encourage new shoots. This eliminates the spring display of white flowers, but for those hooked on those thorns (so to speak), the flowers are of no moment.

My favorite species rose to use as an ornamental shrub with multi-season interest is *Rosa roxburghii* f. *normalis,* from China. This rose boasts all the characteristics you might want from a large ornamental shrub to locate in the place of honor in your garden. It flowers in the spring with white to shell pink single blossoms much beloved by bees. The flowers are followed in late July and August by some of the strangest fruit in the rose family, resembling the bristled horse chestnuts

The brilliant mingling of thorn and sepal, *Rosa sericea* f. *pteracantha* with the dark red *Clematis* 'Niobe'. In Jill Schatz's garden in Portland, Oregon.

known as "conkers" by British children. One might also call them "ankle turners," since these solid, 1- to 2-in. hips turn gold and fall to the ground, making walking beneath the rose briefly treacherous. The ferny-textured foliage turns yellow in the fall and in the winter the decorative exfoliating bark adds even more distinction to this paragon of roses. This rose is erect, growing to 10 ft. tall, and could easily be trained as a small tree by removing low-growing limbs. *Rosa roxburghii* f. *normalis* has, bar none, the strongest wood of any rose I have ever met, anywhere. It is easily able to hold up several medium-size clematis at once or to be the intermediary link between a *Clematis montana* form and a taller tree.

In my garden *Rosa roxburghii* f. *normalis* consorts with three different clematis who bloom at three different times. The season starts with *Clematis macropetala* 'Mountaindale' in the Atragene Group, a newly marketed, exceptionally crystalline blue selection of that species. This cultivar has shaggy double bells and in an extended cool spring will still be in flower when the rose blooms. At ground level the grape hyacinth *Muscari armeniacum* 'Valerie Finnis' echoes blue back up at the clematis (another "deck design" revelation). Later in the spring the dusty purple large-flowered hybrid *C.* 'Perrin's Pride' provides interest as the rose hips develop. This clematis is listed in some sources as being in the Viticella Group, but it has too large a flower, with a portly profile, to be very closely related to *C. viticella.* It doesn't attain the girth of the viticellas, but it can be hard-pruned just as they are. *An Illustrated Encyclopedia of Clematis* (Toomey and Leeds 2001) lists the parentage as *C.* 'Jackmanii' × *C.* 'Ville de Lyon', so we shall leave it to the experts to sort it all out. In the meantime, *C.* 'Perrin's Pride' is a fine clematis that should be better known. In my garden it has grown to the street side of its rose, greeting passersby.

Lastly, *Clematis serratifolia* opens its pale yellow bells in late August, giving *Rosa roxburghii* f. *normalis* one last appearance of being oddly in flower just before the end of the growing season. This clematis species has silky seed clusters that lengthen its time of appeal, but they should be removed before they shatter or you will have seedlings *everywhere.*

THE LAST WORD

Where gardeners run into problems with roses is at the crossroads where the exhibition rose grower's mentality collides with the common wishes of gardeners with less ambition for their flowers. There simply isn't enough information available to gardeners about growing roses that don't need constant spraying or that needn't be on a rigid pruning schedule. These kinds of roses—call them landscape roses or shrub roses or what you will—are available by the hundreds and more easy-care cultivars are introduced every year. The joy is the search, and any color combination you can dream of can be realized. It simply takes research and then finding the source for your rose. If we expect of roses the same seasonal versatility we require of other ornamental shrubs, then roses too will join the ranks of woody shrubs that enhance and are enhanced by clematis.

TEN FAVORITE CLEMATIS FOR ROSES

Clematis 'Anita': She has delicate, out-facing, small white flowers produced over a long season with ladylike foliage.

Clematis 'Barbara Dibley': This is a very large, large-flowered hybrid of a particularly carrying pink.

Clematis 'Chalcedony': Poised and densely double, this large-flowered hybrid is crisply ice blue.

Clematis 'Kiri Te Kanawa': This is a very double large-flowered hybrid, dark rich blue when buds develop during hot weather.

Clematis 'Snow Queen': This is an elegant, white large-flowered hybrid with dark anthers.

Clematis tangutica 'Golden Harvest': This small-flowered cultivar has yellow lantern-shaped bells, summer to fall.

Clematis 'Venosa Violacea': Yes, I *do* have a favorite: white with strong purple-burgundy veining to a solid outline.

TEN FAVORITE CLEMATIS FOR ROSES (continued)

Clematis 'Ville de Lyon': This old French large-flowered hybrid is outlined heavily in raspberry red with a paler central brush stroke.

Clematis 'Warszawska Nike': Just say "war-saw knee-kay" and people will know what you're trying to say; a plum-colored large-flowered hybrid that is redder in some climates.

Clematis 'Westerplatte': This is large-flowered hybrid of a particularly throbbing shade of red with a persistent velvet sheen, nonfading.

TEN FAVORITE ROSES FOR CLEMATIS

Rosa 'Betty Prior': A venerable old broad with bright pink, single flowers that fade much less in the sun than that other old tart, *R.* 'Dainty Bess'.

Rosa 'Buff Beauty': This Hybrid Musk is usually grown as a climber, with larger, more double flowers than the rest of its group. They are buff colored, as luck would have it.

Rosa 'Ghisline de Félingonde': Flower clusters open butterscotch to gold, then fade to cream; a climber with clean foliage.

Rosa 'Jacques Cartier': Mid-to-pale pink, very fragrant and very double; repeat flowering and a good size for small gardens.

Rosa 'Leander': A peach-scented rose, peach to apricot in color, for which we are all indebted to Englishman David Austin.

Rosa 'Phyllis Bide': The only repeating rambler, its clusters of yellow-to-apricot flowers are very long-lasting, and then you get more!

Rosa 'Robin Hood': One of the original Hybrid Musk Group, this one produces huge panicles of small cerise flowers on a large, lax shrub; repeats.

Rosa 'Rose de Rescht': Little cerise "cookie-size" double flowers freely produced on a short shrub; repeats.

Rosa 'Sombreuil': This old tea-scented climber is said to be somewhat tender, although I have never seen it anything less than sturdy and productive; aroma of roses blended with peaches on a warm summer morning; very double, creamy white.

Rosa WISE PORTIA™: Fragrant, double, bright mauve flowers (the color of *Geranium sanguineum* 'Dilys' in chapter seven) on a short, bushy plant; repeats.

CHAPTER 5

CLEMATIS WITH WOODY SHRUBS

*E*minent woody plant expert Roger Gossler once said to me upon spying *Clematis* 'Candida' growing into *Magnolia stellata* 'King Rose' in my garden, "Get that darned clematis out of that magnolia!" Happily, I can report that Roger has changed his tune. When I visited his marvel-filled garden recently, he was eager to show me all the clematis he has added to his mixed shrub borders.

It is my sincere belief, and I am not alone in this, that all woody plants were put on Earth to hold up clematis. As gardeners, all we have to do is decide which clematis we want to use with which woody shrubs and trees. We can consider all the options: texture combinations; flowering time of the clematis; background color selections; whether the shrubs should be deciduous or evergreen, broad-leafed or coniferous; and matching mature clematis size with shrub size. The possibilities are unlimited.

We speak of shrubs and trees as the bones of the garden, and this is certainly true of clematis gardens. What a hopeless tangled mass of a mess the garden would be without woody plants to bring order to the chaos. These plants define our spaces by making hedges, anchoring corners, providing riveting specimen plants as focal points, and giving an upper limit to the garden's highest layer. They can provide fragrance and flower just as any other group of plants. The structure of woody plants

We know conifers add much-needed texture to the garden, but they can also add color. This is *Clematis* 'Prince Charles' with *Chamaecyparis obtusa* 'Tetragona Aurea' in the blue-and-yellow garden at Heronswood Nursery, Kingston, Washington.

gives us a variable canvas on which to paint with annuals, herbaceous perennials, and, of course, clematis.

THE CONIFERS

Just because we most often speak of conifers as good background plants doesn't mean they have to be boring walls of unbroken green. Coniferous evergreens are becoming more popular both as bold specimen plants displayed at the center of an island bed or as components of fascinating tapestry hedges where contorted and colorful forms sit cheek by jowl to create a multitextured and multicolored three-dimensional garden feature instead of merely a utilitarian boundary. There is certainly a dwarf conifer coming to a mixed shrub border near you.

Every shade of green is represented by the conifers, from near-black yews (*Taxus ×media* forms) to the pale yellow-green of deodar cedars like 'Cream Puff' (*Cedrus deodora* forms). The contrast of light and dark can be had on the hemlocks *Tsuga canadensis* 'Gentsch White' and 'Summer Snow' (among others) when their white new growth shines against the dark green mature needles. The various Hinoki cedar varieties can be lustrous velvet green to ice blue or vivid gold (*Chamaecyparis obtusa* and *C. pisifera* forms especially).

In England we can see yew hedges used to great advantage. They use *Taxus baccata* 'Fastigiata', the columnar or Irish yew, for this purpose. At famous gardens like Sissinghurst Castle, the greatest share of the garden's structure comes from such hedges, forming long axial alleys, defining the round lawn that divides the rose garden in half, and directing the eye to sculptures that act as focal points around the garden.

In smaller American gardens, hedges are more often created with arborvitae (genus *Thuja*) than with yew. Yew can be a costly initial investment and is slow growing. Arborvitae is inexpensive, and it certainly takes no time at all to make a hedge requiring yearly pruning. It has become commonplace and is quite taken for granted. I find that a tall, sturdy arborvitae hedge is just the thing for the *Clematis montana* clan. The bright, healthy green of the hedge's new growth makes a sprightly combination with either the white or pink cultivars and especially *C. montana* var. *wilsonii*, with hot-cocoa-scented white flowers

Clematis in conifers can be selected for maximum textural contrast. Here the fuzzy
Clematis fusca shows off in *Chamaecyparis obtusa* 'Fernspray Gold' at Collector's
Nursery in Battleground, Washington.

produced in masses two to four weeks later than its other montana relations.

The second benefit of using big clematis in hedges (and I'm speaking of plants you won't need to prune much) is that they act as natural baling wire. Arborvitae will often split apart in snowy or icy weather—indeed even in heavy rain—with tall limbs peeling away from their brethren and hanging akimbo from the vertical plane of the hedge. This is nothing a mature *Clematis montana* form can't control. In my own 40-ft.- long hedge (which is 10 ft. tall), I have *C. montana* var. *wilsonii,* the pink double *C. montana* 'Broughton Star', *C. montana* 'Elizabeth', and *C.* 'Kermesina' (a viticella form). They are joined by *Lonicera* ×*tellmanniana,* a golden orange-flowered, shade-tolerant honeysuckle. All these vines are pruned only when the hedge is pruned and as much as the hedge is pruned. It is a beautiful relationship.

If I had a large garden, I would grow many more *Chamaecyparis* and *Cryptomeria* than the dwarf forms I limit myself to in my urban space. Both these genera of conifers come in many exciting forms and often take on bronze or gold or even purple coloration when exposed to a winter frost. Some of the dwarf cultivars are too small to consort directly with clematis (although the errant draping vine may brush a needled cheek from time to time), but *Cryptomeria japonica* 'Elegans', a feathery-textured tree that turns puce in the winter, will get 75 ft. tall in its native Japan. This form strikes a convenient bargain with the winter-flowering *Clematis cirrhosa* and its cultivars if you live in the enviable climate that gives you enough cold to produce color in the tree but not too much cold to kill this somewhat tender group of clematis. Early and hardy large-flowered hybrids such as *C.* 'Guernsey Cream' (with large, round, creamy flowers), *C.* 'Miss Bateman' (white with dark purple stamens like overly mascaraed eyelashes), or *C.* 'Moonlight' (with palest yellow, narrow-sepalled flowers) open early enough to accent the cryptomeria's color before it makes the transition back to its summer green.

The Hinoki cedar *Chamaecyparis obtusa* 'Blue Feathers' is a particular favorite of mine. This is a slow-growing form with exceptional blue-tinted new growth. The juvenile foliage is bright blue-green. This conifer

The very early flowering, shaggy *Clematis macropetala* 'Jan Lindmark' is contrasted with the dark green of *Chamaecyparis obtusa* 'Nana Gracilis'. In the author's garden.

creates an oasis of cool in the midst of a hot color border, providing not only respite for the eye but also a softer texture foil for such warm-toned clematis as *Clematis* 'Sunset', *C.* 'Monte Cassino', *C.* 'M. Koster' (syn. *C.* 'Margot Koster'), or *C.* 'Brocade'. A similar effect can be achieved with *Chamaecyparis pisifera* 'Curly Tops', with its blue-gray foliage and contorted needles for added textural interest.

Another chamaecyparis to look for is *Chamaecyparis pisifera* 'Golden Mops', the yellow thread-leafed Hinoki cedar. This shrub is vivid yellow when grown in full sun and can be shorn to an appropriate shape or left to wave its branches about like a dowager covered in fringe. The year-round yellow color makes this plant an ideal structural element in a blue-and-yellow harmony border. A mature *Chamaecyparis pisifera* 'Golden Mops' left unpruned will be well complimented by the soft blue, large-flowered hybrids such as *Clematis* 'Fujimusume', *C.* 'Perle d'Azur', *C.* 'Prince Charles', and *C.* 'Will Goodwin'. It should be stressed that *Chamaecyparis pisifera* 'Golden Mops' wants full sun to be truly golden. The shrub will be bright to medium green in partial shade.

The white small-flowered *Clematis* 'Anita' has many virtues. It has a particularly long flowering season and develops its wispy spun-silver seed heads as it continues to bloom. The flowers are delicate and the foliage is lacy in the way that many tangutica cousins of *C.* 'Anita' can be. This is a good clematis to use with a dark green background, such as *Pinus strobus,* or to be seen through the bluer needles of *Abies koreana. Clematis* 'Anita' can be hard-pruned or left alone to attain some height.

We needn't limit ourselves to small conifers. I have already explained about Ernie and Marietta O'Byrne's use of *Clematis* 'Étoile Violette' in a Douglas fir, *Pseudotsuga menziesii* (chapter two), but I want to return to that point. If the host plant for your clematis is sufficiently muscular and the clematis needs to grow large to be in scale, then don't prune it. If your home is on a hill and your garden flows down a gentle slope, you may find you can let clematis attain their mature size so that—as the theater crowd says—they play to the back of the house (literally). Sometimes the common pruning wisdom just isn't practical.

WELCOME TO RHODY WORLD

It never ceases to amaze me—the bad plant habits a gardener will put up with simply because the plant is evergreen. There are rhododendrons everywhere in my hometown and therefore you can see them misbehaving and poorly grown anywhere in the city. The large trusses of bloom, which last only three weeks in a good year, are easily fried by unseasonably warm weather (a particular 90-degree April 29th leaps to mind). The trusses are often spoiled by excessive rain, which turns the crisp

There is no reason for the spring garden's colors to be pastel and muted. Here *Rhododendron* 'Leo' is enlivened by *Clematis* 'Bees' Jubilee'. In Mike Snyder's garden, Beaverton, Oregon.

bells into sodden brown blobs of mush. For the rest of the year, rhodies are green, and although there are a precious few with intriguing foliage (the purple-leafed *Rhododendron* 'Ebony Pearl' is notable), the common hybrids are simply big green lumps, usually found around house foundations where they can look very unhappy because of the lime leaching into the soil from the concrete, raising the pH too high for them. This simplicity, this boredom-inducing monotony, makes just the sort of situation in which clematis can be shown to their best advantage.

Allowing a summer-flowering large-flowered hybrid or species hybrid clematis to romp over the top of them will not hurt your rhodies in the least. In the fall, when the vine becomes dormant, simply cut the clematis to about 1–2 ft. tall, just above a large leaf node, and roll the detached vine off your shrub like taking a comforter off your bed. The rhododendron will go on about its business, forming flower buds through the fall and winter, and will bloom at its normal time.

It is certainly possible to select a clematis that will bloom with a rhododendron, and the early atragenes make an interesting blossom texture foil for the big bells of most rhodies. The colors of the *Clematis alpina* and *C. macropetala* hybrids are delicate and some rhodies scream, so your color choices will take some thought. Although we often mistakenly read that this group of clematis should never be pruned, quite the opposite is true, and the best time to groom them is right after they flower when 3–4 ft. of vine (or more if you've got a tangle) can be removed at the same time you are deadheading your rhody.

With May- and June-flowering rhododendrons, repeat-flowering large-flowered hybrid clematis will bloom as companions for your shrub, then give a late-summer to autumn display to liven up an otherwise stagnant space in the garden. Like the atragenes, these clematis can be groomed immediately after blooming—or even just deadheaded—and given some fertilizer and they will start preparing their next display.

BROAD-LEAFED EVERGREENS

Of course, rhodies are not the only broad-leafed evergreens to be complimented by clematis. Gardeners in USDA Zone 7b and above, with a Mediterranean climate defined by dry summers, should try the numerous

You can decide if you want a clematis that blooms with your rhododendron or occupies its space later in the season. Here is *Clematis* 'Floralia' at Catswalk, the garden of Joanne Thomas, Portland, Oregon.

pittosporum forms coming onto the market. Where summers are hot, these will want partial shade. I can personally recommend *Pittosporum tenuifolium* 'Purpurea', with shiny purple-brown foliage. This shrub is delicate in texture but can grow to 10 ft. tall, easily pruned to stay a bit shorter. The new foliage is chartreuse, lighting up the older leaves and black twigs. The whole will be dark by midsummer. When the new foliage starts to develop purple spots, fear not. This is simply the transition to the glossy near-black phase.

As I said, this shrub is dainty, with slender branches, so it won't manage a heavy clematis well. However, such refined clematis as *Clematis* 'Brunette', *C.* 'Betina' (now called *C.* 'Red Beetroot Beauty' officially, but we can ignore the new name if we all agree we like 'Betina' better), *C. ianthina* var. *ianthina,* and *C. pitcherii* will not be too hefty. All the clematis mentioned have dark chestnut-to-purple bell-shaped flowers that will be in proper proportion to the leaves of this charming pittosporum and thus make a subtle monochromatic display. And just so you know, this pittosporum makes a long-lasting cut foliage.

The bay laurel (*Laurus nobilis*) and its California relative (*Umbellularia californica*) are of an unusual, off-beat shade of yellowish green. This peculiar color makes a great background for striking red clematis such as *Clematis texensis* and its hybrids, perhaps *C.* 'Gravetye Beauty' or *C.* 'Sir Trevor Lawrence'. Colors that work well with the true laurel must be of strong hue. Weak colors against the drab green are simply lost. In my bay laurel I have the early large-flowered hybrid *C.* 'Mrs. N. Thompson', her brilliant purple sepals drawn with a vivid cerise bar. Later in the season *C.* 'Princess Diana', an intensely pink texensis form, blooms with the tulip shape characteristic of the near hybrids of her texensis parent. *Laurus nobilis* is a shrub that is often seen in herb gardens because of its aromatic and culinary uses. It is another Mediterranean plant wanting a hot summer, good winter drainage, and shelter from cold and drying winter winds. When mine was young I used to wrap it with bubble wrap—a lovely sight in the winter! It has outgrown the need for swaddling.

Well worth inclusion in this mélange of leafy evergreen shrubs is *Loropetalum chinense* and its named forms. This is the Chinese witch hazel, and indeed its flowers do bear a strong resemblance to the hamamelis tribe, but the loropetalums bloom a bit later in spring. The frazzled flowers of the species are white and the foliage is green. The flashiest named forms, *L. chinense* 'Plum Delight' and *L. chinense* RAZZLEBERRI™ have purple foliage and shocking magenta flowers. Hardy to USDA Zone 7, these shrubs appreciate partial shade in hot summer. The best-grown specimens I have seen were in dappled shade from deciduous trees overhead at the Memphis Botanical Garden, giving them full sun in early spring when they bloom. Only the earliest clematis would flower when these shrubs do, such as *Clematis alpina* 'Constance', who is roughly the same color but more subtle. If subtlety is not your forte, the brighter *C. sibirica* 'Riga' is your option. Not yet common in the trade, *C. sibirica* 'Riga' is creamy with a cerise eye where the flower stem attaches to the blossom. It is well worth looking for.

The purple foliage of the named forms of *Loropetalum* gives the gardener food for the imagination. After the flowers have gone, the shrub,

Clematis macropetala 'Pink Flamingo' reaches for a dance partner, *Loropetalum chinense* RAZZLEBERRI™. In the author's garden.

which gets 5 ft. tall by 5 ft. wide (larger in warmer southern climates) and is somewhat twiggy and lax, will serve as a challenging companion for shorter clematis in white, lavender, red, or pink. In late April, my *Clematis macropetala* 'Pink Flamingo' likes to loll out of its tree and tease the leaves of this shrub. The purple-leafed loropetalums are particularly effective at enhancing the pajama-striped clematis such as *C.* 'Nelly Moser', *C.* 'Lincoln Star', or *C.* 'Bees' Jubilee'. These clematis flower well in partial shade and hold their color better there than if grown in full sun.

DECIDEDLY DECIDUOUS

My garden, and my clematis, would be much the poorer without the many deciduous shrubs and small trees I use for structure, flower, fruit, and fragrance. In a larger garden I would collect *Philadelphus* (mock orange) like a mad woman; its fragrance intoxicates me. The same could be said for *Syringa* (lilac). These plants deserve pride of place, even though their blooming season is relatively short.

The earliest genera to bloom in winter gardens are the hamamelis (witch hazels) and the viburnums. If you live where the cultivars of the clematis species *Clematis cirrhosa* are not tender (USDA Zone 8 and above), you can arrange to have a clematis bloom with *Viburnum ×bodnantense* 'Dawn' (imagine it with the aptly named *C. cirrhosa* 'Wisley Cream') or red-flowered *Hamamelis ×intermedia* 'Diane' (try it with *C. cirrhosa* var. *balearica*).

Once the hamamelis are through blooming, usually early March, their leaves appear, and the handsome vase shape of these majestic shrubs can be further decorated with an atragene selection to provide color well into May. A mature witch hazel can easily bench-press several clematis to provide a succession of bloom with, for instance, a *Clematis alpina* form followed by a *viticella* form, perhaps the powder blue *C.* 'Emilia Plater' with an elegant *C. tangutica* cultivar such as 'Bill MacKenzie' or 'Golden Tiara' bringing charming touches of gold and silk to the colorful brocade of witch hazel autumn leaf color.

How much fun can one gardener have with just two plants? Lucy Hardiman explores the possibilities with an out-of-bloom witch hazel (*Hamamelis ×intermedia* 'Arnold Promise') and *Clematis alpina* 'Constance'.

VA-VA-VIBURNUM

There are many, many viburnums from which to choose. These can be selected from a whole menu of characteristics. Once your choice is made—a composite of time of bloom, fragrance, fruit production, mature shrub size, among other options—you will have the fun of selecting just the right clematis to match your viburnum. A favorite form of mine, the common *Viburnum tinus* (formerly called *Laurus tinus*) has become boring to shrub collectors, but it is a plant of many virtues and therefore many uses. This particular species is evergreen, carries little nosegays of slightly fragrant pale-pink-to-white florets in early spring, has clusters of metallic blue berries that are often on the shrub when the new flowers open, and can be pruned to make it a key element in a tapestry hedge. The easiest cultivar to find is *V. tinus* 'Spring Bouquet'. The variegated form, as luck would have it, is called *V. tinus* 'Bewley's Variegated'. The variegated form is more compact than the plain green. Any medium-to-small-size clematis will mingle effectively with *V. tinus*. The dark purple large-flowered hybrids, such as *Clematis* 'Edomurasaki', *C.* 'Lady Betty Balfour', *C.* 'Romantika', *C.* 'Viola', and *C.* 'Rhapsody', are especially effective with the variegated form. Truth to tell, my eyes see *C.* 'Rhapsody' as distinctly bright blue rather than purple.

The Korean spice viburnum, *Viburnum carlesii,* has a thrilling fragrance redolent of cloves and heirloom garden carnations. This plant and the remaining viburnums I will mention are deciduous. *Viburnum carlesii* makes a large shrub that should not be pruned, thus avoiding excessive and awkward new growth. Let this shrub attain its full size at its own pace. This deciduous viburnum will get 10 ft. tall and slightly less wide and should be halfway to those proportions before a clematis is added to the mix. This shrub blooms when the alpinas and macropetalas bloom and makes an admirable partner for them. Newer clematis cultivars such as *Clematis macropetala* 'Purple Spider' (a flower well described by its name) and the clear blue *C. alpina* 'Frances Rivis' would be perfect choices to escort the dense clusters of bright white flowers of the shrub.

A dwarf form of Korean spice viburnum is *Viburnum carlesii* 'Compactum'. Another dwarf viburnum that I grow for fruit rather than flower is *V. opulus* 'Compactum', with its radiant clusters of Chinese-red berries that add so much to my hot-colored border in the fall. This shrub loses its leaves early, highlighting the remaining berries still further. Late-blooming small- and large-flowered clematis find their way into this shrub and a particularly glaring, yet somehow likable, combination is the second wave of flower from the Polish introduction *Clematis* 'Warszawska Nike'. This large-flowered hybrid has glowing plum-colored flowers (redder in some climates), making a challenging partner with the orange-to-red shiny berries of this viburnum. They make a nice wake-up call on a crisp Indian summer morning.

This isn't meant to be a comprehensive guide to viburnums, but there are a few more selections that are hard to resist. Called "guilder rose" by the British, the snowball viburnum, *Viburnum opulus* 'Roseum' is a huge shrub, noticeable while in bloom covered with 3- to 4-in. balls of creamy

Large-flowered *Clematis* 'Lord Nevill' makes a plump and comely mate for *Viburnum opulus* 'Roseum'. In Mike Snyder's garden in Beaverton, Oregon.

florets, a blizzard when these thick spheres shatter to the ground. A stout old snowball viburnum, such as you might inherit when buying an old house and garden, will reach 10–12 ft. tall, with a canopy as wide. Trunks emerging from the ground will be as thick as your upper arm or more. This crown of stems could easily be 3 or 4 ft. wide at the ground level. If sufficient inroads can be made into the soil near the crown, plant any early large-flowered hybrid to make an admirable marriage with the shrub. Earlier clematis forms will bloom with the viburnum, later- and repeat-flowering selections will occupy the green space later in the season.

Many a spring landscape, especially in public plantings and large gardens, will boast a few of the doublefile viburnums—with their ranks of paired white blossoms like *Viburnum plicatum* var. *tomentosum*. Although this viburnum is a true herald of spring, these are monotonous shrubs through the summer until they start to show the colors of their fall fruit and foliage. All the Viticella Group will bloom at just the right time to enliven the summer doldrums for you. Any clematis showing

At Kinzy Faire in Estacada, Oregon, the richly purple *Clematis* 'Sano-no-murasaki' is combined with May-blooming viburnum.

some white in its flowers, such as the viticella forms *Clematis* 'Minuet', *C.* 'Tango', and *C.* 'Venosa Violacea' will refresh the vast expanse of the doublefile viburnum that is taking a siesta.

THE BOYS OF SUMMER

Although spring, with all its possibilities, is my favorite season, I have come to appreciate the summer-flowering shrubs all the more for carrying us into autumn thoroughly entertained. Some of these gems routinely fall in and out of fashion, such as the hydrangeas and fuchsias do, and others, like the hypericums, are only now being explored.

That florists have taken to using hydrangeas as cut flowers in a big way attests to their beauty, range of color, and longevity even when disconnected from their plant. On the plant the buns of florets on a mophead will last for three to four months, in most cases gradually changing colors all the while. The Japanese have created delicate double-flowered lacecap forms (from the species *Hydrangea serrata*) that are slowly making their way into the American market and have everyone panting after them. The mopheads (*H. macrophylla* var. *hortensis* forms) are the old showgirls, flouncing around the foundation of your grandmother's house in their vivid colors, the hues easily manipulated by gardeners adept with aluminum sulfate (to produce blue flowers) and lime (to produce pink). The lacecaps (*H. macrophylla* var. *normalis*), although not so baroque as the hortensias, are perhaps more in scale—both in plant size and floral volume—with smaller urban gardens. It is all a matching game, and hydrangeas have something for everyone. There are even small forms for the container garden, such as *H. macrophylla* 'Todi' and *H. macrophylla* 'Pia' (both varying shades of pink). *Hydrangea macrophylla* 'Pia' takes a long time, several years, to reach its 3-ft. mature size.

Just as we combine the most buxom roses with the most comely clematis, there is nothing like a large-flowered hybrid to enhance a chesty mophead hydrangea. Because many hydrangeas prefer partial shade, the softer-colored clematis with curvy textures are the ones I choose to escort their blowzy heads. These are the clematis with colors that might bleach to white if given a southern, full sun exposure. *Clematis* 'Nelly Moser'–type striped flowers appreciate this treatment and will produce their second wave of bloom when the hydrangeas are at their full glory. Other clematis cultivars to try with partial-shade-planted hydrangeas are C. CLAIRE DE LUNE™ (creamy white with a lavender-blue edge), C. 'Silver Moon' (well-named with luminous gray-lavender flowers), C. 'Peveril Pearl' (a big flower, soft lavender with quiet touches of pink and rose), C. 'Lady Northcliffe' (Wedgwood blue and plump), C. 'King Edward VII' (pink stippled with lavender), or the exquisitely iridescent C. 'Blue Ravine'.

Although subtlety is not my long suit, I do like to combine clematis of more refinement with the lacecap hydrangeas. Here is an ideal use for petite small-flowered species hybrids. We need to remember, however, that although a clematis has diminutive flowers, the vine may eventually become a brute; research is key here. Some sort of speed bump, like an out-of-bloom broad-leafed evergreen, may be necessary to slow down the approach of a rampant clematis, so that only the flowering branch ends reach the lacecap hydrangea you've chosen. This type of hydrangea tends to be of shorter stature than the bigger mopheads, but of course there are exceptions to this. (The variegated form of *Hydrangea macrophylla* 'Mariesii Variegata' gets massive.) Such *H. macrophylla* cultivars as 'Blaumeise' (which can be intensely blue) and 'Taube' (which wants to be pink) as well as *H. serrata* 'Bluebird' (which has the lacecap form) can be combined with clematis such as *Clematis* 'Duchess of Albany' (tulip-shaped and pink), C. 'Helios' (yellow lanterns with a flip hairdo), or C. *pitcherii* (silvery purple urns with plush purple interiors) to produce mannered partnerships that invite closer inspection. This delicate detailing adds a welcome sense of introspection to a garden and reveals greater depths of creativity in the designing gardener.

Anyone can be splashy, but elegance takes forethought.

In my garden the hardy fuchsias are staging a slow coup d'état. As the garden matures and woody shrubs and small trees begin to create more shade, my beloved roses become wan, and I have been replacing them with hardy fuchsias. You cannot kill a clematis with shade, but you can sentence a rose to a slow death if it doesn't get its daily dose of direct sun. The hardy fuchsias revel in partial shade and take over the clematis-lifting from the departed roses. *Fuchsia magellanica* is the typical

Hydrangea macrophylla 'Mariesii Variegata' makes a loaded-with-lace partnership with *Clematis ×jouiniana* 'Praecox'. In the author's garden.

species you see, with its dancing-lady flowers having a body and over-skirt of red and an underskirt of purple. A similar cultivar with bigger flowers is *F.* 'Pat's Dream' and there is a form with tinier flowers called *F.* 'David'.

In partial shade *Fuchsia* 'Pat's Dream' flowers through the whole summer with *Clematis* 'Arabella' providing occasional counterpoint. In the author's garden.

Plant breeders are creating more striking variations on this theme, so watch for foliage variations and variegations. A favorite of mine, first seen in the garden at Kiftsgate near Hidcote in the English Cotswold District, is the variegated *Fuchsia magellanica* var. *molinae* 'Sharpitor'. This selection comes in two forms. *Fuchsia magellanica* var. *molinae* 'Sharpitor' is understood to have small gray-green leaves edged in white, while *F. magellanica* var. *molinae* 'Golden Sharpitor' (sometimes seen as 'Sharpitor Aurea') has a distinctly yellow outline. The flowers on both of these are pale pink, and the whole picture of either form in bloom will add sparkle to dappled shade in late summer.

Other variegated forms include the more colorful *Fuchsia magellanica* var. *gracilis* 'Variegata' that adds a random touch of pink to its gray-green and white leaves, with flowers like the straight species. The most striking leaf form is that of *F. magellanica* var. *gracilis* 'Aurea', with bright golden leaves carried on red stems—an arresting combination for the hot color border. *Fuchsia magellanica* var. *gracilis* 'Aurea' can stay smaller (3 ft. by 3 ft.), but I have seen plants get bigger than printed specifications suggest. If only plants could read.

Older, mature hardy fuchsias can easily manage small- to medium-length clematis (up to 12 ft.), but clematis needing hard pruning are preferred because even the hardiest fuchsias may loose a bit of height after a cold winter and may need some early spring shaping. This is more easily accomplished if the clematis is simply cut back to the lowest developing buds before making the fuchsia presentable for the coming summer season by removing its deadwood. This caveat still leaves us with lots of clematis options, including the viticellas, the texensis, the summer-blooming large-flowered hybrids, the tanguticas, and those fascinating North Americans, *Clematis crispa, C. pitcherii,* and *C. viorna.*

The one problem with recommending hardy fuchsias is that they are hardy only to USDA Zone 7. As a group, they love coastal gardens with mild temperatures enabling them to handle full sun if given sufficient water. If you live in such an idyllic circumstance, the fuchsias will grow happily with clematis as long as the clematis don't get too large and the soil isn't completely sandy.

All hypericums (the St. John's worts) have yellow flowers, and not all of them are voracious ground covers that you're sorry you've planted the minute you've done it. Larger shrubby forms make excellent garden plants, with a long period of bright yellow flowers, often followed by exceptionally fine fruit. The foliage of these taller shrubs (most will achieve 5 ft. in height and spread) varies with the cultivar chosen. As a clematis gardener, you have the option of working with the simple yellow flowers, the foliage color, and the autumn berries as you select your clematis.

If you just want large (to 3 in. wide) yellow flowers produced over most of the summer, look for *Hypericum forrestii.* I marvel at the amount of substance the flowers of this hybrid have. This shrub blooms for two months starting in late spring, takes a brief rest while I prune it modestly if it has gotten beyond itself, and will then flower well into the autumn.

The second bloom cycle for *Clematis* 'Allanah' makes an autumn combination with *Hypericum* ×*inodorum* 'Elstead'. In the author's garden.

In my garden it has formed a handsome monochromatic trio with the English Rose *Rosa* 'Symphony' (but *R*. THE PILGRIM™, *R*. HAPPY CHILD™, or *R*. GOLDEN CELEBRATION™, all of them English, would do just as well) and the petite tangutica form *Clematis* 'Helios'.

The foliage of these larger hypericums has been selected for interesting color variations. Widely grown, but not without its flaws, is *Hypericum androsaemum* 'Albury Purple' (sometimes mislabeled "Aubury Purple"), with intensely purple new growth. The color persists for about two months before turning dark, dull green, and the small yellow flowers are followed by clusters of shiny brown-to-purple fruit (oval and up to ½ in. long). The drawback to *H. androsaemum* 'Albury Purple' is its tendency to attract rust diseases in climates with summer rain or humidity. Young plants do not seem as bothered as much as plants four to five years old. If you don't mind replacing *H. androsaemum* 'Albury Purple' from time to time, its rich foliage makes a striking partner for red clematis that tend toward the claret shades, such as *Clematis* 'Niobe' and *C*. 'Westerplatte', which will bloom early enough to take good advantage of the purple-burgundy foliage of the shrub.

The showiest variegation appears on *Hypericum androsaemum* 'Glacier' (3–4 ft. wide and tall), with its scattered splatters of white and cream over a bright green leaf. The foliage will sunburn if grown in full sun without sufficient water. In late summer and fall this form has bright red fruits. When combining this plant with clematis, be sure to look for vines whose flowers are a solid color. With such busy foliage variegation, a striped clematis with this cultivar would cross your eyes!

Plants with chartreuse foliage continue to grow in popularity, and *Hypericum* ×*inodorum* 'Summergold' is a shrub to look for. Its new foliage is sunny yellow with lime-green brush strokes, looking like yellow covered by a sheer wash of green. It does flower and its fruits are unprepossessing, so to prolong the showiness of the new foliage, I prune the plant slightly when the leaves start to turn a duller green in mid- to late June. This incites another round of new growth of blinking brightness. Clematis in any shade of purple or blue will be well enhanced by *H.* ×*inodorum* 'Summergold'.

TREES FOR SMALL GARDENS

It would be remiss of me not to mention at least a few trees that are happy conspirators with clematis. Fruit trees, both functional and ornamental, have long been used to house roses and clematis, honeysuckles and other vines. Fruit trees are not for everyone, however, and folks with small gardens sometimes avoid them as being too much trouble.

I am not one of those folks. My garden contains, among other trees, two apples and two sweet cherries. Each apple has three clematis, and each cherry has one—but that could easily change. In addition to the fruit trees, we should mention a couple of ornamental trees that ought to be more popular, *Styrax japonica* (Japanese snowbell) and *Halesia tetraptera* (formerly *H. carolina,* the Carolina silverbell).

Both these trees stay rather small for a tree and both have delicate white bell flowers produced in the spring (although the Carolina silverbell is earlier). Both perform well in a wide range of climates. They produce light or dappled shade and can be used at woodland edges in larger gardens. The styrax has the added advantages of a delightful scent and a particularly graceful form at maturity (20 ft. or so). I have paired mine with the pale blue large-flowered hybrid *Clematis* 'Will Goodwin', which blooms in May with the styrax, as well as the later-flowering *C.* 'Star of India', which is a rich violet-purple adorned with a slight red bar. (The bar is sometimes more impressionistic than actual.) My silverbell blooms in April in partnership with *C. montana* 'Tetrarose', but you want to be sure your halesia has much of its growth (to 25 ft., with a rounder canopy than the styrax) before planting a largish clematis such as this. To keep the halesia happy, you will have to prune *C. montana* 'Tetrarose' right after it blooms. Later in the spring, and again in August or so, *C.* 'Nadezhda', a dusty pink-barred large-flowered hybrid, adds more color to my Carolina silverbell. *Clematis* LIBERATION™ is similar to *C.* 'Nadezhda' in both color and habit and may be easier to find.

In many parts of the country, the crape myrtles (genus *Lagerstroemia*) are the dominant small ornamental tree, and they get overlooked where they are common. In the Pacific Northwest at the edge of their hardiness range, we treasure them but have a devil of a time getting them to bloom during a mild summer. Crape myrtles do want their heat and sunshine, and I think that in cool summer areas they benefit from having a vine that requires regular feeding grown into them, so the consistent application of fertilizer reminds them to bloom.

Crape myrtles can be pruned to become small trees or they can be multitrunked shrubs. In either case they are quite twiggy and very strong, well able to provide stability for more than one clematis at a time. It is easy to be fooled into thinking your crape myrtle is sick or dead because the new foliage—which is briefly bronze in some cultivars—emerges later than we think it should. An early-flowering clematis will fill the spring void. I use *Clematis montana* 'Freda', the darkest pink of that group, for this very purpose. I follow *C. montana* 'Freda' with the summer-blooming large-flowered hybrid *C.* 'Madame Grangé', a red-to-plum large-flowered hybrid, which—in my usual rebellious fashion—I rarely prune, so that lengths of blooming clematis branches will glide down the face of the crape myrtle for summer interest. *Clematis* 'Madame Grangé' has boat-shaped sepals with rolled-up edges revealing a handsome gray underside until the flower flattens at maturity. The young flowers give a two-toned appearance, very appealing as they float in the summer breeze.

Once a crape myrtle gains some height (mine is now 15 ft. tall after 10 years), it can hold up a sweet autumn clematis (*Clematis terniflora*) to bloom when the crape myrtle does. This clematis should be hard-pruned once it becomes dormant in the late autumn. To leave it unshorn is to invite the sinking of any small tree under it. The sweet autumn clematis is rumored to be somewhat invasive in the southeastern United States, so care should be taken when growing it there that it not go to seed. Of course, in that climate, where crape myrtles bloom all summer, the range of clematis that will bloom when the crape myrtle does is much broader, so why chose a vine that might be dangerous?

RANDOM SHRUBS

There are just too many great woody shrubs to try to cover them all, but here are a few more favorites that I haven't mentioned yet. Rather than make an extensive list of their habits, I will confine myself to describing select examples of shrubs and the clematis that work with them. Some of these suggestions are from my garden and some are from gardens I visit often and with which I am well acquainted.

At Kinzy Faire a secret garden hides the lovely pond you hear throughout the oldest part of the garden. As you sit facing the pond in the armchairs provided for the purpose, to your back is a warming swathe of woody shrubs and perennials in shades of red—either foliage or flowers. The red-leafed barberry *Berberis thunbergii* 'Rosy Glow' is prominent among the other shrubs, and winding through it is the large-flowered hybrid *Clematis* 'Lincoln Star'. This clematis has two long bloom periods, and the pale, pearly pink flowers with their dusty rose bar are larger and more pointed in the spring. In the fall the flowers are plump and rounded in appearance, although smaller in overall diameter. In the spring such perennials as daylilies (genus *Hemerocallis*) and *Anthriscus sylvestris* 'Ravenswing' round out the red display. In September hardy fuchsias and hydrangeas apply additional rouge.

At Kinzy Faire in Estacada, Oregon, *Clematis* 'Lincoln Star' figures in both spring and fall color stories. In the fall the main partner is *Berberis thunbergii* 'Rosy Glow' and in the spring the handsome filler *Anthriscus sylvestris* 'Ravenswing' joins them.

In western Oregon and Washington we are blessed with the fabulous native vine maple (*Acer circinatum*), which proclaims the arrival of autumn with a shocking color pageant, the first of the natives to adorn itself in orange, scarlet, and magenta. It makes a versatile garden plant, grown as a shrub with multiple trunks or treated as a small tree. Vine maple can, however, seem a bit boring in the spring and summer, so we can take a lesson from the Royal Botanic Gardens, Kew, England, to combine this maple with the engaging *Clematis koreana*. This clematis is not terribly large, and its bell-shaped flowers are in scale with the leaves of the *Acer*. Named hybrids of *C. koreana,* such as *C.* 'Brunette' and *C.* 'Betina' (which has that new name we don't like, 'Red Beetroot Beauty') might be too dark for this purpose, getting lost in the foliage. Pinker-flowered atragenes, such as *C. macropetala* 'Markham's Pink', *C. alpina* 'Jacqueline du Pré', *C. alpina* 'Willy', *C. macropetala* 'Alborosea', and *C. macropetala* 'Pink Flamingo', would also be good choices with the fresh green foliage of this shrub.

In the pink: *Clematis* 'Duchess of Albany' blooms with *Buddleja* 'Pink Delight'. In the author's garden.

Gardeners like buddlejas (butterfly bushes) for many reasons, not the least of which is the wide range of color, their attractiveness to butterflies and bees, and the heavy honey scent of many of the forms. This genus is another of the summer-blooming shrubs we look to for brightening the upper layer of the garden in July and August, and deadheading them keeps the show going. It is as if the *Clematis texensis* hybrids were bred specifically to compliment buddlejas, especially *C.* 'Duchess of Albany' (the same shade as *Buddleja* 'Pink Delight') and *C.* 'Gravetye Beauty' (the molten red is a perfect contrast for *B.* 'Black Night' or *B.* 'Plum Purple'). This is garden showmanship at its finest, and everyone can get hard-pruned at the same time in late winter.

The dogwoods (genus *Cornus*) are grown everywhere, and justifiably so. This is a multifaceted group of plants, including plenty of dramatic variegation, flower, and fruit options and variations in size and usage. The bright blonde variegation of the recent introduction *Cornus sericea* 'Hedgerows Gold', from Hedgerows Nursery in McMinnville, Oregon, has attracted many fans. It is a delightful host to richly purple clematis such as *Clematis* 'Viola' and *C.* 'Romantika' or the dustier purple of *C.* 'Perrin's Pride', any of which can be hard-pruned (or not). In the O'Byrne garden in Eugene, Oregon, the shrubby habit of *Cornus mas* 'Variegata' is paired with *Clematis* 'Viola', a large-flowered hybrid with a long period of bloom.

THE LAST WORD

And speaking of the O'Byrnes' *Cornus mas* 'Variegata', standing next to it is a winged euonymous that has ceased to thrive. Even in death this once stately shrub provides an admirable structure for *Clematis viorna,* an aristocratic North American native species. In my own garden a native snowberry (*Symphoricarpos albus*) lives on only in the occasional sucker that appears 3–5 ft. away from the original plant, which for unknown reasons has grown tired of life. Nonetheless, the snowberry still provides a jungle gym for the early-flowering, purple-skirted *Clematis* 'Pruinina' (from *C. fauriei* × *C. sibirica*).

If a shrub dies, it has not necessarily lost its primary function—to lift clematis to new heights.

Variegated shrub foliage is one of the best accents for dark-flowered clematis. Here we see *Clematis* 'Viola' with *Cornus mas* 'Variegata' at Northwest Garden Nursery in Eugene, Oregon.

TEN CLEMATIS THAT LOVE SHRUBS

Clematis 'Candida': This white large-flowered hybrid is especially adept at making magnolias appear to be in bloom when they are not.

Clematis chiisanensis 'Lemon Bells': Two-inch-long ridged yellow bells with nutmeg dusted on their shoulders make this a handsome addition to out-of-bloom rhodies.

Clematis 'Duchess of Edinburgh': This large-flowered hybrid has tight, extra-double white flowers sometimes as thick as they are round; reliable once established and grand against a yew or other dark green host.

Clematis 'Étoile de Paris': This blue-lavender large-flowered hybrid is snazzy with any shade of hydrangea when the clematis reblooms in the summer.

Clematis 'Étoile Violette': If you look up the phrase "tall, dark, and handsome" in a lexicon, you will find a picture of this clematis. Like a classic string of pearls, it goes with everything.

Clematis 'Fujimusume': A blue large-flowered hybrid of singular beauty when combined with yellow-foliaged woody shrubs whether leafy or coniferous—makes even gold-dust plant, *Aucuba japonica* 'Variegata', look downright exotic.

Clematis 'Gravetye Beauty': Some say this is the truest red clematis; tulip-shaped flowers that open flat as they age.

Clematis 'Hagley Hybrid': A large-flowered hybrid that is reliable, versatile as to pruning, and compact, this plant is still the best pink cultivar readily available, remaining popular since its introduction in 1956.

Clematis macropetala and its newly named selection 'Mountaindale': The species is blue with purple tints, the named form is unclouded azure.

Clematis 'Purpurea Plena Elegans': Buoyant little pom-poms of dusty rose—they simply are *not* purple—are prolifically produced on a big vine that should be hard-pruned annually; excellent partner for beauty berries, genus *Callicarpa*.

This is what happens when favorites collide: *Clematis alpina* 'Pamela Jackman' with the only striped-flowered lilac, *Syringa vulgaris* 'Sensation'. In the author's garden.

CHAPTER 6

THE HERBACEOUS CLEMATIS

*I*t has been to hard to hold myself back from discussing this wonderful group of plants before now, but I feel they are especially deserving of their own chapter. Because my first pang of desire for clematis was sparked by that preeminent herbaceous species, *Clematis integrifolia,* it is impossible for me to be anything less than wildly enthusiastic when discussing these diminutive cousins of the large-flowered hybrids. If you are truly desperate to grow more clematis, these plants will give you a whole new range of options. Having a small garden needn't hinder you from growing the many herbaceous cultivars. They fit everywhere.

Gardeners new to the clematis world often have their heads turned by the outrageous flash and glamour of the large-flowered hybrids, and it is hard to convince them that the herbaceous perennial clematis are the best place for the beginner to start with the genus. These plants are absolutely foolproof. You dig a hole, amend it with some good organic matter, put the herbaceous clematis in, water and fertilize, and stand back to watch a successful plant in action. Slap a couple of sturdy shrubs on either side, maybe a ground cover in front, and you've got a great composition.

There are relatively few gardenworthy herbaceous perennial species and related cultivars of clematis compared to the volume of large-flowered hybrids on the market. This is unfortunate because the shorter nonvining forms *are* so easy to grow—just as easy as any other type of herbaceous perennial. These are long-blooming plants and rebloom is easy to

Clematis integrifolia can be a vital component of any perennial border. Seen here at Northwest Garden Nursery in Eugene, Oregon.

induce. They are versatile plants, varying in length from 18 in. to 6 ft., that can be tied up but are better allowed to find their own way through their near neighbors. They occasionally invent their own combinations, sneaking through the understory of your garden and popping their flowers into the sun to surprise you and baffle your garden guests.

You'll hear this: "*That's* a clematis?"

THE INCREDIBLE INTEGRIFOLIA

The first clematis I ever owned was *Clematis integrifolia,* and this original plant, I am pleased to announce, still grows happily in the garden of Fred and Lucy Hardiman where my husband and I were renting a flat when I was bitten by the clematis bug. Planted in 1988, it was divided once when I moved to a garden of my own and could provide a home for a piece of the primary plant. Because it is an herbaceous perennial, this clematis (18–36 in. tall) can be divided in early spring by digging up the entire plant and, with a sharp knife, cutting the crown—with attached roots—into sections, making sure new shoots can be seen on each piece. These pieces should be replanted immediately, either in the ground or in pots.

Unlike the large-flowered hybrids whose stems are subject to environmental damage and disease, *Clematis integrifolia* and its hybrids needn't be buried deeper than they are seated in the pot in which you bought them. They rarely get diseases (certainly not if properly sited), and they don't support masses of old vine and big flowers, so they don't need the extra encouragement of deep planting to rejuvenate themselves when something untoward happens. They do appreciate a front-row seat in a sunny border (more so than most of the large-flowered hybrids, the integrifolias will pout in partial shade). Once their May-through-June wave of bloom is finished, the plant can be deadheaded or even sheared to the ground. This should be followed by a long drink of water and some fertilizer. New growth will materialize quickly, and the plant will bloom again in August and September.

The flowers of *Clematis integrifolia* are a mellow, silver-tinged blue, with variations within the species including lighter and darker shades of blue, pink, and white. All forms have four sepals, initially bell-shaped but opening wider as the flowers mature. Forms with extra-long sepals

There are several intriguing pink *Clematis integrifolia* forms, including this one, *C.* 'Hanajima' blooming with peony *Paeonia lactiflora* 'Sarah Bernhardt' and the hardy *Geranium pratense* 'Wisley Blue'. In the author's garden.

and with a flippant curl in the sepals are often given a cultivar name, since they are selections of the species. Both *C.* ×*diversifolia* 'Olgae' (actually a cross with *C. viticella*) and *C.* ×*diversifolia* 'Coerulea' are seriously twisted and of a slightly darker blue than the species. The centers on all are creamy pale yellow.

The pink forms of *Clematis integrifolia* are graceful plants with less recurve in the sepals. The selection *C. integrifolia* 'Rosea' is the tallest of the named selections (meaning those forms that appeared in print as *C. integrifolia* 'Whatever' before the 2002 *Clematis Register* was produced), up to 4 ft. in my garden, and the flowers are more formally bell-shaped than the blue type. My *C. integrifolia* 'Rosea' finds its way up through the low-growing *Ceanothus* 'Point Reyes', giving the shrub's shiny green foliage some additional floral liveliness in midsummer. *Clematis integrifolia* 'Pangbourne Pink' forms a handsome mound that I surround with a green wire support ring to help the plant keep its integrity in the face of late spring rains that could flatten the top growth, exposing the stemmy center of the plant. I use this form to cover the bare legs of the old moss rose *Rosa* 'Goethe'. The lavender-colored hardy *Geranium* 'Salome' wanders into *C. integrifolia* 'Pangbourne Pink', proving that one good perennial deserves another. The Japanese have made some excellent seedling selections, and *C.* 'Hanajima' is a handsome paler pink form with exceptionally long-lasting flowers. *Clematis* 'Hanajima' requires full sun and doesn't mind summer's heat.

The white forms of *Clematis integrifolia* tend to carry a bit of fragrance, spicy and light. When garden writer Rand Lee, the self-avowed fragrance fanatic, visited my garden in 2001, he detected a touch of spicy cedar in the Japanese cultivar *C. integrifolia* 'Hakuree'. It is a foggy white, ridged bell, and most flowers will develop a touch of pale blue on the aging sepals. In the case of my plant, the pale blue starts as a bar on the reverse of the sepal (the outside easily seen). With other plants of the same cultivar, ice blue slowly infuses the entire blossom in maturity. *Clematis integrifolia* 'Hakuree' stays fairly short, to 18 in., but the height can vary from plant to plant depending on the garden situation. You can count on the light perfume being present.

Clematis integrifolia 'Hakuree' makes an excellent shorter companion to such an elegant flower as *Iris sibirica* 'White Swirl', but the clematis

The white *Clematis integrifolia* hybrids tend to be fragrant. Here *C. integrifolia* 'Alba' makes a textural blend with *Veronica* 'Pink Damask' at Heronswood Nursery in Kingston, Washington.

will stay in bloom much longer than the iris. This cultivar is useful where you want a shortish plant with white flowers that won't be glaring. Its brand of white is diffuse and gentle. It also makes a soft textural contrast with small herbaceous treasures such as *Erodium chrysanthum*—lacy gray foliage, pale yellow flowers—or short mound-forming campanulas such as *Campanula garganica.*

Clematis integrifolia 'Alba' is taller than *C. integrifolia* 'Hakuree', with longer bells and greater vigor. Its flowers are a brighter white and even the fragrance is a little stronger. The height for *C. integrifolia* 'Alba' runs 24–36 in., so it can be trussed or allowed to wander. This form is handsome wandering through smaller, lax forms of *Deutzia,* such as *D. gracilis* 'Nana', again for a monochrome effect. This would be a good clematis to use in a black-and-white garden scheme, perhaps with black-dark annual *Centaurea cyanus* 'Garnet' (bachelor buttons) planted around its feet.

LARGER INTEGRIFOLIA PROGENY

Often the first *Clematis integrifolia* form new gardeners try is the justifiably popular *C. ×durandii* (sometimes written as 'Durandii'). Introduced in France by the brothers Durand in 1870, this is a superlative garden plant that has won two Awards of Garden Merit from the Royal Horticultural Society during its long history of cultivation. Although the recipe for this hybrid is now only theoretical, it is generally agreed that the original cross was *C. integrifolia* with *C. lanuginosa* in the form of *C.* 'Jackmanii'. Looking at the flowers of *C. ×durandii* in full bloom, you see traits of both parents, which are each distinctive in their own right.

This is the largest—in both height and bulk—of the bigger *Clematis integrifolia* varieties but, true to that parent, *C. ×durandii* does not grasp other plants or nonliving supports with its petioles (leaf stalks). The vigorous new shoots burst from the ground in early spring and seem to head for the sky, reaching 5–6 ft. tall, straight as a stick. One day they are there, and the next day they're gone. They have swooned. Quick investigation will find that the wind has blown the canes over and they have settled immediately into a comfortable life on some fainting couch you have provided in the form of a shrub rose, weigela, viburnum, or other supportive woody neighbor. The stems of *C. ×durandii* will sort themselves

A partnership that lasts nearly all summer, *Clematis ×durandii* with *Weigela florida* 'Variegata'. In the author's garden.

The best clematis for most any occasion in your garden, *Clematis ×durandii* loves to lean on roses. Here the rose is the old Floribunda, *Rosa* 'Betty Prior'. In the author's garden.

throughout their host plants and, by the time the fuzzy buds open, casual observers will be hard put to see where the clematis is actually planted.

I can think of no other clematis that is so clever at making its own way and suggesting its own combinations. I know this sounds too cute, but it is true. I have had my single plant of *Clematis ×durandii* in bloom among the bright and showy leaves of *Weigela florida* 'Variegata', with other branches cavorting with the single pink Floribunda *Rosa* 'Betty Prior' and lower canes in flower amid the hardy geranium, *Geranium clarkei* 'Kashmir Purple'. Any larger hardy geranium would do, especially the *G. pratense* forms such as 'Blue Cloud', 'Striatum', 'Mrs. Kendall Clark' (or the plant that goes around by that name in the United States), or the double forms. More on this is in the next chapter.

And such flowers. The color of the 4- to 5-in.-wide blooms has been described variously as wisteria blue, royal blue, indigo blue—you get the idea. To my eye, the flowers open rather more purple than blue and the blue tints develop as the flower matures. The color holds well in full sun, which is a good thing because the only time you see *Clematis* ×*durandii* growing poorly is when it is in too much shade. The new flowers have a velvety sheen, a silvery shine that plays over the surface of the sepals, highlighting the two or more grooves down their length. The reverse is shiny, with a navy blue wash over the ribs. The white filaments in the center carry pale yellow anthers, giving a complimentary focus for admiring the wide sepals with their curvaceous poise. A fabulously true-to-life—so rare with clematis—photograph taken by Jan Lindmark appears on the cover of *An Illustrated Encyclopedia of Clematis* (Toomey and Leeds 2001), but even this does not fully capture the glow.

Given enough sun, *Clematis* ×*durandii* is going to look quite smart wherever you place it. The standard interpretation of the traditional color wheel suggests that these flowers are going to want a background of yellow and chartreuse foliage and most variegations. If you like jewel-tone combinations, the burgundy or purple leaves of *Physocarpus opulifolius* DIABOLO™, *Cotinus coggygria* 'Royal Purple', and *Sambucus nigra* 'Guincho Purple' will give you the opulence you seek.

Like all its *Clematis integrifolia* relatives, *C.* ×*durandii* has a long period of bloom. It may take a midsummer rest, but deadheading and consistent applications of fertilizer will keep it going or get it back into bloom quickly.

Two lovely versions of *Clematis* ×*durandii* have been slow to make their way into the North American market from their European origins, but are well worth seeking out. The eldest of the two is *C.* 'Sizaia Ptitsa', introduced in 1980. I have had the pleasure of seeing this plant in bloom at the Seattle garden of the late Steve Antonow and can report that its primary difference from *C.* ×*durandii* is that it is much more purple, making the flowers appear darker. The other variety to look for is the Uno Kivistik introduction *C.* 'Juuli', which came from Estonia in 1990. This is a sturdy plant, getting 4–5 ft. tall with light blue flowers occasionally touched with a soft red-to-pink brush stroke. The flowers are up to 3½ in. in diameter—smaller than *C.* 'Sizaia Ptitsa', but prolifically produced.

Similar to *Clematis* 'Juuli' is the English introduction *C.* 'Arabella'. This cultivar can get taller than *C.* 'Juuli', is more delicate in weight, and has flowers very similar to the Estonian form, although they open more purple, maturing to midblue. *Clematis* 'Arabella' is less stiff in its growth and so is the more willing of the two forms to ingratiate itself with nearby plants and create its own plant combinations. It is particularly effective with hardy fuchsias, hydrangeas, and other summer-blooming deciduous shrubs. The variations in the fully open flowers of the two forms are subtle, and only garden testing will reveal exactly

Clematis PETIT FAUCON™ looks like the falcon's wings it is named for. It adds detail to the fragrant *Philadelphus* 'Belle Étoile'. In the author's garden.

Clematis PETIT FAUCON™ is shown to great advantage against the foliage of *Cornus sericea* 'Hedgerows Gold'. At Northwest Garden Nursery in Eugene, Oregon.

what those differences prove to be. *Clematis* 'Arabella' may have a darker base color, and the intensity of any pink bar is weather-dependent in both cultivars.

An equally vigorous but more delicately flowered herbaceous clematis is Raymond Evison's modern (1995) introduction, *Clematis* PETIT FAUCON™ (the *c* is pronounced as a *k*, not as an *s*). Its cultivar name is the unfortunate *C*. 'Evisix'. Much nicer to think of this plant by its translation—little falcon—and indeed the sepals are as slender and graceful as a falcon's wings. Of the many of Raymond's introductions I have grown, this is by far my favorite because it is truly unique and marvelously robust in its growth.

The flowers of *Clematis* PETIT FAUCON™ are dark purple, although catalogs will persist in trying to make it look more blue and showing the flowers as pendulous. In fact, the blossoms face upward. This can be quite a shock if you have never seen the plant in real life and go strictly by pictures intended to induce sales. Evidently, the folks setting pictures in the catalog art department assume all small-flowered clematis face downward and to place it right side up seems wrong to them. But it isn't wrong. These flowers wink right up at you.

After a midwinter scalping at the ground, *Clematis* PETIT FAUCON™ will set to work making itself bushy within its host shrub. Its ebony flowers can be a bit hard to see if they are not given a light background. At Northwest Garden Nursery the vivid *Cornus sericea* 'Hedgerows Gold' is used to excellent effect, illuminating *C.* PETIT FAUCON™. In my garden, the mock orange *Philadelphus* 'Belle Étoile' provides a more subtle host and midspring blooming companion.

THE UKRAINIAN SISTERS

By discussing the cultivars *Clematis* 'Alionushka' and *C.* 'Pamiat Serdsta' together, I run the risk of making readers as confused about these two plants as I am. Both cultivars are from the Ukraine, so presumably there they can tell them apart. In my garden, where they are separated by 25 ft. of pathway and garden, it seems they are the same, with the following few differences. Both are large plants by *C. integrifolia* standards, getting 5–6 ft. tall. In my garden *C.* 'Pamiat Serdsta' is the taller of the two—sometimes stretching itself to 7 ft.—and has a tendency to produce darker flowers of lavender-pink. It also seems to have a longer period of bloom than *C.* 'Alionushka'. Both have flowers with four sepals that are flattened and broaden at the tips and can be curled or twisted to some degree. *Clematis* 'Alionushka' has lighter, pinker flowers, but seasonal climatic variations can render these plants twins.

Saying I cannot always tell the two plants apart is not meant to discredit them. This could just as easily be an indictment of my lack of attention to detail. However, it makes me nervous to think that clematis breeders are now introducing plants that have precious little difference one from another. We see plants introduced from the shallow end of the gene pool, especially large-flowered hybrids, that are difficult to tell apart for the average gardener. I believe gardeners want distinctive plants, with unique and easily identifiable traits that make plant selection easier. How many pajama-striped large-flowered hybrids do we need? How many short dark purples? I mention this because the lovely Japanese *Clematis* 'Sano-no-murasaki' is, florally speaking, identical to

Clematis 'Alionushka' blooms with a fringe of volunteer feverfew at its feet. At Northwest Garden Nursery in Eugene, Oregon.

the equally lovely British introduction *C.* 'Burma Star'. And both plants tend to stay short, although they do climb. In such a vast gene pool as the clematis have, one hopes modern hybridizers will swim to the deep end and not tread water.

Now that I've had my say, let's move on to a few of the more adventurous *Clematis integrifolia* progeny.

"VITICELLIC" INTEGRIFOLIAS

In scholarly works on clematis (which this book does not pretend to be) and according to the 2002 *Clematis Register,* the progeny from crosses of *Clematis integrifolia* and *C. viticella* are known as *C. ×diversifolia* followed by 'Cultivar Name'. There is no such naturally occurring species as "*C. diversifolia.*" *Clematis ×diversifolia* is a created name for a man-made group of plants. The two clematis I am about to mention (and a couple already mentioned) could properly be written with the designation *C. ×diversifolia* 'Olgae', for instance. Because the new—or, in some cases, very old—cultivars do tend to take after one parent or the other, I find that the designation ×*diversifolia* doesn't tell me enough, nor do I ever see it on plant tags at nurseries.

A couple of certifiable antiques in the *integrifolia* × *viticella* group— both first documented in the 1830s—represent this different cross (×*diversifolia*) and therefore have a somewhat different look from those clematis mentioned in the previous section. Long before *Clematis integrifolia* was crossed with *C. lanuginosa* (or some form of it), it was crossed with *C. viticella,* creating plants popular enough to keep collectors searching for them more than 160 years later. Like any plants exposed to taxonomists and committees of nomenclature over a long period of time, their botanical names have changed, but not their admirable qualities.

For the sake of our conversation here, I will refer to the two plants by their modern cultivar names, *Clematis ×diversifolia* 'Eriostemon' and *C. ×diversifolia* 'Hendersonii'. Just as often you will see them listed as named forms of *C. integrifolia.* They are two fine plants by any name.

We shall discuss *Clematis ×diversifolia* 'Eriostemon', the older plant, first. In flower size and color it bears a striking resemblance to *C. viticella.*

It is hard to beat *Clematis ×diversifolia* 'Eriostemon' for beauty and grace of habit. The rose is *Rosa* PINK MEIDILAND™. At Northwest Garden Nursery in Eugene, Oregon.

The flowers remind me of pagoda roofs—four-sepalled flaring flowers of a rich blue-purple, silvered at the margins of the reverse. The growth habit is pure *C. integrifolia,* with short sturdy petioles that do not grab their hosts, but lean affectionately. *Clematis* ×*diversifolia* 'Eriostemon' can get at least 6 ft. tall and is rather more lightweight than *C.* ×*durandii.* This cultivar has a long period of bloom and will span the time from spring's old garden roses to summer's early hydrangeas. This plant would be a perfect choice for enshrouding a resting rhododendron or gallivanting over the top of shrubby lonicera and boxwood edgings.

Of the two plants, *Clematis* ×*diversifolia* 'Hendersonii' is the more difficult to procure. The flowers look more "integrifoliaceous" than "viticellic." The sepals are a darker and truer purple, fold back on themselves lengthwise, and can have a half twist. This is considered the shorter of the two plants by English gardeners who have grown them both, and it has narrower leaves. The buds of *C.* ×*diversifolia* 'Hendersonii' form long cones before opening, and the sepals do not show a silvered edge as *C.* ×*diversifolia* 'Eriostemon' does. Although the flowers are smaller in *C.* ×*diversifolia* 'Hendersonii', I feel they are even more abundantly produced and have a more lively personality.

These two have a much younger (1947) Canadian sibling, *Clematis* ×*diversifolia* 'Blue Boy', which has lighter, soft blue flowers and a definite *C. viticella* attitude. This is the tallest of the three forms, and all three are exceptionally winter hardy.

AUDACIOUS INTEGRIFOLIA HYBRIDS

In France in the 1850s, *Clematis integrifolia* was crossed with the delightfully fragrant *C. flammula* creating *C.* ×*aromatica.* The normal flowers of *C. flammula* are tiny, with four white sepals totally overshadowed by a crown of creamy stamens. The size of the flowers is made up for by their volume, the mass allowing us to get a noseful of the heady scent of the vine when in full flower. As so often happens when using *C. integrifolia* as a parent, the ability to hang on to the nearest stationary object is lost in the children. The flowers of *C.* ×*aromatica* (occasionally seen written 'Aromatica') are still small, but they are purple rather than white, providing a more dramatic background for the substantial fringe of stamens and pistils at the center of each floret.

The scent of *Clematis ×aromatica* is most effective when the plant is grown in full sun. In a long, mild growing season, the plant will get 6–8 ft. tall, blooming in midsummer. It is best used covering the trunky legs of climbing roses or old *C. montana* forms that have run to top growth and no longer bloom from the ground up.

Another early *Clematis integrifolia* hybrid full of whimsy is the silly yet charming *C. ×cylindrica*. If you are familiar with *C. crispa,* the other parent of this form, you can predict the playful outcome: ridged, purple flowers on a nonvining plant—characteristics contributed from the *C. integrifolia* parent—with sepals variously curled, twisted, waved and rippled—that's the vining *C. crispa* parent having the last word. Not widely available, but well worth seeking for the extra texture.

The Japanese clematis breeders, such as Kazushige Ozawa, are willing experimenters and have tried marrying North American native species with *Clematis integrifolia.* The most popularly successful of these trials produced *C.* 'Rooguchi' (or 'Roguchi', depending on your method of transliterating Japanese, but both ways are pronounced the same, "row-guu-chee"). The North American parent is *C. reticulata,* which has as uninspiring a little flower as you could ever hope to overlook. Yet this simple, small, bell-shaped flower, with a purple wash over a green base color, has imparted surprising elegance and grace to its famous offspring. The flowers of *C.* 'Rooguchi' are what Scarlet O'Hara would have called "dangle-bob earrings." Or so I imagine. The bells are 2 in. long, straight-sided to the sepal points, which recurve, but not too much. The flowers are purple to purple-blue, certainly much more purple than *C. integrifolia* itself, and show strong ridges. A healthy *C.* 'Rooguchi' growing in full sun will clothe itself in hundreds of these flowers, a show that will last two months. I mention health because this cultivar, if grown in even partial shade, is bound to get powdery mildew in all but the very driest summer climates. I am sorry to say I would not attempt it in areas with consistently high summer humidity.

Joy Creek Nursery, of Scappoose, Oregon, was the first in the United States to bring *Clematis* 'Rooguchi' to market, and it was at their display garden that I first saw it in bloom, covering an old maple tree stump with flowers draping down into variegated hostas. Ten years later, I still visit this plant every spring on the nursery's opening day to make sure the multiple shoots of their original plant are bursting from the ground, and I check on its progress with each visit throughout the season.

We are all pilgrims in our own way.

I have seen *Clematis* 'Rooguchi' supported by *Rosa glauca,* flowing down a retaining wall amid annual *Cerinthe major* 'Kiwi Blue' seedlings, and scrambling up a bamboo lattice to about 4 ft. tall before ending its fight with gravity to turn back down in a waterfall of bells, effectively

Easily the most popular *Clematis integrifolia* hybrid introduced in recent years, *C.* 'Rooguchi'. At Northwest Garden Nursery in Eugene, Oregon.

covering the lower stems of *C.* 'Polish Spirit' or *C.* 'Huldine' at Northwest Garden Nursery in Eugene, Oregon. This is a plant with endless possibilities.

CLEMATIS AS FILLER FLOWERS

And, since we're speaking of Northwest Garden Nursery, let me mention the inventive way Marietta O'Byrne uses herbaceous clematis in repeated patterns in the display garden to carry the viewer along as you stroll the pathways. The plant she uses most often is *Clematis recta* or the dark-leafed form, *C. recta* 'Purpurea'. The froth of tiny cream-to-white flowers, produced at anywhere from 4–7 ft. tall, bubbles over the top of the plant and neighboring shrubs and perennials. After their first inflorescence, these clematis are sheared to the ground, and they arise rejuvenated to flower again, somewhat more modestly, through autumn.

The fluffy clusters of *Clematis recta* make an admirable filler for hot colors at Northwest Garden Nursery in Eugene, Oregon.

It is said by some that the *Clematis recta* forms are fragrant. I believe this can vary widely from plant to plant and nose to nose. Usually the scent will be strongest in clematis grown in full sun.

Clematis recta makes an excellent cut filler flower and serves the same function in the garden, blending colors and filling gaps. It can be grown thickly to provide a lace curtain effect to screen or soften a scene and is effective to mollify clashes in a hot color border. As other herbaceous clematis do, *C. recta* can hide the bare legs of tall roses and other shrubs. It is an uncomplicated plant, but very useful.

As promised, the *Clematis recta* 'Purpurea' form has dark purple new foliage that lightens to dull green by the time the flowers open. New

The impressive new foliage of *Clematis recta* 'Purpurea' is given special treatment at Catswalk in Portland, Oregon.

growth is always purple, so it is certainly best to shear the plant after flowering. Dark-foliaged cultivar *C. recta* SERIOUS BLACK™ has been selected for holding its color longer, but hard pruning will always revitalize the desired foliage effect.

THE HERACLEIFOLIA SHRUBS

Because my first clematis was herbaceous, I was especially predisposed to buy any such clematis I came across early in my garden's history. During the summer we looked for a house, I started buying plants, and my *Clematis heracleifolia* var. *davidiana* moved to the new place with us the following winter and shortly thereafter was planted on the southeast corner of the house. Over time—as many of the *C. heracleifolia* forms do—it built for itself a woody crown about 18 in. tall and as the years go by, when hard-pruned in the winter, this crown bursts forth with many new buds. The florets are reminiscent in shape of pale blue hyacinths, but are carried in whorls and have only a light scent. The species itself has darker flowers, and the hybrid *C.* 'Wyevale' has noticeably larger flowers of a singular shade of midblue.

As so often happens, there is now some puzzlement over what is a cultivar of *Clematis heracleifolia* and what comes from *C. tubulosa*. The cognoscenti could tell you the differences, but now that all three plants are involved in hybridization efforts (*C. heracleifolia, C. heracleifolia* var. *davidiana,* and *C. tubulosa*), it is perhaps best to speak of the named cultivars directly by their given names rather than add to the confusion. The foliage on all three is large and coarse, very different from other herbaceous clematis groups, and all form a woody base that turns them into shrubs over time. All are upright in their growth.

Clematis 'Edward Prichard' is a combination of one of the above with *C. recta* and is yet another case where the individual flowers are worth seeing only in their mass display. Rather than being tubular, the flowers are thin-sepalled and flat, and they are touched with mauve, making them quite sparkly in a way that carries their presence some distance. These little flowers compose a chorus that plays to the back of the house. *Clematis* 'Edward Prichard' is lax in its growth, like its anything-but-erect *C. recta* parent. This clematis is perfect as a filler in the mixed border.

A much larger plant is the cultivar *Clematis ×jouiniana* 'Praecox', or just 'Praecox'. The small, tubular, ice blue flowers are produced over most of the mid- and late-summer season. This form does not have grasping leaf stems, but does form long heavy canes fully capable of running roughshod over anything in its way. Similar to it, but adding *C. virginiana* into the genetic mix, is *C.* 'Mrs. Robert Brydon'. This clematis has larger leaves and a later flowering season. *Clematis* 'Mrs. Robert Brydon' is less likely to want to lean upward into small trees or large shrubs and makes a fine, vigorous ground cover. This plant is most useful when used to cover the waning foliage of spring bulb displays, filling in a 6-ft.-by-6-ft. area with its handsome leaves, then bursting into silvery blue bloom in late summer. It would take few of these plants to cover a large area. In late fall when the clematis is thoroughly dormant, it can be hard-pruned to 12-in.-tall stumps, leaving the field clear for tulips, narcissus, early alliums, and other summer-dormant spring ephemerals.

There seems to be little controversy over *Clematis stans,* similar to *C. heracleifolia* but with distinct differences. *Clematis stans* becomes a woody-based shrub, hard-pruned in the winter and rebounding each spring. Of this group of clematis, it is the earliest to bloom and it has the longest period of bloom, up to three months at a stretch. It is shorter (rarely taller than 3 ft.), and the tubular flowers are smaller than the rest of this group. But it makes a merry plant, by far superior to other plants used to blend disparate colors or textures or to cover the unsightly.

TO STAKE OR NOT TO STAKE

If it is a clematis, it must be grown vertically, right? As I've said earlier, letting plants do what they want to do usually gives the best results. The taller *Clematis integrifolia* relatives—like *C. ×durandii, C.* 'Pamiat Serdsta', *C. integrifolia* 'Rosea', *C.* 'Rooguchi'—are better left to wander where they will. It is difficult to keep them upright, and they will keep you busy all summer tying them onto any vertical object you've chosen for them. Shorter cultivars can be supported by metal rings available for the purpose, since these rings will become invisible while keeping the plant within its circumference in the desired mound shape. Taller forms have a way of looking trussed up and unnaturally bound into a foreign and awkward pose. If you feel that *C. ×durandii,* for instance, has become ungainly, hard deadheading when the initial flush of bloom is finished is always a good idea. In addition to taking off spent flowers, clip off an additional 24 in. of each stem that has had flowers. Follow this with fertilizer and water and you'll have a branching plant ready to get back to the business of blooming in late summer and fall.

Most of the *Clematis heracleifolia* shrubs have strong upright growth to 4 ft. tall and can be treated like any other woody shrub you plan to hard-prune in the winter—as you do with cotinus, sambucus, or buddleja. The big, lax cultivars such as *C. ×jouiniana* 'Praecox' can be leaned into a sizable upright and subtly tied into place. I have had this particular plant raise itself up to 7 ft. tall, resting in a bay laurel (*Laurus nobilis*) but creating havoc when dislodged by late-summer winds. If your plant wants to grow up and has sufficient support for its weight, a little human intervention in the form of a few well-placed ties will not detract from the picture your clematis wants to create.

Don't feel you have to stake these plants, but if you do, for goodness sake be sly about it.

If you are naturally shy of pruning anything, use the herbaceous clematis to practice on. They can be pruned anytime after they go dormant, so the timing is easy. Once you've had to tidy an overgrown and unkempt herbaceous clematis, you won't let it happen again!

WANDERING FURTHER AFIELD

It would be remiss of me not to mention the fine, feathery foliage and abundant creamy blooms of *Clematis angustifolia,* which has recently found its way to prominence among other herbaceous perennials in Northwest garden centers. The slender, dissected foliage is its chief charm. If given pride of place in full sun, it will bloom in May and June at about 36 in. tall. It is best grown next to roses or other large-foliaged plants, so the more delicate clematis foliage has a textural foil.

Some charming herbaceous perennial clematis just happen to be North American native plants. I won't try to mention all of them, as some are not particularly gardenworthy (they're just too fussy or inconsequential) and some will be mentioned in the chapter on growing clematis in containers because of their soil needs. But a few of these plants are well worth seeking for their grace and charm.

Closely related to *Clematis texensis* is the nonvining *C. addisonii.* It has stout burgundy-pink bells on a short bushy plant with tender, bright green, rounded leaves. Its stems can be pink also. The flowers flip back at the sepal tips, giving a "granny's bonnet" impression, and the margins and interior are cream-colored, outlining and highlighting the thickness of the sepals. (It is hard to resist the urge to bend over and chuck this little flower under its chin and tell it how sweet it is.) Deadheading can produce a second flush of bloom. This plant must be grown at the front of the border in full sun, since it relishes rich soil and good drainage. *Clematis addisonii* will appreciate the warmth of a gravel mulch, but this does not mean this is anything like a drought-tolerant plant. The one drawback to *C. addisonii* is a tendency toward powdery mildew, but there are now effective organic methods for controlling this fungal problem. Once you have seen the bewitching flower, you will forgive the occasionally flawed foliage. *Clematis addisonii* is also willing to rebloom if the early wave of flowers is removed before they set seed. If you want to both collect seed and have the plant rebloom, plan to collect seed from the second batch of flowers.

Clematis ochroleuca is more closely related to *C. integrifolia.* Unlike its cousin though, it has soft green-to-cream-to-pale yellow bell-shaped flowers. And when I say soft, I mean it literally because the flowers are coated with tiny hairs. There is often a purple stain where the flower attaches to its stem and the inside of the sepals is lime green. This clematis makes a sturdy mound of green, fuzzy foliage and will rebloom easily if deadheaded before the seeds can set. A bit of lime (calcium phosphate) or placement on the sunny side of a new home foundation will meet this plant's needs admirably. Or a chunk of old concrete can be buried in the soil of a container to provide lime. *Clematis ochroleuca's* first bloom usually occurs in late April or early May. This species can be brought back into bloom by deadheading the first batch of flowers. Full sun is a must.

To recap, the herbaceous perennial clematis (as opposed to the woody vining forms) are a uniformly virtuous group of plants, ranging in height from about 15 in. to 10 ft. They can be grown as front-of-the-border jewels, clever wanderers placed behind and growing through medium-size shrubs, or as large, trained, upright plants able to hide (for the summer at least) the bare legs of their upwardly mobile vining cousins or climbing roses without trunk foliage. These are among the best clematis for beginners with the genus because they are rarely susceptible to disease, are agreeable to a variety of exposures, and are free flowering. They practically come with a warranty, "guaranteed to grow."

THE TEN BEST HERBACEOUS CLEMATIS

Clematis 'Arabella': This is a pleasing shade of blue, lighter than *C.* ×durandii and with a more delicate shape, and quite the little wanderer if left unguarded.

Clematis ×*diversifolia* 'Blue Boy': This plant can get huge, covering a 6-ft.-by-6-ft. area with a mass of stems and a proportionate volume of gunmetal blue bells.

Clematis ×*diversifolia* 'Eriostemon': The Oriental poise of the dark blue sepals and their demure nodding habit make this antique cultivar perfect for gardens where subtlety is the theme.

Clematis ×*durandii*: You will find this plant on any clematis grower's list of plants everyone should have. Easy to grow, floriferous, beautiful.

Clematis fremontii: Of the herbaceous perennial North American clematis species, this is the easiest to make happy. It loves life in a trough.

Clematis integrifolia: There are both historic and sentimental reasons to grow this plant, not to mention that it has a tractable nature, long period of bloom, and flowers of quiet charm. We never forget our first true love, do we?

Clematis integrifolia 'Alba': The flowers are graceful, eloquent, and fragrant. Place it in your garden where you won't miss it.

Clematis recta 'Purpurea': This clematis has many virtues, the main one being that it is compliant. You can grow it for its dark foliage and use it as a cut-flower filler. It revitalizes itself after a midsummer pruning. What more could you ask?

Clematis stans: This bushy clematis is upright and "architectural," to use clematis collector and scholar Brewster Rogerson's apt word. The flowers are pale blue flared tubes, produced over a long season.

Clematis 'Wyevale': Let the experts sort out the nomenclature of this plant; we can go on growing it for its striking Mediterranean blue, hyacinth-shaped flowers.

The shorter second bloom of *Clematis recta* is accented by volunteer seedlings of golden feverfew at Northwest Garden Nursery in Eugene, Oregon.

CHAPTER 7

CLEMATIS WITH HERBACEOUS PERENNIALS

*Y*ou will no doubt have realized by now that I am an unrelenting, unrepentant color addict. The best way to turn up the color volume in a quiet border is to add clematis to every level—ground, middle, and canopy. Surprisingly, many large-flowered hybrids are happy to spread along the tops of herbaceous perennials. Those clematis with up-facing flowers just naturally look better grown this way. Although the backs of the sepals of some clematis have interesting bars of color or perhaps veining, it is the upper surface that is bred to be showy. How disappointing to have the vines get so tall we can't see the brightest color. Encouraging a lower rambling habit is a sure way to enjoy these blossoms and to get the most of combinations with herbaceous perennial flowers.

It is with the herbaceous perennial group of plants that most gardeners find the greatest satisfaction. These are the plants we use to clothe the garden in swathes of color, making tonal connections that knit different garden strata together and giving the whole a sense of cohesion. To use a fashion metaphor, a small tree might be the dress, with a vining clematis supplying stockings and a jacket. The herbaceous perennial plants add matching shoes, handbag, and jewelry. All are necessary for a finished, polished look. Heaven knows, we don't want our gardens seen in public looking as if they got dressed in the dark.

It is this concept of color as the skin over the bones of your garden, no matter if you like a monochromatic or a contrasting palette, that

One good herbaceous perennial deserves another: *Clematis integrifolia* with *Allium cristophii.* In the author's garden.

makes any well-chosen planting into a showstopper. Because clematis are themselves members of a family of plants made up primarily of herbaceous perennials (the Ranunculaceae), it makes sense that they combine easily with their cousins. The nonvining clematis are completely at home in a mixed perennial border.

If you are a collector of certain herbaceous perennials, such as the hostas (family Liliaceae), corydalis (Fumariaceae), or hardy geraniums (Geraniaceae), you will find that the wide variety of clematis sizes, shapes, and colors allows you to grow them with your collection to free your garden from looking like an educational institution without much joy. Plants like to commingle in gardens as they do in the wild, and nobody has more fun doing it than clematis.

THE RANUNCULACEAE

It has been said, and I've said it too, that all the best herbaceous perennials are of the family Ranunculaceae. Not only does the family include clematis, but also delphiniums, hellebores (which have developed an undying following), anemones (wind flowers), cimicifugas (snakeroot, bugbane), aquilegias (columbines), and the thalictrums (meadow rue)—and this only scratches the surface. All these plants look well together. Their colors all seem to harmonize, and the widely divergent structural forms ensure that an all-ranunculoid garden would not be in the least boring. In temperate climates this one family might give you flowers all year-round.

Given their vast differences, you might well ask what uniting element keeps these plants together in one family. As I understand it, the common factor is flower structure: Many of the Ranunculaceae do not have petals, letting their stamens gain full exposure to pollinating winds and insects. Often their petals or their sepals have spurs, structures that Mary Toomey calls "shoulder pads," which we can easily see in the aquilegias, delphiniums, and the well-named *Clematis ranunculoides*. Other clematis with visible rudimentary spurs include *C. koreana* and *C. chiisanensis*. Our mission here, though, is not to be botanists, but to be gardeners. The similarities in flowers can help explain why certain plants just seem to want to be together, and knowing who the near relations are helps it all make sense.

My favorite clematis relatives are the thalictrums, also known as the meadow rues. I've never met one I didn't like. These are the lace curtains of my garden, with airy stems populated by flowers made up almost entirely of stamens. Not surprisingly, the leaves of this genus strongly resemble columbine foliage, and there is even a species so named, *Thalictrum aquilegiifolium.* Many of the meadow rues reach 3–4 ft. tall and, with their gauzy inflorescence consisting of puffy panicles of colored stamens (usually lavender, yellow, or white), they can be used midborder to partially screen something intriguing behind them (just as lace curtains do) or to soften what might otherwise be a harsh color combination. This genus is most effective in partial shade, making them ideal consorts for the soft-colored clematis that would fade if grown in the sun. The meadow rues *can* be grown in full sun, but will need a ready supply of water to prevent sunburned foliage and shriveled flower buds.

Although all in this genus appear to be gardenworthy, I particularly seek those species and cultivars that hang on to their sepals (like clematis, the thalictrums do not have petals). The flower buds of the meadow rues are spherical, like little beads, and in *Thalictrum rochebruneanum* and *T. delavayi* and its hybrids the sepals hang on once the flower opens, forming little cup-shaped structures that give the flowers more substance and color. In some cases the fringe of stamens is yellow and the sepals are bright mauve—suddenly there is more to these flowers than an interesting texture.

Although the meadow rues have tiny (quarter-inch-wide) flowers carried in a mass, the species with the largest flowers is worth seeking. It is *Thalictrum diffusiflorum,* with each floret a half-inch wide—or more—and of a gentle shade of pale lavender-blue. The flower stems reach 2–3 ft. tall. Like many plants we covet and then fret over once we own, it is slow to increase and needs rich soil. This is a creature that will fill you with plant lust the first time you see it.

The hellebores are such good garden plants, blooming as they do in partial shade and at a time of year when anything with flowers is welcome. In temperate gardens the flowers persist for three months, although the colors lose their vibrancy and become uniformly greenish with age. The longevity of the flowers (particularly the *Helleborus orientalis* tribe) gives us ample opportunity to overlap their season with the end of the *Clematis cirrhosa* winter flowers and the early spring season of the Atragene Group. Although hellebores do not come in blue—as *C. alpina* and *C. macropetala* do—the whites, pinks, and purples can all be matched or contrasted with some hellebore form or other. Happy hellebores indicate you have a somewhat neutral soil, which clematis prefer over an acidic soil if given a choice. Another indication of well-established hellebores is the arrival of seedlings, which you will want to monitor to see if you've developed the next big thing in hellebore breeding through benign neglect.

It has long been my ambition to design and grow a black-and-white garden, simply as an exercise and because I am drawn to plants with very dark foliage or flowers. I am able to occupy my mind with such daydreams on long plane rides, thus suppressing the urge to throttle the parents of screaming children. The clematis that is first on my list for this flight of fancy is *Clematis* 'Alba Luxurians'. Its white flowers often start the season touched with green and their anthers are dark. Standing in front of this clematis would be the striking dark-foliaged form of the elegant Ranunculaceae member, *Cimicifuga simplex* 'Brunette', with its bronze-black foliage and sinuous white flower spires. Conversely, the clematis could be the dark partner; perhaps *Clematis* 'Romantika' could be persuaded to be the dusky backdrop for the green-leafed, prolific-flowering *Cimicifuga simplex* var. *matsumare* 'White Pearl'. In *my* black-and-white garden, I could certainly have it both ways.

A BIT OF DEBUNKING

We often hear it said that clematis like their feet in the shade and their heads in the sun, but you'll notice I haven't repeated this old wives' tale until now. Certainly I've mentioned plenty of clematis that prefer growing completely in dappled shade (what they call "high shade" in the American Southeast) as well as late-flowering varieties that won't bloom well unless they can absorb full sun from the ground up, such as *Clematis terniflora* and *C.* 'Lady Betty Balfour'. That does leave some middle ground for discussion. It is generally assumed that shady soil is moist soil, and clematis need fairly moist but not soggy soil. The new-to-clematis gardener assumes that if a clematis has its feet in the shade, it won't need as much water. If you put a rock over clematis roots to shade them, they can cook if the rock gets too hot, and water doesn't flow freely through rock. A well-watered rock does not translate into a well-watered clematis. There is such an affliction as dry shade and most clematis hate it.

A deeply planted large-flowered hybrid clematis will be much happier with a shallow-rooted herbaceous perennial over its feet than with a rock, whether or not the pair are planted together in full sun, in shade from the waist down, or in uniform partial shade. Chances are, the perennial will ask for water sooner than the clematis will, but they will both actually want a drink at the same time. The clematis is just too polite to trouble you all the time, to its peril. By the time the average clematis looks like it is begging for water, you have most likely damaged the roots and should think seriously about reducing some of the leafy upper growth of the vine to help those all-important roots recover.

Some clematis do like to emerge from a host shrub to bask in the summer sun (*Clematis* 'Comtesse de Bouchaud' and her cream sport *C.* 'John Huxtable', for instance), but others will sunburn if hot weather arrives all of a sudden (*C.* 'King Edward VII', *C.* 'Royalty', and *C.* 'The President' are examples) even when given ample water. Watch your plant and observe what it is trying to tell you. If the leaves sunburn (they brown and turn crackly), having its head in the sun is not your vine's idea of a good time. It will prefer wandering through a broad-leafed shrub without any taller support to tempt it further upward, it will be happier under a lath house or similar structure providing dappled shade, or it will be more at home growing in a situation where the hottest afternoon sun is blocked by house shadow or a hedge. You can decide which situation you can most easily provide. The Montanae do not seem to sunburn unless they are drastically dry at their roots.

SHARING THE SHADE

Canadian plantsman Thomas Hobbs speaks of gardens as jewel boxes, and indeed they are. Made up of colorful gemstones, the herbaceous perennials afford us many baubles to plant in gilded settings with clematis. The plants I've selected to feature here, the genus *Corydalis,* are examples from my own garden that have given me great satisfaction and offer little destructive root competition for clematis.

Just as I've never met a thalictrum I didn't like, I've never met a corydalis I didn't like either. Vaguely related to the genus *Dicentra* (which we call bleeding hearts), this genus has delicate foliage—similar to maidenhair fern without the black stems—usually bright green, with a mounding habit of growth. Some corydalis grow from fleshy tubers (*Corydalis solida,* for instance), making them strongly summer dormant, but I find that the nontuberous species and cultivars have the longest garden impact. Plant snobs consider the bright yellow *Corydalis lutea* to be beneath contempt because it is common and spreads itself around by seeds, but I like it and it seems to like me. Of course, it is telling that my numerous original *Corydalis lutea* plants were housewarming gifts from Lucy Hardiman, who encouraged me to dig as many as I wanted. "No really, take more," she said.

Corydalis lutea will colonize retaining walls, venturing into full sun and partial shade with equal vigor. Its shallow roots mean that errant seedlings are easily moved or removed. The bright golden mounds are about 15 in. tall and 20 in. wide unless starved in a wall crevice. It grows over the feet of the purple large-flowered hybrid *Clematis* 'Guiding Star' at the foot of my front retaining wall, and the clematis appears to not know its companion is there. *Clematis* 'Guiding Star' is adept at making new growth from its roots, emerging right up through the corydalis with no harm done. And I don't see any complaints from *Corydalis lutea* plants that have clematis running riot over the top of them. These are, all in all, complacent little plants, just pleased to be a small part of your grand scheme.

Every gardener I know has different successes and failures with the blue corydalis, the ever-increasing number of named selections from *Corydalis flexuosa.* These are the garden's sapphires. You have no doubt heard their names: *C. flexuosa* 'Blue Panda', *C. flexuosa* 'China Blue', *C. flexuosa* 'Père David', *C. flexuosa* 'Purple Leaf', and *C. flexuosa* 'Golden Panda', to cite only a few. Lucky is the gardener who can get any one of these to seed itself around the place. Although I have occasional good

Two dazzling plants: *Corydalis lutea* braving the full sun to bloom with the lower stems of *Clematis* 'Venosa Violacea'. In the author's garden.

fortune with one or two of these, they can take time to establish and not all are equally long-lived. On the other hand, Bruce Wakefield, of Old Germantown Gardens in northwest Portland, has a 4-ft.-by-3-ft. patch of very successful *C. flexuosa* 'China Blue' that would make anyone think these blue-flowered varieties will spread like wildfire. Unlike their yellow cohort, *C. lutea,* which will tolerate sunny exposures fairly well, the blues need partial shade. These *C. flexuosa* cultivars are all more or less the same size as their yellow kin and don't mind a bit if a clematis vine wanders through.

A generally tougher plant—wafting the scent of gardenias through the air—is *Corydalis elata.* It is more erect than mounding, with its small electric blue flowers carried on spires up to 2 ft. tall. The flower stems are red, and its bright fernlike foliage can have tiny red dots. *Clematis elata* is more reliable for me than any of the other blue forms, although I am enjoying a run of good luck with *C. flexuosa* 'Blue Panda' (knock on wood).

The last corydalis cultivar I want to mention is the hybrid known as *Corydalis* 'Blackberry Wine'. This is my living amethyst. It makes the largest hummock of any of the easy-to-find corydalis, and the flowers are reddish-purple, as the name suggests. *Corydalis* 'Blackberry Wine' has a long period of bloom, from early spring (late March) through the end of June and even longer if the spring is mild. Clematis that are hard-pruned to the ground, such as the Viticella Group, or that die back on their own—the integrifolias—have no trouble emerging through the foliage and flowers of *Corydalis* 'Blackberry Wine'.

The genus *Pulmonaria* also provides some good foot warmers for clematis in the spring. This is the lungwort clan of low-growing ground covers, some with white-spotted foliage and some—like *P.* 'Benediction'—with arresting blue flowers. These cope well with the cultivars of *Clematis alpina* and *C. macropetala*. The pulmonarias need shade and make the ground level interesting under a tree with a *C. montana* form blooming up in it. The lungworts can get powdery mildew, which I control by cutting the plant back very hard after it has bloomed (thus deadheading too). The new foliage will be fresh and clean.

Since we are speaking of plants that prefer some shade, we cannot leave out hostas. I have mentioned growing clematis and roses together (ad nauseam, perhaps), and clematis can make a shady habitat beneath themselves that hostas will appreciate. Hostas are grown for the variety of their foliage variegations, and making careful selections of a variety of forms and colors will go a long way toward filling a shady nook that has been vacated by sun-loving plants that are no longer getting enough light. Clematis, though, adapt well to areas where shade slowly overtakes the sunny spot where they were initially planted.

Blue hostas are particularly fascinating because of the waxen powder coating that makes the leaves appear blue-gray to human eyes. If you wipe this surface off, you will have just another green hosta, but why would you do that? The color blue adds misty depth to any shade garden, yet those blues that are nearly silver (such as *Hosta* 'Blue Moon') light up in a dark setting. The other value of a blue hosta is the anecdotal evidence that suggests that blue-leafed cultivars are not as appetizing to

Two handsome shade plants glow together, *Clematis* 'Peveril Pearl' with *Hosta* 'Devon Blue'. In the author's garden.

slugs and so are spared some of the damage that can deface other forms. This has certainly been true in my garden.

FAVORITE BLUE HOSTAS

Hosta 'Abiqua Drinking Gourd' (large)
Hosta 'Blue Arrow' (medium to small)
Hosta 'Blue Diamond' (large)
Hosta 'Elvis Lives' (medium)
Hosta 'Hadspen Blue' (medium)
Hosta 'Hadspen Hawk' (small)
Hosta 'Hadspen Heron' (small)
Hosta 'Lakeport Blue' (very large)
Hosta 'Osprey' (small)
Hosta 'Pearl Lake' (medium to small)

All hostas form clumps that are quite dense in the ground. Therefore, they are not the best choice for a companion to place right over the crown of a newly planted clematis. Hostas are better as near neighbors, and we need to allow enough space around them so they will achieve their full mature diameter without crushing innocent bystanders. Low-branching clematis can send their flowering stems over to the hostas to play.

SUNNY DISPOSITIONS

Alliums (ornamental onions) do not form heavy mats like hostas do (admittedly a handful do), and their small bulbs are easy to insert into the garden in the tight spaces between plants where bare earth needs filling. Their umbels are variously sized domes, in sizes fit for troughs (*Allium thunbergii,* autumn blooming, 8 in. tall in cultivation, rosy color), up to the giant alliums (*A. giganteum,* spring blooming, 4 ft. tall). Colors vary widely, including white (*A.* 'Mount Everest', *A. nigrum, A. karataviense* 'Ivory Queen'), bright yellow (*A. moly* 'Jeannine'), several shades of pink (*A. pulchellum, A. unifolium, A. senescens*), blue (*A. caeruleum*), and various shades of purple (*A. aflatunense* 'Purple Sensation' and *A. sphaerocephalon*).

The herbaceous clematis are especially effective when used in the foreground, backed by a chorus of bobbing round allium heads. The winsome blue bells of *Clematis integrifolia* make a superb textural contrast to the jovial *Allium cristophii* (known as star of Persia) that is silvery lavender in color. Many alliums lose their foliage as—or just before—they bloom, so their base is an unsightly snarl of dried foliage. Short herbaceous clematis hide this admirably. Because *C. integrifolia* can be convinced to bloom on and off all summer, a variety of alliums can be planted behind it (as I said, they won't take up too much space) to vary the color harmony from late spring to autumn, depending on which allium cultivars you select. *Clematis integrifolia* prefers full sun and alliums need it to thrive, making them ideal perennial partners.

The pink perennial bachelor buttons, *Centaurea dealbata* and *C. hypoleuca,* should be grown in the opposite way, in front of taller clematis rather than behind short ones. These are easy species, and we would be remiss not to mention their best-known cultivar, *Centaurea hypoleuca*

Clematis 'Sunset' makes a sunglassworthy hot combo with *Centaurea hypoleuca* 'John Coutts'. In the author's garden.

'John Coutts'. These herbaceous perennials reach 18–24 in. tall when blooming, when the rosy pink-fringed flowers (which tend to be paler or white in the center) rise above the handsomely dissected foliage—which can be quite gray, especially on the reverse. In my garden the form *Centaurea hypoleuca* 'John Coutts' will bloom in two or three waves, usually timing itself to make a showy underskirt for the large-flowered *Clematis* 'Sunset'. Some folks might say this is an excessively dissonant color harmony, but I quite enjoy it. For folks who mutter and shake their heads over such things, I would recommend any white large-flowered hybrid instead. Because these centaureas have repeated periods of bloom, do select a clematis companion that will bloom in both spring and fall. *Clematis* 'Duchess of Edinburgh' would be one option, with her thick, creamy pom-poms looking like vaguely similar giant versions of the centaurea flowers. There I go again, suggesting a blowzy, unrefined duet, but the centaureas are anything but formal.

Oriental poppies (*Papaver orientale*) bloom at the same time as the spring-flowering large-flowered hybrids, and it is wise to make the most of this opportunity. Cultivars in new colors of this poppy are arriving in garden centers every year, with *P. orientale* 'Patty's Plum' making a big splash in the market. In the Pacific Northwest "Patty" has met with varying degrees of success, and Marietta O'Byrne, of Northwest Garden Nursery in Eugene, Oregon, suggests this poppy be grown in partial shade to keep the muddy mauve color fresh for as long as possible. I have tried this and I get fewer, but nicer, flowers.

The other Oriental poppies have brilliant colors. Even the white and peach varieties usually have black basal blotches that make the open flowers dashing. To get the most of the clematis-poppy combination, a third party must be enlisted to cover the bare spot left by the poppies as they go briefly dormant after flowering. Later-blooming herbaceous perennials, such as Japanese anemones or fall-blooming asters will hide the poppy corpses until their new crown of foliage emerges in mid- to late summer.

In the spring, though, the poppies play their part with dynamic vigor and scene-stealing color. There is no truer red in the plant world than *Papaver orientale* 'Beauty of Livermere' or *P. orientale* 'Tuerkenlouis'. I

The popular Oriental poppy *Papaver orientale* 'Patty's Plum' picks up the bar color of *Clematis* 'John Warren'. In the author's garden.

am partial to the screaming pinks, *P. orientale* 'Watermelon' and *P. orientale* 'Raspberry Queen', which are exceptionally good with early, white, large-flowered clematis—such as *Clematis* 'Guernsey Cream', *C.* 'Gillian Blades', or *C.* 'Miss Bateman'—that will bloom from the ground up, making the perfect backdrop to reflect these strong pinks back into the garden. Keep a pair of sunglasses ready when approaching the poppy *P. orientale* 'Prince of Orange', a real shouter that combines well with early purple clematis such as an unshorn and therefore early-blooming *C.* 'Viola' or the naturally vernal double *C.* 'Kiri Te Kanawa' (quite a showstopper in her own right). Do make sure that whichever purple or dark blue clematis you choose has the same intensity of color as *P. orientale* 'Prince of Orange' or the clematis will be an extra in your production rather than earn star billing with the poppy.

The plant family Campanulaceae affords us many perfect companions for clematis. I try to avoid both those that are tall and tend to flop

(*Campanula pyramidalis,* the chimney bellflower, for one) and those that form heavy root mats that new clematis shoots cannot break through (*C. glomerata,* the globe bellflower). This leaves us countless other species and cultivars to plant over or near clematis.

Some of my favorite full-sun ground covers are campanulas, and even those that spread wide and flat have smaller crowns than their surface would suggest, making them excellent flowering mulch over clematis roots. The tidy *Campanula garganica* blinks up at you with up-facing star-shaped flowers, its bright white eyes surrounded by Mediterranean blue. I have not found this species to be an aggressive spreader, but I have read that it may be. In my garden the low (5-in.) mounds reach a foot wide, so several plants are needed to fill in a square yard of bare soil. The golden-leafed form of this species, *Campanula* 'Dickson's Gold', has remained popular and maintains your interest when not in flower. A bit of dappled late afternoon shade doesn't hurt either form. This species makes a fetching lap rug for the blue *Clematis integrifolia* cultivars, since the campanulas gaze up and the clematis look down. Adorable.

Two other campanula ground covers are difficult for me to keep straight because of their tongue-twisting names, *Campanula portenschlagiana* and *C. poscharskyana.* Try to avoid having to speak these names aloud in public unless you can get a running start at them. Both are blue-flowered and drape decoratively over retaining walls. If anything, *Campanula poscharskyana* is the more aggressive of the two, spreading wider, and its flowers are much more star-shaped than its cousin. *Campanula portenschlagiana* has cupped flowers and forms a shorter, though still spreading, mound. If these plants are not side by side, it is hard to remember their differences, but both make lively partners for flowing ground-cover clematis, such as the pale yellow *Clematis chiisanensis* 'Lemon Bells' or the large-flowered white *Clematis* 'Marie Boisselot' (pronounced "bwah-sell-oh"), which likes to face up and so is best used where it has no support and can therefore ramble on top of such things as unpronounceable campanulas.

The upright campanulas are legion, making a vast throng at specialty nurseries and garden centers, and most are worth trying, although I do like to avoid those varieties that might crush herbaceous clematis or

Clematis chiisanensis 'Lemon Bells' drapes with *Campanula portenschlagiana.* In the author's garden.

break the canes of vining clematis should the campanula topple. Although I have resisted actually collecting campanula species (showing uncharacteristic restraint), I have grown a number of them and now stick to old choice varieties with a few newer cultivars that peak my interest. The peach-leaf bellflower (*Campanula persicifolia*) and the scented milky bellflower (*C. lactiflora*) can always be recommended.

Peach-leaf bellflower has out-facing bells that are chubby cups (to 1 ½ in. wide). The typical color is a clear faded-denim blue, but this can vary in a seedling batch. There are white forms and double forms, and I like them all. The flower stems are thin, wiry, and very strong, to 3 ft. tall (the doubles can be shorter), and the bells open in random order up and down the spire. I think all blues go together (others might disagree) and like to see such large-flowered hybrids as *Clematis* 'Fujimusume', *C.* 'H. F. Young', *C.* 'Lasurstern', or *C.* 'Will Goodwin' wandering toward this campanula when everybody blooms in May and June. There is better flower production if this species is grown in full sun, but the bright whites do sparkle in partial shade, a lovely effect. A recent *Campanula persicifolia* form with which I am favorably impressed is 'Chettle Charm'. It has white flowers with a subtle outline of lavender. English plantsman Christopher Lloyd describes white as a "staring color," but the manicured margin of pale mauve to lilac saves this cultivar from being just another white blob in the full-sun garden.

The milky bellflower (*Campanula lactiflora*) is so named, in part, because of its milky sap (although it isn't the only campanula with latex in its veins) and also because its color is pale blue with a creamy center (certainly this is skim milk). The individual florets are small, but arrive in great panicles (pointed, branched flower clusters) in plants 4–6 ft. tall. It is rarely mentioned, but this plant breathes the scent of incense into the summer's evening breeze. This perfume quite surprised me when I first encountered it and waded into the mixed border hunting its source. *Campanula lactiflora* is one of the best species for partial shade, which helps this dreamy inflorescence last longer.

The milky bellflower has strong, tall stems, rarely requiring staking unless positioned in a windy site. I'm not sure I would ask it to carry the weight of a large clematis, but in my garden it makes an admirable backdrop for the similarly colored, double, large-flowered *Clematis* 'Louise Rowe', who sits in a large container at the corner of a path with the campanula behind it. Double *Clematis* 'Veronica's Choice' or the extremely fine *Clematis* 'Chalcedony' (pronounced, I am told, "cal-SAID-o-ny" and rhymes with "pony") would do as well in this dappled-light position. A pinker form of *Campanula lactiflora* named 'Loddon Anna' is equally attractive and not at all uncommon. Allowing nearby clematis to wander into this plant, while the vine's weight is borne by a woodier host, is the best plan if you want the clematis to flower right into the campanula.

HARDY GERANIUMS

As I said, I have resisted collecting the genus *Campanula*, but I have not been so lucky with hardy geraniums (genus *Geranium*). Their common name is cranesbill because of their elongated, pointed seed pod, which matures to a certain level of dryness, then bursts open, propelling the tiny seeds all around the place. Hardy geraniums have more or less bowl-shaped flowers (to 1 in. or slightly more in diameter); some appear starry because the five petals do not overlap or are pointed. Every time I think I've bought or been given the last choice geranium cultivar I will ever need, I find another. I justify this because many cranesbills are perfect plants to grow at the feet of clematis, and some of the rambling forms will cover bare legs nicely. Hardy geraniums also look quite chummy interplanted with herbaceous clematis. It pays to learn the young leaf distinctions between the geraniums so you can decide which seedlings—and you *will* have seedlings—you want to save or transplant and which you want to strangle at birth. I tend to spare the hoe for any seedlings that are from the *Geranium phaeum* clan (common name, mourning widows), but there are some that I remove immediately upon seeing their true leaves because I know their true colors.

Before we go much further, I want to broadcast the reminder that these are much different plants from summer's tender perennials, the genus *Pelargonium.* New gardeners get all excited when they hear the phrase "hardy geraniums," which conjures visions of vividly colored window boxes blooming all through winter with plants that never need

Clematis 'Sano-no-murasaki' matches *Geranium phaeum.* In the author's garden.

replacing. It would save a lot of confusion indeed if the common name for the pelargoniums were something other than "geranium," wouldn't it? But no such luck—the true geraniums must be called "hardy geraniums." The pelargoniums deserve nothing better than some newly made, "olde" English-sounding epithet, such as "Tender Toms" or "Here Today, Gone Tomorrows."

Not that I would suggest for a minute that there are no gaudy versions of the hardy geranium. These plants can be insolently bold, and certain forms can be grown in containers, too, for that matter. It's just that none of them are red or orange. Hardy geraniums don't scream at you; they wave and beckon in a much friendlier way, asking for your attention rather than demanding it. So your back is turned—you are lulled into a false sense of security—as certain species of hardy geranium take over your garden.

What is rampant in my garden may behave itself in yours, but I will issue a few warnings, knowing that I will have to argue later with gardeners who have taken offense. Keep in mind that I have a small garden and would rather have many select forms of hardy geranium than drifts of just a handful of cultivars.

The geranium I am most sorry to have ever planted is *Geranium nodosum*. It has shiny, bright green lobed leaves and is commonly sold for the shade garden, but will seed itself in full sun or dappled shade with equal verve. Its flowers, which are pink to lilac with a silver sheen in full sun, are produced over a long season. The plant forms a knot of underground rhizomes from which the leaves and flower stems arise, and this fibrous ganglion enlarges as the individual plant grows, forming a deep, coarse mat that no bulb or clematis or trowel can penetrate. This nasty rascal will germinate right into a clematis crown and is difficult to extract if you don't pull the seedling out the very moment you first see it. Herbicides take repeated applications—usually at least two—to kill this plant, and the colony you've just killed will reappear if you leave even the smallest piece of rhizome in the ground. There is no more thuggish plant in my garden, bar none.

The offspring of *Geranium endressii,* especially the cultivars *G.* ×*oxonianum* 'Wargrave Pink' and *G.* ×*oxonianum* 'Claridge Druce', will engage in orgies of seed production and you will have illegitimate babies of dubious gardenworthiness everywhere inside a year unless you are a vigilant weeder. Furthermore, there are entirely too many similar cultivars in this shallow end of the geranium gene pool, as any investigation of a specialty nursery's geranium list will prove. I am sure botanists, and those wishing to make a profit on new plant introductions, can enumerate the slight differences between, for instance, *G.* ×*oxonianum* 'Claridge Druce', *G.* ×*oxonianum* 'Lady Moore', and *G.* ×*oxonianum* 'Winscome'. I can't tell them apart out in the melee of the garden, and I have quit growing geraniums from this group. It took a concerted search-and-destroy effort to remove all but one demure (because I keep it that way) clump of *G.* ×*oxonianum* 'Wargrave Pink'. This remaining plant is hard-pruned to the ground immediately after flowering so it cannot set seed, thus getting itself into a family way.

Now that the grievances have been aired, let us consider some of the many, many extraordinary hardy geraniums that make good neighbors for clematis. The meadow cranesbills (*Geranium pratense*) are good plants, but some get too big for small gardens. The aforementioned mourning widows (*G. phaeum*) are especially well suited to partial shade, and the bloody cranesbills (*G. sanguineum*) are loose mat formers for full sun that are the best "beach umbrellas" for clematis crowns. A series of *G. clarkei* progeny are certainly gardenworthy, and they, in turn, have spawned distinct and charming selections of their own. *Geranium himalayense* imparts remarkable shades of blue to its children, and for howling magenta, any form including *G. psilostemon* in its lineage will give you the blast of color your garden may need. It could be said there are too many hardy geraniums being introduced from any species, but in all fairness, for every plant that doesn't merit our attention, there is another new geranium worth making space for.

We gardeners are generally enamored of any double flower, and there are a few really good double hardy geraniums. My preference is for the double *Geranium himalayense* 'Plenum', which is a reliable repeatbloomer and is not bothered by mildew. It is also known as *G. himalayense* 'Birch Double'. At only 12 in. in height, it is an edge-of-the-border plant that gives good value for its space. In addition to *G. himalayense* 'Plenum', there are several rewarding single forms from this species. *Geranium himalayense* 'Gravetye' is compact, sun loving, and a unique shade of sky blue. *Geranium himalayense* 'Baby Blue' has a paler hue and also stays a manageable size.

Geranium pratense has three commonly encountered double forms—*G. pratense* 'Plenum Album', *G. pratense* 'Plenum Caeruleum', and *G. pratense* 'Plenum Violaceum'—which get a lot taller (to 24 in.) and wider (to 36 in.) than *G. himalayense* 'Birch Double'. The downside to these double pratenses is that they can take too long to establish themselves, limping along for years barely blooming while all around them other types of plants, and other geraniums, are thriving. If you have traveled to see gardens in England, you will have seen these pratense doubles and been overcome with desire. At Waterperry Garden School in Oxfordshire, they grow the blue and purple double forms right next to each other, demonstrating that there is, in fact, a significant difference between the two.

As seen earlier in this book, the O'Byrnes have paired *Geranium* 'Ann Folkard' with the equally floriferous *Clematis* 'Étoile Rose', a flamboyant conflagration that gives a punctuation mark to a long border of mixed clematis, other vines, and a skirting of herbaceous perennials at Northwest Garden Nursery. In my own garden *G.* 'Ann Folkard' finds many partners, and I especially like it when she meets up with the superlative roaming clematis, *C. ×triternata* 'Rubromarginata'. You often see this clematis cascading down the front of a tree, but in my garden I leave the plant to its own devices among old garden roses, hydrangeas, *G.* 'Spinners', and *Thalictrum rochebruneanum.* I prefer to see the spidery little flowers of this clematis up close, instead of viewing the mass waving at me from on high.

Undoubtedly, I have neglected to mention *your* favorite hardy geranium, but the species and hybrids recorded here are not terribly scarce and they know how to pull their own weight in the carefully controlled chaos that is a mixed shrub and herbaceous perennial border. Although often thought of as essential plants for cottage gardens, the versatile new cultivars of hardy geraniums, like *Geranium phaeum* 'Samobor', are stylish enough to find wider currency with modern garden designers and a more minimalist aesthetic. And they are great leg warmers for the clematis garden.

FILLING A TALL ORDER: LATE-SEASON COMBINATIONS

Certainly we can't complete a survey of all the herbaceous perennial plants that combine well with clematis, but there are a few more groups I want to mention briefly. These are common plants that tolerate, and perhaps even enjoy, having the blooming ends of clematis branches travel through their spot in the garden, making artful compositions that we gardeners might not expect.

Susan Saxton's garden in Gresham, Oregon, contains a thoughtfully selected and beautifully grown array of roses, clematis, and herbaceous perennials. At Susan's front gate you are met at the height of summer by the first of her many charming vignettes, the cool mauve duo of *Agastache* 'Blue Fortune' (pronounced "ag-gah-sta-key") and *Clematis* 'Star of India'. This is an antique large-flowered hybrid with an impeccable heritage. It is an early hybrid from *C.* 'Jackmanii', very like its

Plump and round, *Clematis* 'Star of India' is well married to the spikes of *Agastache* 'Blue Fortune'. At Harmony Hill, Susan Saxton's garden in Gresham, Oregon.

Luscious lilies flower with *Clematis* 'Royal Velours'. At Harmony Hill in Gresham, Oregon.

auspicious parent, but including a dashing wash of deep red down the center diffusing into the purple at the sepal edges. The bushy agastache easily covers the lower clematis stems in the full-sun site Susan has selected for them. The weight of the clematis is carried by an arch that guides you through the gate from the sidewalk to the garden proper.

Lilies have a role to play, and Susan has deftly combined Oriental Hybrid lilies with *Clematis* 'Royal Velours'. This smaller-flowered clematis can have very dark flowers, though they will appear brighter red in full sun. This clematis is luscious with the heavily scented lilies, and Susan has selected a subtle, white lily cultivar with pink spots for maximum contrast with the vivid clematis. At Old Germantown Gardens, plantsman Bruce Wakefield has used the large-flowered *C.* 'Ville de Lyon' in combination with the dark red Asiatic Hybrid *Lilium* AMERICA™. This is an exciting hidden alliance, found only in Bruce's secret garden. *Clematis* 'Ville de Lyon' is, truth to tell, more raspberry pink than red, but clematis fanciers take great license with both what is truly red and what is truly blue. (Shhh—don't challenge us about this; it makes us cranky, just like telling daffodil growers that their pink-trumpeted cultivars are actually peach. And let's not get started talking about what daylily people perceive as lavender, purple, and blue.)

Since we are speaking of Old Germantown Gardens, I will mention an autumn association that caught my eye there. The second blooming of *Clematis* 'Candida', a plump, white, large-flowered hybrid, rambles over a clump of *Crocosmia* 'Norwich Canary', which is just one of many late-blooming crocosmias now available. The spring bloom of *Clematis* 'Candida' fuses with the English Rose *Rosa* 'Constance Spry'. In the fall, the clematis blooms on shorter stems from behind its supporting arch, mingling with autumn-blooming herbaceous perennials in dappled shade. *Crocosmia* 'Star of the East', *Crocosmia* 'Constance', and *Crocosmia* 'Emily McKenzie' are three other excellent forms.

If you want a multipurpose herbaceous perennial that blooms in late summer, I will always recommend the brown-eyed Susan, *Rudbeckia triloba*. This plant grows 4–6 ft. tall, producing many thin stems that end with one to three 1½-in.-wide golden daisies with dark centers. Indeed, *R. triloba* has the smallest flowers of all the species of *Rudbeckia*. It is an

Glowing embers in a secret garden: Asiatic lily *Lilium* AMERICA™ with the French introduction *Clematis* 'Ville de Lyon'. Sublime détente. At Old Germantown Gardens in Portland, Oregon.

Late summer glitter: *Crocosmia* 'Norwich Canary' accents *Clematis* 'Candida'.
At Old Germantown Gardens, Portland, Oregon.

excellent cut flower, and it won't reseed much because winter foraging birds know it as a food source. Color combinations I would shun as gaudy in the spring I welcome in the fall, and when the pink-barred large-flowered hybrid *Clematis* 'Doctor Ruppel' makes its way into this aura of brilliant gold, I do not shudder. I am delighted. The brown-eyed Susan will also catch the last flowers of *C. ×durandii,* making the classic blue-and-yellow association recommended so often by People of Taste. Or you can put pink and yellow together and grovel with the rest of us.

Blue salvias are a weakness of mine, and many sold as half-hardy perennials have been long-lived in my USDA Zone 7A garden if placed carefully. The second bloom of *Clematis* 'Viola' (a multivirtued, Estonian-bred, large-flowered hybrid clematis) coincides with the pro-longed autumn display of *Salvia guaranitica.* Because *C.* 'Viola' is hard-pruned after flowering in the spring, the second wave of bloom appears on relatively short growth, only 5–6 ft. tall. The height of the clematis corresponds perfectly with the height of the salvia, and both plants lean into a sturdy lilac tree.

The second flowering of *Clematis* 'Doctor Ruppel' finds its way into *Rudbeckia triloba,* the brown-eyed Susan. In the author's garden.

Salvia patens, the gentian sage, is a searing, electric blue, calling sala-
ciously to you with its rudely extended liplike petals. This is a tuberous-
rooted salvia, so a clematis should be planted a few feet from it to avoid
the passage of its new shoots being blocked by the thickened salvia

Hard-pruned after its first flowering, *Clematis* 'Viola' will rebloom in time for
an unexpected partnership with *Salvia guaranitica.* In the author's garden.

roots. If you are unsure of your abilities with color, any bright white clematis (try the small starlike *Clematis* 'Anita' or the large-flowered hybrid *C.* 'James Mason') will make an adequate compliment to the salvia. If you are daring, aim a glowing clematis at *S. patens,* such as *C.* 'The Vagabond' (bright purple color, smaller flowers than most large-flowered hybrids), the glossy purple *C.* 'Kosmicheskaia Melodiia' (just say "Cosmic Melody" if your Russian is rusty), or the rich pink of the tall *C. integrifolia* form *C.* 'Zoin' (trade name INSPIRATION™) from Dutch clematis breeder Wim Snoeijer.

The salvia clan also offers us many purple forms that create drifts of color that clematis like to wander over and through. *Salvia nemerosa* 'East Friesland', *S. nemerosa* 'May Night', *S. nemerosa* 'Amethyst', and *S. verticillata* 'Purple Rain' all provide dense spires of true purple, violet, and bluish purple, and all are around 2 ft. tall. Drifts of salvia can be interspersed with drifts of any of the shorter *Clematis integrifolia* forms, and the salvias can also be used to cover the lower legs of a taller clematis that will carry the color harmony you've chosen to a higher level.

Many dazzling herbaceous perennials can be combined with clematis. To decide how best to merge the perennial with your clematis, try to see the plant growing in a display garden or in a friend's garden. Check out the crown of the plant at the ground, making sure the perennial has a loose root habit a clematis can work through if you want to use the plant as clematis footwear. Taller, sturdier perennials can stand side by side with clematis as long as there is no mortal root combat. Shorter-growing clematis, and those that prefer life on the horizontal rather than the vertical plane, can be planted behind the perennials and will meander into, around, and over the top of their shorter fellows.

Herbaceous perennials are sometimes disparagingly called the window dressing of the garden, as if that which is colorful is somehow not worthy of deeper consideration. Quite the contrary, I feel the versatile and kaleidoscopic herbaceous perennials give a garden personality and help me understand the garden maker's heart. Think of your garden as a layer cake, with structure (trees and woody shrubs) to give it dimension,

A little something for red-and-yellow fans, *Clematis* 'Monte Cassino' blooms with *Phlomis russeliana*. In the author's garden.

leavening to make it rise (clematis), flavoring to give it interest (garden art, seating, built structures), and frosting (herbaceous perennials) to cover its seams and make the parts appear whole. Some folks just don't care for icing, considering it insipid and unnecessary. I prefer my cake with the frosting on, the thicker and richer, the better. After all, the message of the cake is written with the frosting.

TEN CLEMATIS TO PARTNER WITH HERBACEOUS PERENNIALS

Clematis ×*diversifolia* 'Hendersonii': This antique *C. integrifolia* hybrid has a graceful, rambling habit, but does not cling. Its flowers are more purple than *C. ×diversifolia* 'Eriostemon'.

Clematis 'Guiding Star': This purple clematis has a medium-size flower for a large-flowered hybrid. I love the twisty sepal points. This clematis gives a good account of itself without hogging the spotlight.

Clematis 'Helios': What did I do for a yellow clematis before *C.* 'Helios'? This is a happy plant: The flowers are large for its type and bright yellow, and the vine can be kept small (to 8 ft.) and is free flowering.

Clematis integrifolia: What could be better with herbaceous perennials than an herbaceous perennial?

Clematis integrifolia 'Pangborne Pink': A well-grown mound of this cultivar would be an asset to any garden. It needs full sun and room to make a large crown of stems.

Clematis 'Madame Edouard André': This red clematis does not fade to the horrible washed-out pink that some reds do (*C.* VINO™ or *C.* 'Beth Currie'), even in full sun. She always sends out some horizontal flowering branches, just to see who might be close by at her feet.

Clematis 'Margot Koster': This is a soft mauve-to-red gappy flower that is lovely in mass. The color is surprisingly blendable. This vine blooms early for a viticella form (even if hard-pruned) and will rebloom easily.

TEN CLEMATIS TO PARTNER WITH HERBACEOUS PERENNIALS (continued)

Clematis 'Roko-Kolla': This cream-white large-flowered hybrid of Estonian origin actually has rather middle-size flowers. The sepals are pointed and the vine doesn't get too tall.

Clematis ×*triternata* 'Rubromarginata': A multibranched but lightweight vine, this tiny-flowered hybrid covers itself in starry blossoms that are white with sepals tipped in rose.

Clematis 'Venosa Violacea': This is my favorite clematis of all. There, I've said it. It has unique and striking flowers, is easy to manipulate by pruning, and is tough as old boots.

CHAPTER 8

ANNUALS, OTHER VINES, AND ANYBODY ELSE WE'VE MISSED THUS FAR

You have a small garden and a big love for clematis. Where do you go next? You have covered your house and all other structures at your command. All your trees and shrubs are carrying as much clematis biomass as possible. Vines are frolicking along the tops of your perennial borders. That leaves you ready for some innovative options. It is time to start thinking outside the arbor.

Each spring I spend at least an hour walking my garden with a pad of graph paper in hand, taking notes. March is the best time to do this because only a precious few clematis are already in bloom and I am not so easily distracted by a pretty face. I jot down possible plant combinations, remind myself of chores, and make rustic sketches of what I hope to accomplish. For the moment, I stop looking at my vines as precocious children and try to assess them with an unbiased eye. What I am looking for is healthy new growth, especially new shoots from the ground. Is the plant in need of one last bit of grooming? Have winter rains washed away soil so the vine's crown is exposed? Is someone overwhelming someone else? Writing down the problems generates a work list, making tasks less likely to be forgotten.

This process often yields an epiphany or two. It was during such an early spring garden evaluation that I had the brilliant idea that the outer edges of the sepals of *Clematis* 'Ville de Lyon' are exactly the same color as ripe raspberries. There was simply nowhere else for another clematis to go (ha! that was a hundred clematis ago), so the invasion of the vegetable garden began. Michael Pollan has written a wonderful book, *The Botany of Desire,* that discusses how plants manipulate humans so the plants can spread and evolve successfully. This is certainly how clematis behave in my garden. Perhaps my attitude can best be expressed as "the botany of desperation."

This desperation is not unique to me. There are many remarkable clematis gardens where the vines and herbaceous forms have been composed with surprising mixtures of plants and where clematis have been allowed to skulk stealthily into a garden party to which they were not specifically invited but to which they are welcome once they put on their party hats. A more amenable group of plants you'll never meet.

Once we have grown clematis with each other, with woody shrubs, with roses, and with herbaceous perennials, it is time to move onward and upward. Annuals, other vines, the vegetable garden, all are rife with possibilities.

Which brings me to why poor *Clematis* 'Guiding Star' was planted amid English ivy, how the much put-upon *C.* 'Ville de Lyon' survived life with raspberries, and where *C.* 'Gillian Blades' ended up after the great rambling rose removal of '96. It amazes me when people say clematis are difficult to grow. I have abused them (mostly unintentionally) in every possible way, and yet they do not merely subsist—they thrive. They flourish. They prosper.

WE'RE ALL VINE

Gardeners are inventive people, and it is great to visit open gardens to see how others solve problems we might have ourselves. The biggest problem might be having a small garden with a big garden's worth of plants. It is the fearlessness of small gardens, and their guiding spirits, that I find fascinating. Amazingly, it is these dear, daft folks—fools like myself—who seem to grow the greatest variety of vines in the smallest possible space. Not just clematis, but anything with tendrils, anchoring suckers, twining stems, and dexterous petioles.

In a bigger garden than my little city lot, I would dabble even more into the world of the honeysuckle (genus *Lonicera*). I would figure out why some get gray aphids so badly that they disfigure and cannot bloom, and yet others, no more than a few yards away, go blithely on with no worries. Their scent is intoxicating and their flavor must be the nectar of the gods for hummingbirds, who cannot resist even the forms that don't have a smell to my human nose.

As long as they don't have to compete for root space and therefore water, honeysuckles and clematis bloom quite happily together. The red tubular lonicera forms *Lonicera sempervirens* 'John Clayton', *L. sempervirens* 'Blanche Sandman', *L. ×brownii* 'Fuchsioides', and *L. ×brownii* 'Dropmore Scarlet' tend to bloom in midspring when the *Clematis montana* forms are hitting their stride and the large-flowered hybrids are coming on in the backstretch. If your *C. montana* cultivar of choice is in need of pruning and has clasped a honeysuckle in an ardent embrace, it will do neither plant any harm to be pruned as much as is needed right after they've flowered.

The *Lonicera periclymenum* cultivars, known as the woodbines, offer several later (June and July) blooming varieties that will combine ably with the redder-flowered selections of the Viticella Group. *Lonicera periclymenum* 'Late Dutch' (also known as *L. periclymenum* 'Serotina') combines in my garden with the fairly early *Clematis* 'M. Koster' (sometimes seen as *C.* 'Margot Koster' and I call her "Margot" when we're at home). The flowers of the honeysuckle are rosy red while closed, opening to reveal a creamy interior. *Clematis* 'M. Koster' is the same shade of dusty red as the honeysuckle buds. Also from this lonicera species is *L. periclymenum* 'Graham Stuart Thomas', and it is a vine as big and influential as the great man himself. There are many plant tributes we can grow in remembrance because there is a multitude of plants of all forms, shapes, and sizes named for him. His namesake honeysuckle has greeny yellow buds that are cream to buff on the inside, then turn golden in their decline. Any blue large-flowered hybrid clematis would be honored to bloom with it. Choose a clematis with as much vigor as possible and plant it at least 6—if not 10—ft. away. I'd try the large-flowered hybrid *C.* 'Rhapsody', which is so intensely blue, or any of the paler blue *C. viticella* forms, such as *C.* 'Prince Charles' or *C.* 'Emilia Plater'.

The Japanese honeysuckle, *Lonicera japonica,* has a purple-leafed form that is an excellent garden vine (*L. japonica* 'Purpurea'). The new leaves are very purple when they emerge in late March just in time to accent a like-minded atragene clematis, and I've chosen *Clematis alpina* 'Constance' as the early dancing partner for the honeysuckle. The creamy gold-to-yellow flowers bring their scent to the party in early June. The leaves become dark green by mid-June, and the vines make a grand snarl that, surprisingly, most clematis charge right on through. *Lonicera japonica* 'Purpurea' would really rather be a ground cover than a high-climbing vine, and that is why an upwardly mobile clematis has no trouble shooting right up whatever vertical structure is available. Standing *C. recta* 'Purpurea' in front of *L. japonica* 'Purpurea' is just the sort of stunt I'd be likely to pull in my garden. The All-Purpurea Revue!

The large and rambunctious grape clan (genus *Vitis*) can be effective with clematis if planted in the same way the lonicera are, with the root systems well separated and only the tops intermingling. The best vine for most gardens is *Vitis vinifera* 'Purpurea' (the purple-leafed grape), which is rarely taller than 15 ft. and has celadon green, downy new leaves that—over the course of the summer—turn various shades of burgundy (how apropos), the color intensifying after a little crisp autumn weather to add random dashes of red and scarlet to the foliage. The wine color infuses the leaves in several different ways, which can be mildly confusing at first; you wonder what on earth your grape is doing. Some leaves will develop pin dots of wine that will enlarge, looking a bit diseased until the color flows together; some of the leaves will develop the dark color along the veins first and this will bleed out to the leaf margins; still others will develop a purple outline that will eventually drift onto the entire leaf surface. All three methods of turning from green to merlot will happen on the same plant at the same time, so that by August the plant is all dusty burgundy. Once a cold night has passed, the color intensifies exponentially and the vermilion streaks and patches show up, making a vivid crazy quilt of the vine. Although deciduous, the leaves will hang on until early to mid-December.

Mature plants will produce small clusters of black grapes, quite decorative in their own right and attractive to foraging birds. In the spring, when the leaves are softly textured gray-green, the foliage is an excellent backdrop for the mauve-blue double *Clematis* 'Vyvyan Pennell', whose long-lasting flowers open a color similar to those of *C.* 'Proteus' but add a blue cast, one might say a blue rinse, to the large flower, making "Vyvyan" ideal for partial shade situations where the colors can develop without fading. In the fall C. 'Vyvyan Pennell' will have single flowers, more mauve than blue, which resonate against the now dark grape leaves.

Related to the grapes is the Virginia creeper, *Parthenocissus quinquefolia,* a big vine that waits for a cold snap to enrobe itself in brilliant shades of red. Purple forms of *Clematis viticella,* such as the species itself, C. 'Blue Belle', or C. 'Étoile Violette', will cast an agreeable smoky haze over the surface of the reddened Virginia creeper if they can be induced to rebloom late by topping the clematis right after their first flowering in June or early July. Cut the whole clematis back by about 5 ft—assuming it has gotten 12 or so ft. tall—fertilize, and keep well watered. In areas with long growing seasons or true Indian summers, the clematis should perform again.

In the O'Byrne garden they don't wait for the Virginia creeper to dazzle them in the autumn. They grow the variegated form, *Parthenocissus quinquefolia* 'Variegata', that has its green five-part leaves peppered with white flecks throughout the summer. This version of the Virginia creeper makes a gentle background for soft colors, and the O'Byrnes have selected the pebble-textured, light blue viticella form *Clematis* 'Emilia Plater' (pronounced "platter," not "plate-er") to make a combination of quiet charm. *Clematis* 'Emilia Plater' has a certain whimsical twist to its sepals—they curl under with a half spin—similar to the red viticella C. 'Madame Julia Correvon', a characteristic that adds a certain feeling of movement and dimension to any composition.

The commonly named potato vine (genus *Solanum*) is proving to be hardier than its zone ratings would have us expect (USDA Zones 8–9). It is widely grown in California for its generously produced purple flower clusters revealing the plant's nightshade family heritage (Solanaceae). Southern gardeners moving to the Pacific Northwest have had no trouble growing it as long as the roots are protected. This is a robust group of vines (some grow to 30 ft. tall and wide if not pruned by you or the weather), and a little winter dieback is not the worst thing that could happen as long as the roots are mulched or are growing against a warm wall. Potato vines appreciate a sweet soil, so placing the roots at the base of a concrete retaining wall or near a concrete pathway will raise the pH sufficiently to make this vine happy. A shy-flowering solanum is simply asking for a little lime to be added to its fertilizer. In a protected garden this vine may be evergreen.

The most popular of the potato vines is *Solanum crispum* 'Glasnevin', which covers itself with clusters of purple florets, each having a perky yellow eye (which is the stamens). *Solanum crispum* 'Glasnevin' will bloom in May, at *Clematis montana* time, and continue flowering well into June. This cultivar is more petite in its habit, reaching about 15 ft. at maturity, and the flowers are followed by yellow fruits that are wisely assumed to be poisonous. The more tender species, *S. jasminoides,* has two interesting forms that are not unusual or really all that fragile. The pale blue-flowered *S. jasminoides* 'Variegata' can get huge in areas with mild winters and will be deciduous in areas regularly nipped by frost. It will succumb in climates where the ground freezes. The plain-leafed *S. jasminoides* 'Album' with its bright white flower clusters makes a handsome foil for dark-flowered clematis that are June-blooming. This really is a smart-looking, crisp, and clean plant when in full flower, and Susan Saxton has combined it brilliantly with *C.* 'The President', a large-flowered antique clematis with royal purple blossoms. The flowers of *C.* 'The President' can show a touch of red or even a lighter brush stroke from midsepal to its point, but Susan's vines get afternoon shade and the color stays rich on her clematis.

Certainly there are many more vines to be considered for clematis partnership. Let your imagination guide you to more interplanting with such options as the climbing hydrangea (*Hydrangea anomala* subsp. *petiolaris*) or fragrant jasmines (*Jasminum officinale,* perhaps the hardiest, or *J.* ×*stephanense* with pale pink flowers) or you could even be daring with wisteria (*Wisteria sinensis* and *W. floribunda,* to name but two)—just be sure to select a clematis that can be pruned as frequently as the wisteria will need to be. I have had wonderful luck with the Viticella Group standard-bearer *Clematis* 'Étoile Violette' in *W. sinensis* 'Caroline'. They don't bloom at the same time; the clematis blooms for a long period after the wisteria has finished, making an excellent chronological partnership. Observe when your flowering vine wants to bloom, and there is sure to

In the Hardiman garden mixed vines provide privacy. Here *Clematis montana* var. *rubens* throws a jovial arm around *Solanum crispum* 'Glasnevin'. In Portland, Oregon.

Nothing makes royal purple look richer than a liberal sprinkling of white. Here it is
Clematis 'The President' with *Solanum jasminoides* 'Album' at Susan Saxton's
Harmony Hill, in Gresham, Oregon.

be not just one but a whole selection of clematis ready to harmonize or to provide color when the other vine is resting.

WHY NOT ANNUALS?

Sweet peas (*Lathyrus odoratus* selections) will be our segue from woody vines into the world of annuals. These quaint and evocatively fragrant plants have been enjoying a renaissance in recent years, thanks in part to Pat Sherman of The Fragrant Garden, originally in Canby, Oregon, and now located on the Oregon coast. (Sweet peas *love* a coastal climate.) Her early fascination with them led her to seek out older forms, and she painstakingly sorted traditional seed mixes as they bloomed, recovering antique named forms from a life of anonymity and making sure she had true seed strains. Her seeds can now be widely found in the spring at garden centers and garden shows.

A word of warning: The plant we think of as wild sweet pea, *Lathyrus latifolius,* which blooms along roadsides in pink, white, or a pearly hybrid of the two, is not a North American native plant. It is actually from the southern reaches of Europe. Despite being lovely (although it isn't fragrant), this plant has a root system that runs deep and wide, fully capable of strangling a clematis cultivar from underground. Do not plant this menace unless you want to have it with you always, and do not plant it near clematis, at least not near one you like.

In the effort to try as many types of plants as possible with clematis, gardeners have been combining sweet peas with the summer-blooming small- and large-flowered clematis cultivars. My vegetable garden includes many flowers for cutting, including sweet peas, and these are allowed to climb *Lilium* 'Casa Blanca' lilies and old leek flower stalks as well as use the three grocery carts parked in the vegetable department much the way a three-year-old child does. There are clematis (usually two) under the carts and they form a heady-scented concoction with the sweet peas. Last summer *Clematis* 'Minuet' formed a delicate framework for the white-outlined-with-lavender sweet pea *Lathyrus odoratus* 'Butterfly'. They were joined by the creamy sweet pea *L. odoratus* 'Mrs. Collier', one of my favorites. *Lathyrus odoratus* 'Butterfly' was actually planted in the ground near the clematis, and *L. odoratus* 'Mrs. Collier' came up from seeds planted in a pot that rode in the cart.

Other gardeners may not be as silly as I am and are certainly more refined in their sweet pea growing. The late Steve Antonow, an ardent gardener and clematis fan from Seattle, Washington, enjoyed sweet peas and used the heirloom variety *Lathyrus odoratus* 'Painted Lady' to hide the structure, of his own devising, that he used to support the herbaceous *Clematis* 'Alionushka'. He avoided the trussed-up look that artificially upright herbaceous clematis can have by giving *C.* 'Alionushka' a casual partner. Sweet peas never can look formal and, by planting them to cover the vertical mechanics, Steve created a beautiful and long-flowering effect. Easy maintenance, too, since both the clematis and the spent sweet pea vines could be removed in the fall.

We can travel again to Susan Saxton's garden to see more sweet peas well combined with clematis. *Clematis* 'Elsa Spaeth' is a popular large-flowered hybrid, long blooming and with a color that firmly straddles the fence between purple and blue. Which color it is depends on which source you are reading. One year, on the opposite side of her garden gate arbor from the previously mentioned agastache and *C.* 'Star of India'

Clematis with sweet peas, the fragrant *Lathyrus odoratus* 'April in Paris' with the large-flowered *Clematis* 'Elsa Spaeth'. At Harmony Hill, Gresham, Oregon.

marriage, Susan combined "Elsa" with the astonishingly fragrant sweet pea *Lathyrus odoratus* 'April in Paris'. What a way to greet your garden guests, inviting them in with sumptuous color and divine fragrance. Certain sweet peas need to be sniffed up close to be appreciated, but *L. odoratus* 'April in Paris' allows any passing breeze to advertise its fragrance to a wider audience.

Next to her front porch, Susan has made a more unusual but nonetheless effective sweet pea-clematis merger. A white sweet pea has been planted to mirror the white trim of her yellow house, but the effect is saved from being a too tidy monochrome by the placement of *Clematis* 'Gravetye Beauty' with its truly red flowers and tulip shape retrieving the ensemble from tedium. *Clematis* 'Gravetye Beauty' is planted near the concrete porch, enjoying the benefits of a slightly sweeter soil as a result and it blooms abundantly to show its appreciation of being so well treated.

Sweet peas are truly annual vines, leaving nothing behind but scattered seeds for the coming year. Other vines said to be annual will survive mild winters, and I call these the not-reliably-tender vines—you cannot count on them to die. *Cobaea scandens,* the cup and saucer vine, is one such example. It makes a handsome showing in one year, reaching 8–10 ft. tall in one summer. If there is no extended or severe frost, by the end of the next summer this will have taken over the front of your house and will be eyeing the next warm wall rapaciously. *Eccremocarpus scaber,* also cited as an annual vine, is now three years old in my garden, and I have taken to pruning it mercilessly whenever I feel like it. It begins flowering, flaunting its orange-to-red tubular flowers at just the same time as the large-flowered *Clematis* 'Daniel Deronda'. The ruby-orange of the eccremocarpus sharpens the lavender-blue of the clematis and makes more noticeable the nebulous touch of peach that sometimes occupies the tips of the clematis sepals.

Of course, annuals that don't flower on vines can be equally appealing with clematis. Most clematis are much heavier and more vigorous than your average annual, so scenarios must be planned where the clematis can just meander over, with the flowering stem ends making the connection with the annual. The annual lavateras such as *Lavatera trimestris* 'Mont

Blanc' and *L. trimestris* 'Mont Rose' are long-blooming plants (to 3 ft. tall) well able to fill temporary vacancies in a perennial border with luminous white or bright pink open trumpets, respectively. Annual cosmos are also very good at this, and those with unusual flower form, such as the rolled-petalled *Cosmos* 'Sea Shells' or the fluffy double *Cosmos* 'Psyche' will be less likely to seed around annoyingly. The green *Zinnia* 'Envy' makes an unusual and surprisingly effective companion for any color of clematis. Clematis make happy unions with dahlias, although it is best if a woody shrub bears most of the clematis vine. In Margaret Willoughby's garden, *Clematis* 'Duchess of Albany' careens over a shrub and lands on a peachy

A rare but effective partnership, white sweet peas with *Clematis* 'Gravetye Beauty'. At Harmony Hill in Gresham, Oregon.

pink dahlia that enhances the elongated pink clematis flowers. This is a long-lasting garden effect, with this "Duchess" blooming throughout July and August as does the dahlia. The vast range of dahlia color and shape gives us infinite opportunity for experimentation.

In my garden most nonvining annuals are planted in containers. They hang in the air, sit clustered on the deck in color schemes that vary from year to year, or occupy large planters that serve as visual anchors and focal points along pathways. Clematis planted in the ground are used to finding a constant change of dance partners from year to year, or even during the growing season as pots are moved or replanted.

A summer romance—the annual *Lavatera trimestris* 'Mont Rose' with *Clematis* 'Royal Velours' at Harmony Hill in Gresham, Oregon.

For many gardeners, dahlias symbolize summer. They bloom here with *Clematis* 'Duchess of Albany'. In Margaret Willoughby's garden, Portland, Oregon.

It is always enjoyable when a clematis hoists itself into a scene with a hanging basket. Plant nurseries have become much more sophisticated in their offerings for shady gardens, and it isn't just fuchsias or impatiens anymore (although I have those too). Hanging baskets for shade include violas, maidenhair ferns, and heucheras with colorful foliage. One of the baskets beside my kitchen windows (which face east, the shadiest side of my garden) hangs over *Clematis* 'Silver Moon' who happily climbs into the suspended planter. Because this clematis (which is planted in the ground) has a very soft color, I avoid combinations in the hangers that are too garish, choosing plants that are colorful but in the pastel or blue and purple range.

In full sun a wire sphere lined with moss was full of intensely purple and blue violas that were hung out in April and thrived until late July heat got the better of them. The bracket for this feature was on a 4 × 4 wooden post that served as the support for the early-flowering large-flowered hybrid *Clematis* 'Miss Bateman' (with her heavily mascaraed

Clematis find annuals that are just hanging around. *Clematis* 'Silver Moon'
blooms with a hanging basket planted for semishade. In the author's garden.

stamens) and was later covered by the creamy white *C.* 'John Huxtable'. *Clematis* 'Miss Bateman' has a long first-bloom cycle and she easily accompanied the viola ball for most of its life.

For the first eight years in my garden, I experimented with the large basket-weave-style concrete containers that sit on either side of the front porch. I've tried tree roses (too thorny), mixed bulbs (ratty foliage issues), and mixed annuals with varied success. The annual that proved best—best meaning showiest, easiest to care for, fragrant—was a shocking cerise *Dianthus* 'Ideal Violet'. While the color of this plant isn't violet by any definition, it is a carrying color that shouts "Hello!" as guests come up the stairs. You can hear it for blocks. Billed as an annual, *D.* 'Ideal Violet' survived three years before finally blooming itself to death. *Clematis* 'Madame Edouard André', a dusky red large-flowered hybrid clematis, was not to be outdone by some upstart annual. Planted in the ground but climbing up into a rose and swinging around the porch, "Madame Ed" made sure to throw a few flowers into the dianthus. The freshly opened flowers of the clematis were a match for the darker central shadings on the dianthus florets. As the clematis faded, the pair was not as well balanced, but this encouraged me to deadhead the clematis more regularly than I might have otherwise. After the demise of the dianthus, a *Fuchsia* 'David' was placed in each pot. These also look great with *C.* 'Madame Edouard André'.

After a gorgeous Chinese garden seat was stolen from the southwest corner of my garden (clearly I wasn't the only one who thought it gorgeous), I determined I would put a huge planted container in its place. Alas, it is not something I can sit on to contemplate that corner of the garden but, on the other hand, it would take a gang to even move it, let alone stealthily carry it away. The container sits in a perfect spot for coleus, and although dubious about the resurgence of this formerly déclassé houseplant, I am now a fan of the hot new colors and increased sun tolerance. These are great plants for filling in for the untimely demise of a key plant in a focal pot right before important visitors are expected. The coleus *Solenostemon scutellarioides* 'Pink Petticoats' attracted the attention of the reliable *Clematis* 'Ernest Markham', a dependable large-flowered hybrid clematis that most folks prune hard in

Clematis 'Madame Edouard André' flings her arms far and wide to find partners, such as the annual *Dianthus* 'Ideal Violet'. In the author's garden.

the winter. I find this plant to have an almost unceasing sequence of bloom without my doing much of anything to it except keep it watered and fertilized. If you are just *looking* for something to do in the garden, you could deadhead what you can reach, but even that is unnecessary busywork. "Good Old Ernest" shares the southwest corner of my house with the thornless old Bourbon rose, *Rosa* 'Zepherine Drouhin'. Although this rose and clematis marriage is consummated high in the air at the eaves of the house, the clematis blooms up and down its length at will and cuddles the newly planted container. The darkest shade of deep pink in the coleus leaves fits *C.* 'Ernest Markham' to a tee.

CLEMATIS WITH ORNAMENTAL GRASSES?

Although all around me constantly sing the praises of ornamental grasses, I seem unable to love them, which makes me out of step with almost every other gardener I know. It's a personal problem that defies solution. I do see the abundant value of grasses in floral design, but why not just venture into an abandoned, overgrown lot and harvest it to your heart's content? The one ornamental grass in my garden, *Pennisetum alopecuroides* 'Moudry', the black fountain grass, adds an interesting texture to a hot color combo in autumn. Poorly placed grasses in small gardens can make the entire ensemble look like an unmade bed no matter how tidy the rest of the garden is. Perhaps my chief complaint against ornamental grasses is that they aren't particularly ornamental in May and June when my garden peaks. Ah, but you say, the reason to grow grasses is so there will be something happening later on. Sorry, I want May and June to go on and on and on.

My friend Lucy Hardiman has tried for years to change my mind and, although she hasn't succeeded, one of her clematis nearly did. Early in her clematis-growing career, Lucy planted the silvery double-flowered *Clematis* 'Belle of Woking' at the foot of a cherry tree. For years the notoriously slow-to-establish plant would climb to the top of the fence, decide the effort wasn't worth it, and collapse back to the ground. When the clematis finally did bloom, Lucy (and I) had long forgotten which cultivar it was, but a quick visit by Brewster Rogerson reminded Lucy it was *C.* 'Belle of Woking'. Suddenly in the spring of 2002, "Belle" took off like a smoking rocket, at last vaulting into the tree and covering her-self with 4-in.-wide pom-poms of palest mauve-silver flowers. She was jaw-droppingly beautiful and was made all the more so by the presence of *Miscanthus sinensis* var. *condensatus* 'Cosmopolitan', only 4 ft. tall when the clematis was blooming, but providing a misty foreground. The grass had become the third element of a silver trio starting at the ground with a stachys (lamb's ear relative), the grass in the middle, and *C.* 'Belle of Woking' presiding over all.

What helped this scene work was that the clematis was actually nowhere near the grass. The perspective made the grass seem as if it were right in front of the clematis, but it wasn't, and a good thing for the grass too. Except for the major thug grasses like *Arundo donax* that, in addition to being invasive in most locales, is extremely straight, most grasses either have an arching habit or are open and airy. Grasses are meant to be sheer and translucent and to wave in the breeze like "amber waves of grain." There is no way that a grass can support even a few feet of clematis vine and flowers without being knocked off balance. Both the grass and the clematis need supplemental support to keep any such composition from interfering with the simple grace of the grass. It is far better for ornamental grasses and clematis to *appear* to be growing together without actually mingling at all.

THE LAST WORD

Yes, I did grow *Clematis* 'Ville de Lyon' in my raspberry patch for sev-eral years and a very happy arrangement it was, too, until the raspberries contracted a virus and had to be destroyed. *Clematis* 'Ville de Lyon' has been pouting in another part of the garden ever since, although the removal of the raspberries did free a wonderful amount of ground for more clematis and other plants too.

The delicately colored *Clematis* 'Gillian Blades' (white with a peb-bled texture and merest whisper of a lavender outline on newly opened flowers) was grown into the rambling rose *Rosa* 'Gardenia'. The rose was much beloved by neighborhood birds, finches and sparrows, who felt protected by the dense twiggy growth of the canes. Of course, birds forage everywhere and before I knew what was afoot, the rose and

C. 'Gillian Blades' had become overrun by Himalayan blackberries. There was nothing to do but dig out the whole area, destroying the clematis and the rose in the process. A low spot in the garden, under *Lonicera similis* var. *delavayi,* received the extra soil from the excavation. Two years later, *C.* 'Gillian Blades' was in flower, peeking out from under the honeysuckle. Only the smallest possible morsel of crown and root could have survived the great blackberry purge, but survive it did.

Desperate for space, the author planted *Clematis* 'Ville de Lyon' into the raspberries—a perfect match. In the author's garden.

At the foot of my front retaining wall, smack in the middle, is an amorphous mass of English ivy, which appears on noxious weed lists around the country. Every year I hack at it, but I am unwilling to spray toxic substances on it. The ivy may even predate the wall, and I suspect the ivy roots may be keeping the cracked areas together. So I just keep pruners handy. In the effort to dress up the no-longer-politically-correct ivy, I planted *Clematis* 'Guiding Star' (I think of it as "purple porch light"), a large-flowered hybrid that is purple with a flippant little twist at the end of each pointed sepal. After six years, *C.* 'Guiding Star' has actually moved its crown closer to the ivy and the clematis foliage covers the ivy foliage. The clematis is pruned very little, really only deadheaded, and it blooms about three times per growing season. Let's let *C.* 'Guiding Star' lead us to my next point.

Do not place any limits on yourself when considering plant combinations including clematis. Challenge yourself to see potential partners everywhere. Look beyond the prevailing wisdom about what will and won't work with what. No one has to live with the finished result but you, and if you think a purple clematis with a circle of 'First Lady' marigolds (*Tagetes*) growing around it is beautiful, then it is. After all, I'm the one smiling whenever I see my shopping carts in my own personal grocery department, loaded with clematis and sweet peas and 'Kentucky Wonder' string beans and with a pot of chives in the kiddy seat.

Who could ask for more?

TEN UNUSUAL COMPANIONS FOR CLEMATIS

Amaranthus caudatus (love-lies-bleeding): This annual is so dramatic draping over other plants or lounging on a retaining wall, a terrific companion for any clematis willing to grow the same way. Look for the green form, *A. caudatus* var. *viridis* 'Green Tails'.

Angelica gigas: In 1988 I heard Holly Shimizu, of the National Botanic Garden, encouraging a national conference of Master Gardeners to grow this plant, so I have been planting this biennial ever since. This is a tall, purple-stemmed herb with a long-lasting purple flower head that all manner of insects will line up to pollinate. It flowers late summer and fall.

TEN UNUSUAL COMPANIONS FOR CLEMATIS (continued)

Bupleurum rotundifolium (hare's ear): This annual is dead-easy to grow from seed (even I've done it). It produces chartreuse clusters of tiny flowers backed by larger bracts on well-branched stems. Your friends will think you have found the coolest new euphorbia.

Cerinthe major 'Purpurescens': The New Zealanders developed a fine named form of this unusual not-reliably-tender annual, 'Kiwi Blue', so now folks think this plant is a Southern Hemisphere native. Actually the species is from southern Europe. Gray foliage, smudged with dull white, and purple-blue bracts surround the pendulous purple true-flowers. Very easy from seed. Very.

Consolida ambigua (annual larkspur): This annual delphinium cousin is actually a clematis relative too. The stalwart spires of crepe-paper textured florets are available in purple shades, pale or bright pink, and fluttery white. If you are lucky, you will have a few volunteers for the next year.

Helianthus annuus (sunflower): The favorite summer flowers for those who are young at heart, a stand of sturdy sunflowers could easily share the job of supporting a not overly vigorous clematis. The cultivar 'Soraya' makes well-branched plants 4–5 ft. tall, with ripe golden flowers 3–4 in. across. Put a bright clematis with it and enjoy.

Lablab purpureus (hyacinth bean): *The* annual plant to grow for people with certain breeds of dog. This plant is purple in nearly all its parts: stems, the underside of the leaves, the flowers, and most importantly, the 3- to 4-in.-long, broad and flat gleaming purple bean pods. Not edible, but visually yummy nonetheless.

Phaseolus coccineus (scarlet runner bean): *Clematis texensis* was for years called *C. coccineus* until the taxonomists got hold of it. Both this and the bean have the same shade of flower, so why not try them together?

Raspberries and cane fruits: I was shocked by how successfully *Clematis* 'Ville de Lyon' competed for root space with raspberries. What about *C.* 'Étoile Violette' with Marionberries or thornless blackberries?

Tropaeolum majus 'Moonlight': An unusually tasteful color for this usually boisterous gang of annual vines (nasturtium). It does not come true from seed, so if you are trying to maintain some sense of decorum, you will have to remove next year's volunteer seedlings and plant fresh seed.

CHAPTER 9

GROWING CLEMATIS IN CONTAINERS

By now you are thinking, is there anything these plants can't do? No, there isn't. Clematis are being more widely grown as container plants, or as the star component in combination planters, than at any other time in the history of their cultivation. We should thank primarily the Japanese clematis breeders for making great strides to produce short climbing cultivars. They have been developed to be gift plants, much as has happened to azaleas, chrysanthemums, and hydrangeas. Careful crosses have resulted in vines that stop climbing at 3–4 ft. tall and turn their attention to prolific bloom production.

Another advantage of growing any plant in a container—including clematis—is that it puts us in charge of the soil environment. If you have a species clematis that needs exceptional drainage or a higher pH than your native soil can provide, it is easy to create a perfect environment in a large pot. Should you need to adjust this custom-made soil, there is less trauma to the clematis root ball in sliding it out of a pot than in risking a mishap with a shovel digging it up from the ground. Special plant treasures sometimes require, and deserve, deluxe accommodation.

NOT ALL CLEMATIS LIKE POT LIFE

Clematis collector extraordinaire Brewster Rogerson, who for many years has grown his vast array of clematis in containers in an unheated greenhouse at a private nursery, will be the first to tell you that not all

Many double clematis, such as *Clematis* 'Violet Elizabeth', are happy to live their lives in large pots. In the author's garden.

clematis are suited to life in a pot. Certain cultivars, such as the well-known, white, large-flowered hybrid *Clematis* 'Henryi' or the purple *C.* 'The President', will try for two or three years and then finally give up. One imagines the questing roots hitting the floor and sides of their cell, finding it all a rude shock, and summarily shutting down. Large species (although with small flowers) such as *C. connata* and *C. rehderiana,* while not having quite as drastic a reaction, will bloom poorly even with excellent watering, perfect exposure, and ample fertilizer.

Any clematis that gets extremely large or puts on 10–15 ft. of growth—or more—every year (even though hard-pruned in the winter or early spring) is a poor candidate for container culture. If you can imagine how much root must be created to support the mass of top growth, you can easily visualize pots being broken and roots escaping drainage holes to find real ground. This means that the large *Clematis montana* forms, the vigorous *C. viticella* cultivars, and the late-flowering large-flowered hybrids such as *C.* 'Gipsy Queen' and *C.* 'Madame Baron-Veillard' will not succeed in pots.

The Atragene Group of clematis, especially the *Clematis alpina* and *C. macropetala* hybrids, will attempt to make a hasty exit from their pots by any means available. After three years in a generously sized vessel in my garden, *C. macropetala* 'Pink Flamingo' is fleeing to the edges and drainage hole of its pink glazed container, with new plants emerging around the rim and out the bottom (more on this later in the chapter). This is typical behavior and I can suggest several courses of action. The clematis can be pruned after flowering to make it easier to manipulate as you remove it from its pot to assess whether the new plantlets have enough root mass of their own to be planted into gallon pots. Once established on their own, these young plants, which are genetic clones of the main plant, can be given to unsuspecting friends. This rearrangement of the root ball is a fairly difficult, labor-intensive method of propagation (requiring two humans to corral a large plant) and not one I recommend. Nevertheless, at this time when the "mother" plant is out of its pot, I can prune its roots and freshen the soil in the bottom and sides of its container before replanting it. This will buy me a year or two before the process is repeated.

Another option for such escape artists is to move the plant into a larger pot leaving the new youngsters in place. This will provide you with a climbing thicket where you once had a modest vine. Over time, the original canes of your clematis will decline and cease to grow, leaving the former babies to carry on in a wider root ball with dead material at its core. Eventually (a point in time that is never as far away as it seems), you will no longer be able to find or afford either a large enough pot or the manpower to move the pot and wrestle with the plant, and you're not getting any younger yourself. We often see *Clematis alpina* and *C. macropetala* forms suggested as good container plants merely because many do not exceed 8–10 ft. in height. In all honesty, this is a short-term proposition at best.

Consider the weight of the plant. Plants in pots are by definition a lot more portable than clematis in the ground. Each spring I generally rearrange my container plants to varying degrees, and there never seems to be another strong back around when the motivation strikes me. The largest clematis in the biggest pots can be scooted around on a hand truck. For the most part, I limit my use of clematis in containers to large-flowered hybrids that are both spring- and repeat-blooming, especially the doubles. It takes a lot of energy to produce those double flowers, and most double forms would rather flower than spend a lot of time growing extra lengths of vine. These rarely make giant, heavy-vined, woody plants like the *Clematis montana* forms do, so the weight is mostly that of the pot and the moist soil. I have a small garden, but even if I had a five-acre estate, I would avoid planting huge clematis in huge pots as focal points. Certain clematis will always do better in the ground. The bigger the mature vine, the less happy it (and you) will be in confined quarters.

Having said this, let me discuss how they manage large containers at Sissinghurst Castle in England. Most of their decorative containers are original pieces collected from France, Italy, and the Middle East by Vita Sackville-West and Harold Nicholson, the couple who created this famous garden. Other vessels were gifts to them. Vita and Harold used giant urns with relatively small openings to display clematis draping over the sides of the containers rather than climbing up a support. The trick is that the antiques are merely sleeves for the clematis. Inside the big (4-ft.-tall) pots are bricks and overturned terra-cotta pots that prop up the smaller pot (usually two-to-three-gallon plastic) that the clematis is actually growing in. The vine blooms when it should, beginning with *Clematis macropetala* in the spring for the start of the garden-visiting season, later to be replaced by *C. viticella* in midsummer. This is a dramatic and successful ruse. When not in bloom, the clematis live in an unseen (by the public) staging area. Individual plants that become unhappy in their regular plastic pot or get too big are eventually replaced by vigorous young plants of the same variety.

We all want our clematis to look happy and prosperous, to bloom well and be healthy. To that end, we must admit that not all clematis can do everything we might ask of them. Most of us do not have undergardeners in our employ to whisk away that which has become unsightly. Let us turn our gaze to what works best.

GOING TO POT

As a general rule, when planting clematis into decorative containers, the depth of the pot is more important than the width. In this way we are assured enough space to bury the crown and the lowest 3–4 in. of the stems if we are using a large-flowered hybrid. If the clematis I am planting is in a gallon pot (averaging in depth about 8 in.), then I look for a pot at least 12–18 in. deep. Clematis roots tend to grow down before growing wide, but this varies from species to species and cultivar to cultivar.

If you want other plants in the pot with the clematis, make selections that are shallow-rooted—annuals are ideal—or select a pot that is nearly as wide as it is deep, so other plants you might include that have deep roots (a rose, for instance) will have their own root space. Clematis don't like to compete too much at the root level, but manage nicely with most annuals and tender perennials such as salvias, fuchsias, and pelargoniums (especially the fancy-leafed and scented forms of the latter).

In small gardens a hodgepodge of different containers—glazed and unglazed, terra-cotta and colored, plastic and ceramic, wooden and metal—can be visually confusing unless all the plants are so bountifully grown that the containers are obscured. I have a small garden and long ago decided I would unify the container display in it by limiting myself to glazed cobalt blue ceramic pots. My clematis seem to like these very well. Another strategy for a gardener with wider-ranging taste in containers than mine would be to group containers by type, so you might have one corner devoted to terra-cotta and another devoted to a certain color, with yet another form of vessels in their own garden room. Using many colors, textures, and shapes together detracts from the plants and, even with my collection of blue pots, it is still the plants I want to feature.

Clematis are uniformly tolerant of many container types as long as the size is adequate. If you worry about clematis getting too hot when their pots are displayed in full sun, group smaller pots around them with sun lovers—annuals, bulbs, and sedums—that will relish the heat and shade the vine's container. Each type of pot seems to have a drawback or two that you need to be aware of to maintain sound growing practices. Plastic, for instance, is nonporous and can hold too much water around the roots, especially with plants that have been in the pots for a long time and the soil is breaking down and becoming compacted. Plastic absorbs heat quickly, but is not a good insulator, so roots can fry on hot days and then be steamed by trapped moisture when you water them in a panic. Thus you have "twice-cooked" clematis, a situation from which the plant may not recover. White plastic pots will reflect away a certain amount of heat, but are not appropriate for every garden or architectural style. Placement and careful watering are key considerations when using plastic.

Wood and unglazed terra-cotta pots are porous, so excessive watering is not the same hazard, but drying out the vine is. My experience has shown that it is easier to rehabilitate a clematis that has been overwatered than to revitalize a plant that is consistently too dry. At least with a soggy plant you can change its soil and mend your ways. Once clematis roots have become thoroughly hot and dry and the top growth shows sunscald, there isn't much hope. Poor-grade potting soils lose their ability to reabsorb water once they are completely dry. This makes an emergency bath unsuccessful. Trying to unpot a clematis with a dry root ball and replace dry soil with fresh moist dirt will tear the roots, throwing the plant even deeper into shock.

In the case of severe drying, plunge the entire container into a larger vat of water (the water should be so deep that the rim of the pot will be underwater and the soil completely submerged), preferably in a shady location, and wait for the pot to sink or weigh it down with bricks or rocks. Leave the pot in the water even after air bubbles have ceased to escape, allowing the plant to drink for several hours. Then you can attempt to unpot it and see if there are enough living roots to make repotting with fresh soil an option. If your clematis is in such a large pot that it isn't practical to plunge it into an even bigger vessel and it has become thoroughly dry, then I hope your summer vacation was worth it and that you fire the person you hired to water your plants in your absence. If desperate, you could make deep holes into the soil with a ¾-in.-diameter length of dowel or a broom handle. Carefully fill each hole with water, then repack the soil with the flat of your hand, add more moist soil if necessary, and hope for the best.

Troughs are not usually included in the list of good containers for clematis, but for lime-loving plants they are just the ticket. Several North American species such as *Clematis fremontii, C. albicoma,* and *C. coactilis* come from the Midwest where the soil is closer to neutral than in most coastal habitats. They like good drainage as well, so hypertufa troughs with a gravelly soil mix will provide both characteristics. The cement in the trough's walls will slough lime into the soil for many years, just as a new house foundation will raise the soil pH in its immediate vicinity.

While we are speaking of container types, it is good to remember that growing clematis in pots changes their ability to withstand winter's cold. The roots are now above ground, away from the protection of sur-rounding soil and a mulch or snow topping. In mild areas, such as coastal climates where winter is rarely severe, this is hardly a considera-tion. Most of the clematis we grow in our gardens are quite winter-hardy, with the exception of the *Clematis montana* forms (down to USDA Zone 7); these are not good container candidates anyway. Most large-flowered hybrids are hardy from Zones 4 to 9 and so will survive outside in a con-tainer with little care. Keep in mind that plastic insulates poorly and thick-walled troughs insulate best, with ceramics and wood falling some-where in between. If you are a worrier and are not overly concerned

North American native *Clematis fremontii* is happier in a trough than in acidic soil. In the author's garden.

about how your garden looks in the winter, you can insulate large pots by wrapping them in the bubble wrap used for packing. This is especially useful in areas with cold, drying winds and the clematis are in unglazed pots. The smaller *C. tangutica* forms, such as *C. tangutica* 'Radar Love' and *C.* 'Helios', are *supposed* to be hardy to USDA Zone 4, but anecdotal information suggests that in containers they become considerably more tender.

Again we have a rule of thumb: Growing a clematis in a container will change its cold tolerance by one full zone. In other words, you may have a large-flowered hybrid that is hardy to USDA Zone 4, but if you plant it into a pot, it will be hardy only to Zone 5. Consider the zone rating of your area and decide if the clematis in question would be all right in a pot or safer in the ground. You can decide for yourself how much winter protection you are willing to provide.

ABOUT THE SOIL

When it comes to a basic thing like potting soil, we truly do get what we pay for. It makes little sense to buy a $25 clematis only to pot it into soil that was on sale at a store specializing in home remodeling or groceries. Cheap soil is cheap because only the most inexpensive and least useful materials have gone into its recipe. You can find bark dust and wood chips, a bit of perlite, and lots of peat moss, but little else. If you plan to mix this with healthy compost of your own making, then you will be doing this stuff (one hesitates to even call it dirt) a world of good. If you use the cheap stuff straight, your clematis will be harmed and they will complain. Bark chips and peat moss are both acidic and neither has any nutritive value. In fact, fresh bark dust pulls nitrogen out of the soil as it breaks down, meaning that it is using the fertilizer you have given your plants for its own evil purposes.

Buy the best quality potting soil you can afford. Look for ingredients such as pumice or sand to lighten the tilth; composted manure (such as chicken) and worm castings to provide minimal nutrients; and kelp meal to provide trace minerals. The best-prepared soils even include ground oyster shells or dolomite lime to adjust the pH. Premium soils will add bat or bird guano for a quick boost of potassium, bone or feather meal for phosphorous and calcium, and a touch of soap or other surfactant to help the soil take up and hold water efficiently. If you are watering your plants properly, this last additive is not critical. Always feel free to mix in your own homemade compost. I use three parts good prepared potting soil, one part pumice, and two parts homemade compost.

I am often asked about the advantage of using water-fixing polymers in potting soil. My own results have been mixed. There is a tendency to use more of these expanding crystals than is recommended (the old "if one is good, two is better" theory is fine for garlic in spaghetti sauce, not so good for plants), and therefore we tend to end up with either plants that are overwatered in rainy climates or plants that are starved for water because we don't think we need to water regularly.

For clematis you want to grow in troughs, be sure to add more sharp sand (builder's grade or heavier) or fine gravel, such as poultry grit or pulverized granite (or perhaps a mix of both), to the potting soil at a ratio of one part sand to two parts potting soil. Add a scant handful of slow-release lime for each five gallons of soil you make. This will ensure the quick drainage that is so necessary for plants in troughs. The smaller-growing New Zealand species and cultivars, such as *Clematis marmoraria* (which is the smallest of all clematis species worldwide), *C.* 'Lunar Lass', and *C.* ×*cartmanii* 'Joe', will also appreciate this same soil mix even if they aren't in a trough.

Clematis preferring sharp drainage seem to also enjoy a top dressing of fine gravel. It captures warmth, reflecting light and heat back up to the plants. Perhaps it just reminds them of their native environment. I say this because *Clematis texensis* grows in gravel near streambeds in its home habitat and, whether in a pot or in the ground, it prefers a gravel surface. To me, gravel looks tidy and it is easy to weed. New shoots have no trouble emerging from crushed pumice, pea gravel, or gravel called "quarter-ten," which is not extremely fine and has been washed. Plan to cover the pot or trough surface evenly with 2–3 in. of gravel.

DRAPING VERSUS CLIMBING

Not all clematis want to grow up (just like some people) and some cannot—they have no mechanism for grasping hold. The just-mentioned

Clematis that need sharp drainage can have the type of soil they desire in a container. Here *Clematis* 'Lunar Lass' drapes down an antique stand. In the author's garden.

Clematis 'Lunar Lass' and *C.* ×*cartmanii* 'Joe' are ideal for pots on plinths (short concrete or wood columns) so their stems of varying lengths can form a drapery that will be clothed in greenish cream (in the case of *C.* 'Lunar Lass') or white (*C.* ×*cartmanii* 'Joe') when they flower in March and April. Both these cultivars have foliage that is similar to parsley, very curly, and quite attractive when the plants are out of flower. They are both proving to be more winter hardy than first expected, *if* they are given quick-draining soil. Either of these plants will decline when grown in acidic clay soil.

If a clematis is given nothing to climb upon (or climb up on), it will drape, as witnessed in the big urns at Sissinghurst. Clematis that can climb will try to do so if they can reach anything higher than themselves, so getting a usually climbing clematis to hang means that the pot it is planted in, or set into, must be positioned well away from vertical temptations. Large-flowered hybrid clematis that face upward are very effective when used this way so we can admire the faces of the flowers instead of seeing their backs when they get too tall. It will be necessary to hard-deadhead the clematis grown in this way, taking off another 1–2 ft. of growth behind the blossoms to encourage further growth and reflowering and to keep the vines from becoming ground covers, leaving you a lot of unsightly stemmy growth at the rim of the pot.

For this very reason, most *Clematis integrifolia* forms (with one notable exception) are poor selections as container cloakers. When they flower, they turn their attention away from their lowest foliage (it often yellows) and so, if in pots, will end up looking like badly grown Boston ferns. Even though they can be cut back to encourage fresh new growth and reflowering, there will be a period of time when the leggy brown stems at the pot mouth detract from the handsome bell-shaped flowers skirting the container. The exception is *C.* 'Rooguchi', that uniformly virtuous plant that is compliant in all things and will bloom from the top of the container to the ground. You will find yourself constantly looking for a higher support for your containerized *C.* 'Rooguchi' to increase the drama of its decent.

In the 1990s a new-to-horticulture clematis, *Clematis fruticosa* 'Mongolian Gold' became available to specialty nurseries. This makes a

Clematis fruticosa 'Mongolian Gold' is handsome draping out of a pot. In the author's garden.

woody shrub 3 ft. tall and wide, with lithe, arching branches ending in pendant flower clusters of shiny, butter yellow chubby bells. It flowers for me in July and August and resents late-season frosts once it has started active growth in March. Thus it should not be pruned until after all frost danger is past and you can see how much dieback there is. In mild coastal areas this clematis may well bloom earlier. The growth habit is reminiscent of curving fuchsia branches and, to further the similarity, I am sure *C. fruticosa* 'Mongolian Gold' would be happiest wintering in a cool greenhouse, getting plenty of light and occasional watering. In any case, this is a good draping plant and the only clematis I will recommend as a candidate for a hanging basket.

SUPPLYING SUPPORT

There are two factors to evaluate when selecting the vertical supports for clematis when you want them to be upwardly mobile even in a pot. Of primary concern is the mature height of the clematis, but we must also consider the size of the container. Proportion is difficult to teach, but most folks can see when it is wrong. Proportion does matter, and when a clematis goes into a pot and is given a staff on which to climb, we have, in a sense, created a floral arrangement visually similar to putting flowers in a vase. It makes us uncomfortable to see poorly designed flower arrangements that look either overbuilt and tippy or as if the flowers are just peeking over the top of their urn. Neither is right. The same principle holds true with all potted plants, and most especially clematis, because they will keep growing after we think our composition complete.

If the vine, loaded as it will be with flowers, looks too heavy, or if the container seems stumpy and the upright too tall, the proportion will be out of whack. Stand back and look at the whole picture when the container is freshly planted and the vertical element is in place. Even if the clematis is young, try to visualize how it will look when fully grown and with any companions included in the pot at their mature size too. If you are one of those souls who cannot do this, ask a friend who can to drop by and inspect your project well before the plants get too comfy in their new lodgings. Most vining clematis will embrace their new support in about twenty-four hours (although this can happen in about fifteen minutes with a robust plant in active growth on a warm day), so that is how long you have to decide if you've got the proper proportion in hand.

The surroundings will affect your sense of proportion too. Where will the clematis in its container be displayed? If taller, more imposing garden elements accompany the container, including its upright, in the sight lines—such as a tall tree in the borrowed landscape of a neighbor's garden or a tall fence as a backdrop, or if the container is glimpsed at the end of a pergola—then an upright that might seem too tall on its own will appear to be a unifying element between the scene you are creating in the pot and the greater garden context.

In floral design the basic rule of proportion is that the total height of the arrangement (the height of the container plus the height of the flowers) should be one-and-a-half to two times the height of the empty pot. This rule of proportion is why it is suggested that a vertical element be included in a pot of annual plants, whether it be a loopy stem of curly willow (*Salix contorta*), a dark and handsome *Phormium tenax,* a casual ornamental grass, or a stately *Lilium regale.*

Now that you know the rule, have fun breaking it.

Often, the mature size of your potted clematis and the proportionately proper height of a support structure in the pot will not be one and the same. This means you won't be the only one playing fast and loose with the concept of balanced proportion; your clematis is better at the game than you are. Most often clematis reach the top of an inadequate upright, then gently fold double on themselves. Sometimes a vine that appears to bloom from the ground up looks that way because it is growing back on itself, so the very newest growth is no longer at its apex, but flowing down the front of the plant. There is nothing wrong with this as long as the plant is healthy. In some ways, the plant will be easier to prune because all we have to do is find the bend, prune at that point, then gently tease the detached growth from its bottom half.

SUPPORTING PLAYERS

The shape, material, and personality of the supports you choose will be as formal and elegant, or as whimsical and enigmatic, as your container and overall garden theme dictates. My selection of things for containerized clematis to ascend is pretty nutty, but there is a method to my madness. Primarily, the uprights should be functional, something your clematis will be comfortable climbing. The leaf stems (petioles, in botanical parlance) emerging from opposite sides of a node like to wrap around fencing, the branches of other plants, and metal tubing or wooden stakes less than 1-in. in diameter. A few clematis with long petioles (such as *Clematis* 'Perle d'Azur') will obviously have more options and can even reach around a 4 × 4 post to grab themselves and shinny up unaided. How convenient that our modern explosion in clematis popularity has coincided with the abundance of functional garden art ready to support our habit (so to speak).

A wide range of support shapes is available: ladders, single shafts with finials, flower bells, tripods, fan-shaped trellises, wattle teepees of woven twigs, you name it. I try to group containers with structures of like finishes (we already know all my pots are more or less the same

Rust-finished uprights carry potted clematis aloft. The dark pink one is
Clematis 'Beth Currie'. In the author's garden.

color). Metal towers with black-powder-coated surfaces are in the same corner, out of the sight line of the many rusty uprights that are the majority. Copper-tubing trellises are likewise segregated unto themselves, merely to draw attention to them and avoid a clash of substances (or "substance abuse"). This is no easy trick in a small garden.

The upward guide for a clematis in a pot does not need to actually be in the pot with the container. The northeast corner of my garden is home to my pink flamingo collection and other flotsam and jetsam that are both tacky and pink, juxtaposed with purple-foliaged plants such as *Loropetalum chinense* RAZZLEBERRI™ and *Rhododendron* 'Ebony Pearl'. What better place to plant *Clematis macropetala* 'Pink Flamingo' to grow into the Rainier cherry that dominates that corner? A quick assay of the soil under the tree revealed that there were too many surface roots to make a hole of sufficient size for the clematis. Undaunted, I searched for a large pink pot. The potted clematis was put right under the tree and happily grew up into it, blooming with the antique miniature climbing rose *Rosa* 'Pompon de Paris', which flowers early enough to partner *C. macropetala* 'Pink Flamingo'. The rose was planted some years earlier before the cherry tree was as well established and it is in the ground, as is the later-blooming large-flowered hybrid *C.* 'Jackmanii Rubra'. Three years later, *C. macropetala* 'Pink Flamingo' was ready for a larger pot. The transfer was tricky and definitely a two-person job, involving the gentle sliding of the clematis out of its pot sideways, the placement of the new pot (alas, burgundy, not pink), and the careful alignment of the vine into its improved circumstances.

With a different potted cultivar, such as *Clematis* 'Mrs. Tage Lundell' (Tage is pronounced "tag"), that is annually hard-pruned, any transplanting from pot to larger pot can happen while the plant is at the manageable stage of its yearly growth cycle. This vine's container sits on a decaying tree stump, and the clematis enlivens the out-of-bloom *Rosa moyesii* in midsummer.

Or, the living support for a containerized clematis can share the pot with the vine. This is going to take a vessel of substantial size, since it is not a combination you will want to have to tackle often. It is likely this will not be an easily moveable ensemble, so choose carefully the plant partnership, the container, and the ultimate site of the planted container.

Woody shrubs that take to pruning are best for containers, such as the spreading and comparatively prostrate *Ceanothus* 'Point Reyes', hardy fuchsias, hydrangeas, roses, viburnums (*Viburnum davidii* or *V. opulus* 'Compactum'), deutzias (*Deutzia gracilis* 'Nana'), *Corokia cotoneaster* (a wacky woody from the Southern Hemisphere with dark contorted stems and tiny leaves), *Sophora microphylla* (with tiny compound leaves), to name only a few.

PLANTING AND MAINTAINING CONTAINERIZED CLEMATIS

Let's imagine you are potting up a new clematis into a glazed ceramic container 18 in. deep and 14 in. in diameter. Your intention is to grow a short, vining clematis with a fringe of annuals to provide color when the clematis is out of bloom, and you've selected the large-flowered hybrid *Clematis* 'Beth Currie' for this imaginary project. This clematis is spring-blooming, a matte red-burgundy (if the flowers develop during cool weather), and the summer blooms show a bit of a bright bar. This is an easy plant to get to rebloom.

You have a rusty metal tripod for "Beth" to climb upon. It should be 36 in. tall (two times the depth of the container), but if it is a bit taller, the clematis will appreciate the additional headroom. Put a rock or broken pot shard over the drainage hole, followed by 2 in. of gravel, assuring that water will not pool in the bottom of the pot. The potting mix is a top-quality soil to which you will add two generous tablespoons of a pelleted, time-release fertilizer formulated for blooming container plants. This will provide a mild initial boost for your new plant without risk of burning the new roots. Layer 3 in. of soil into the pot.

Your selection is in a one-gallon pot with a few roots showing out the drainage hole. Remove your clematis from its pot, leaving the stake in place if this can be done without harming the plant. If the stake is loose, detach any ties that bind it to the vines, and remove it completely. A flopping stake will work against you as you try to control the clematis when you situate it in the new container. If you have the plant out of the pot without a stake, hold the root ball in one hand while supporting the top growth with the other or lay the top growth over your shoulder. Sit the plant into the pot to see how deeply the stems will be buried. Now is the time to loosen a few roots if you can do so without tearing them.

Ideally, you want to submerge about 3 in. of stem and remove any leaves that will be buried so they won't rot into the fresh soil. If you need more soil, remove the plant, laying it horizontally on the ground if you've taken away the stake, and add enough soil to properly level the plant. Now replace the clematis in the pot (either in the center if the pot will be seen from all sides or toward the back if the pot will be sitting against a wall). Start filling the pot with soil until the root ball is covered, then insert the tripod.

Now the original stake can be removed (if you were able to leave it in until this point), and the top growth can be pruned by a third to encourage the crown of the plant to produce more stems and branching from the nodes below where you cut. Tie the plant *tightly* to its new brace so it doesn't slide down and bow out, increasing the chance of snapping the fragile stems. You should tie it more than once if it looks at all necessary. Once the clematis is secure, add more soil to bury the crown and lower stems. Pack the soil lightly (I do this by lifting the pot and setting it down again with a brisk thump). Water the clematis until there is seepage at the drainage holes. Now finish the project with three or four annuals (perhaps the coleus *Solenostemon scutellarioides* 'Molten Lava' or 'Pink Lemonade', a white wave-type *Petunia* to drape over the edge of the pot, and an erect *Nicotiana,* perhaps of the Domino strain, for scent), all planted so the soil is an inch or two below the spill level of the pot. Planting right to the rim ensures that soil will be accidentally washed out (making a mess of the sides of the pot), and you want to be able to create a bit of a puddle in the top of the pot that will give the plants a thorough drink whenever you water. Water the pot again with the annuals settled in place, and carry the pot (with help if necessary) to its permanent site if you haven't planted it in situ.

Water the pot every two to three days in cloudy but nonrainy weather and as often as every day if the weather is hot. Four to six weeks after planting, start giving the pot a blossom-booster type of fertilizer once a week, employing the same formula used on other pots of annuals in the garden. Stop fertilizing when the buds have set. Plan to remove spent blooms from the clematis, and excessive new growth can be pinched back at the same time.

This pretend clematis that you have just planted into a handsome container (might as well dream big!) will not need to be repotted or have its roots disturbed in any way for two to three years. This doesn't mean that some maintenance shouldn't be done annually, and early spring is the best time to do it. Begin by removing any spent annual plants and weeding the soil surface. Check the clematis stems and crown for signs of new shoots breaking from the crown and leaf buds unfolding out of the nodes on the stems. Cut off any lengths of dead clematis stem so the plant looks tidy and ready for the coming growing season.

Finally, scrape away the top 3–4 in. of old potting soil—which can be added to your home compost bin. In a large bucket combine equal parts fresh potting soil and your good homemade compost or purchased composted manure. Stir in a few generous handfuls of bone meal or a tablespoon or two of the pelleted slow-release fertilizer you used when the vine was planted. Use this fresh mixture to top-dress the pot, adding new soil up to the level it had been. This process will happen about two months before you decide whether to let the clematis fly solo or if you want to add annuals again for the summer.

CULTIVARS COMFORTABLY CONTAINED

Thumbs get a lot of use, what with rules being made of them all the time, but still I will relay yet another rule of thumb about selecting clematis for containers. Look for early-flowering clematis that seem to want to bloom from the bottom up and like to produce lots of healthy new shoots every year. Remember, you can prune a containerized clematis in layers (prune part of it hard, shorten part by only one-third, and leave a few stems longer) to create this effect if the plant isn't doing this naturally. Clematis that grow to only 8 ft. tall or less make the best container plants, *if* they will bloom on short lower branches as well as at their tops. Most double-flowered, large-flowered hybrids are good container plants because they put a lot more energy into those deliciously dense flowers than into reaching for the stars. Most late-season large- or small-flowered hybrids get too tall to be effective in containers. Herbaceous clematis will need all-around support to keep from flopping over the edge of the pot, revealing their bare-stemmed interiors, so clippings from twiggy shrubs or an in-container woody companion will hold them up naturally.

Try the *Clematis alpina* and *C. macropetala* forms in containers advisedly because these can be rowdy plants who resist confinement—they are escape artists. Repotting these can be tricky when they become mature.

Because growing clematis in containers is rather a new concept to most gardeners, and because there are many, many cultivars—with more new ones coming all the time—that have not been tried in pots, let us simply end the chapter with a series of lists rather than a ten-best-list enumerating those I have tried or seen in containers.

CLEMATIS THAT LIKE TROUGHS OR SHARP-DRAINING SOIL

Clematis albicoma: Nonclimbing, herbaceous.
Clematis ×*cartmanii* 'Joe': Rambling or draping, evergreen.
Clematis coactilis: Nonclimbing, herbaceous.
Clematis fremontii: Nonclimbing, herbaceous.
Clematis 'Lunar Lass': Rambling or draping, evergreen.
Clematis marmoraria 'Aoife': Mounding, evergreen; pronounced "ee-fa."
Clematis texensis: Climbs to 8 ft., lightweight.

DOUBLE LARGE-FLOWERED HYBRIDS FOR CONTAINERS

Clematis ARCTIC QUEEN™: White; can be hard to establish.
Clematis 'Belle of Woking': Silver-mauve-blue; slow to establish.
Clematis 'Blue Light': Said to be a blue form of *C.* JOSEPHINE™, but its center can be just plain odd. If you don't like *C.* 'Multi Blue', then this one will certainly give you the yips as well.
Clematis 'Daniel Deronda': Purple-blue; random lighter, weather-related markings; usually not double at second bloom.
Clematis 'Duchess of Edinburgh': White pom-pom type; said to be touchy, although mine isn't.
Clematis 'Duchess of Sutherland': Very double, red; not free flowering.

Dramatic clematis in containers don't need companion plants to steal the show. This is *Clematis* 'Westerplatte' in the author's garden.

DOUBLE LARGE-FLOWERED HYBRIDS FOR CONTAINERS (continued)

Clematis florida var. *flore-pleno*: Greenish-white; fussy; about the
only way it can be successfully grown *is* in a container.

Clematis florida var. *sieboldiana*: White with purple staminodes;
fussy; see *C. florida* var. *flore-pleno* above.

Clematis JOSEPHINE™ (*C.* 'Evijohill'): Pink, with darker bar on
outer sepals.

Clematis 'Kiri Te Kanawa': Rich purple-blue; slow to bloom freely
but worth the wait.

Clematis 'Louise Rowe': Pale lavender to blue; very crisp flowers.

Clematis 'Multi Blue': Blue to purple with a spiky doubled center.

Clematis 'Royalty': Dusty royal purple.

Clematis 'Veronica's Choice': Color varies with weather, silvery
blue or lavender; larger flower than *C.* 'Belle of Woking'.

Clematis 'Violet Elizabeth': A pretty pink-lavender; very crisp
pose and nice poise.

Clematis 'Yukiokoshi': White, can be touched with pink;
dramatic; hard to find in the trade.

Double large-flowered hybrids that are too vigorous and heavy for
containers: *Clematis* 'Jackmanii Alba', *C.* 'Sally Cadge', *C.* 'Proteus', *C.*
'Vyvyan Pennell', *C.* 'Mrs. Spencer Castle', *C.* 'Countess of Lovelace'.

EARLY LARGE-FLOWERED HYBRIDS FOR CONTAINERS

Clematis 'Asao': Pink, with lighter pink sepal centers.

Clematis 'Baltyk': Very large-flowered, purple-violet.

Clematis 'Bees' Jubilee': Light pink with dark pink bar, luminous.

Clematis 'Beth Currie': Dark pink to burgundy, color weather
dependent.

Clematis 'Blue Ravine': Delicate lavender with blue tones; must
be well-pruned to stay compact.

Clematis 'Burma Star': Dark bright purple; flowers identical to
the Japanese cultivar *C.* 'Sano-no-murasaki', equally compact.

Clematis 'Edward Desfossé': Wide flower; medium lavender-blue.

Clematis 'Fujimusume': Matte periwinkle blue, must be seen to be appreciated.

Clematis 'Gillian Blades': White, early lavender tones; pie-crust edge.

Clematis 'King Edward VII': Pink stippled over lavender, a unique flower.

Clematis 'Lemon Chiffon': Palest yellow-cream; think evening garden.

Clematis 'Luther Burbank': The largest of the large-flowered hybrids.

Clematis 'Miss Bateman': White with black-purple stamens; flowers not terribly large, but loads of them.

Clematis 'Mrs. N. Thompson': Purple with dark red bar, vivid but not garish; repeats easily.

Clematis 'Niobe': Burgundy with pale yellow stamens; reliable.

Clematis 'Piilu': Lavender to pink with dark pink bar; allegedly double, but I have not had it bloom double in three years, so I list it here with the singles.

Clematis 'Rhapsody': Quite an electric shade of blue by clematis standards; bushy growth.

Clematis 'Sano-no-murasaki': Rich royal purple; quite short growing; amply rewards kind treatment; difficult to find.

Clematis 'Snow Queen': White flowers with red anthers; very clean looking blossom.

Clematis 'Special Occasion': Pretty shade of pink-lavender, sepals can be paler in their middles.

Clematis 'Sunset': Dark hot pink, some would say red; its vigor is variable from year to year.

Clematis 'Toki': White, large flowers appear from the ground up.

Clematis VINO™: New flowers are claret-colored fading to a bland medium pink; haven't tried it in partial shade, but that may save the color; very reliable nonetheless.

Clematis 'Westerplatte': Rich red with persistent velvet sheen.

Different gardeners may have varying results with other large-flow-ered hybrids in containers, but I find many vines want to head straight up for a goodish while before flowering and no amount of pruning dis-suades them. Of the late-flowering large-flowered hybrids, there are not any I would wholeheartedly recommend for containers. We often see the mature height of *Clematis* 'Comtesse de Bouchaud' greatly underesti-mated at 6–8 ft. Try putting a 1 in front of both numbers (16–18 ft.) and you'll be closer to reality.

Clematis VINO™ provides a major garden focal point and repeats its flower cycle three times. In the author's garden.

SMALL-FLOWERED HYBRIDS FOR CONTAINERS

Clematis 'Brunette': Dark mahogany-burgundy bell-shaped
   flowers produced over a surprisingly long season.
Clematis 'Helios': Bright yellow flowers that flip back wildly;
   sometimes blooms precociously in May.
Clematis 'Rooguchi': Large dark purple ridged bells; try allowing
   this one to flow down rather than trussing it up in a corset.
Clematis montana 'Jenny Keay': Double cream-pale pink flowers
   on a shorter vine; the longer I know it the more I like it.

Clematis 'King
Edward VII' can
easily be brought
back into bloom and
grows well in a con-
tainer. In the
author's garden.

CHAPTER 10

GARDEN DESIGN: THE BIG PICTURE

My flirtation with being a professional garden designer was fleeting. After quickly realizing that creating other people's gardens kept me from working in my own, I gave up the effort. Having said that, I admit I have always been happy to render a requested opinion about someone else's gardening efforts, especially where the use of vines is concerned. Consulting with and educating my fellow gardeners about proper cultivation and plant placement, and suggesting plant and color combinations with my clematis and anyone else's, will probably occupy the rest of my days, whether anyone is paying me or not!

For most of us, though, the garden already exists and we have our own ideas about how to fix or change it. Some basic outline or structure of our garden's current incarnation was present when we came on the scene. Most of what I call garden design happens as we walk around our mature borders with a new plant, giving it a tour of its new home and hoping it will whisper, or in some other way indicate, where it would like to be planted. (*Clematis* 'Kardynal Wyszynski' actually caused me to stumble in front of *Rosa chinensis* 'Mutabilis', nearly dropping from my arms in its effort to effect immediate partnership with the rose it had chosen for itself. In the chapter on roses you've seen the result of this clematis stating the obvious to me, the oblivious gardener.) This sort of by-the-seat-your-pants designing may induce a domino effect: "Well, if I put you there, then that will have to move there, and I was going to take

Clematis 'Duchess of Albany' makes a lively partner for *Hydrangea serrata* 'Bluebird'. In the garden of Larry Neill and Craig Quirk in Portland, Oregon.

that out anyway, so that could go there. . . ." And on and on you go until you've rearranged some large part of your garden all by surprise.

Even a brief walk around an established garden will reveal many places for clematis. A blank spot in the perennial border could be filled by a *Clematis integrifolia* form. A hydrangea may look like an undifferentiated blob of blue in midsummer, and a wandering *C. texensis* hybrid with striking floral texture, such as the long-blooming *C.* 'Duchess of Albany' could enliven the picture. A handsome *Magnolia stellata* that has been pruned to become a small tree would be the perfect support for the large, white *C.* 'Candida', duping passersby into believing your magnolia is blooming out of season.

Clematis can play many roles in our gardens. As gardeners, we identify the tasks we need plants to perform (in addition to being pretty) and, in a genus as vast as clematis, there is bound to be a perfect plant of the color, size, texture, and timing we deem correct to meet the garden's needs. Clematis can serve as refreshing backdrops; they can enliven a focal point; short forms and nonclimbers can provide the ground-level border with an eye-catching edge. Clematis can animate the inanimate, and vining and rambling clematis can knit a scene together, literally and figuratively. Your choice of clematis will project a message about you to everyone who visits your garden, just as all your other plant selections do. Therefore, it is fair to say that clematis allow you greater artistic expression while empowering you to solve your garden's problems in many flower-filled, colorful ways.

SET DRESSING: THE BACKGROUND

In both large and small gardens, there are occasions when a vertical space just needs to be filled quickly. Not many of us will be faced with the dilemma of Sissinghurst Castle's curved brick wall at the end of the rose garden. The wall makes a half circle and in front of it is a bench where every tourist in the world wants to sit and be photographed. It is important that the space be covered with flowers for as much of the summer as possible. The problem has been solved by the installation of eight plants of *Clematis* 'Perle d'Azur', a large-flowered hybrid known for its luminous periwinkle blue, pebble-textured flowers typically dis-

played in great masses. Together these clematis form a blue wrap, con-
toured around the photo opportunities of the garden-visiting throngs.

What can we mere mortals learn from the vast canvas of
Sissinghurst? I learned that *Clematis* 'Perle d'Azur' is a sufficiently
bulky vine that one specimen—rather than eight—is ample to cover my
garden shed. In the O'Byrne garden one plant provides the inviting
enclosure for a simple weathered-blue bench. Garden visiting is one of
the best ways to learn garden design. Most people who grow *C.* 'Perle
d'Azur' have also learned that it is impossible to capture its rare shade
of blue on film. This plant is always more beautiful in person.

Clematis 'Perle d'Azur'
doesn't need to be
famous to be effective.
At Northwest Garden
Nursery in Eugene,
Oregon.

There are those among us who do have large gardens. Old Germantown Gardens in northwest Portland, the garden of Bruce Wakefield and Jerry Grossnickle, sits on a five-acre site, with three acres under cultivation. While the whole garden was not designed around clematis, a special clematis has been given an equally special structure upon which it forms the garden's autumn crescendo. The sweet autumn clematis, *Clematis terniflora*—at least that's what the taxonomists are having us call it *this* week—is, as its grower Bruce says, "the dollop of whipped cream on the fall garden." As it sweeps up, across, and over the garden's largest structure, a black wrought-iron folly, the scent of this clematis in full bloom fills the garden. All the fall colors, both floral and foliar, play against the billowing creaminess of the myriad tiny flowers. It catches the daylight—and the moonlight—from wherever you are in the garden. At Old Germantown Gardens, *C. terniflora* is both the autumn focal point and the background.

At crucial points throughout Old Germantown Gardens, black wrought-iron obelisks enfold roses and clematis, protecting them from the severest predations of local deer and providing mini focal points echoing the larger gazebo in style and substance. These mark crucial turning points in pathways and signal where to walk as one lawn swirls into another around island beds and peninsulas of perennials. A pair of these structures separates upper from lower lawns, noting the elevation change by their very verticality. *Clematis* ×*jouiniana* 'Praecox' is the summer- and fall-blooming clematis used in this pairing and the rose is *Rosa* 'Darlow's Enigma'. Together they make a bold presence in understated colors that do not clash with surrounding daylilies and asters.

In small gardens the appropriate background is even more important. Mike Snyder's cottage garden in Beaverton, Oregon, has the goal "to create the kind of garden my grandmother should have had, but didn't." To give definition to an island bed approaching a flower-bedecked arch, he has chosen an antique clematis any grandmother would love, the white, double, large-flowered hybrid *Clematis* 'Duchess of Edinburgh'. In Mike's garden we see the clematis blossoms behind a layer of blushing lace provided by campion *Lychnis flos-jovis* and *Pimpinella major* 'Rosea'. The haze of small pink flowers would be just

Wrought-iron supports embrace *Clematis ×jouiniana* 'Praecox', marking key locations in Old Germantown Gardens, Portland, Oregon.

Clematis 'Duchess of Edinburgh' provides an appropriate background for a pink lace vignette. In Mike Snyder's garden, Beaverton, Oregon.

so much busy detail in a very full garden without the calming background of this clematis, each white pom-pom touched—or sometimes smeared—with green.

I would imagine Mike Snyder purchased his pimpinella from the O'Byrnes at Northwest Garden Nursery in Eugene, Oregon, since they are the only reliable and relatively local source for it. In Northwest Garden Nursery's display gardens, the backbone of the facing double perennial borders is provided by clematis. The plants are supported by various structures, including bamboo fencing and metal obelisks topped with orbs. The clematis include *Clematis* 'Huldine' (creamy white flowers 3 in. across with a mauve bar on the back of each sepal) and *C.* 'Polish Spirit' (amethyst-purple flowers, 3–4 in. wide). Both these make large plants that prefer full sun, have a lengthy period of bloom, and are hard-pruned in late fall when they have become dormant. Elsewhere in the garden, *C. recta* is allowed to grow and flower when tall, at 6 ft. high, filling metal spheres with fluff. Shorter puffs of flowering *C. recta* stems are mixed with numerous herbaceous perennials, such as *Alstroemeria ligtu,* Asiatic lilies, various crocosmias, ornamental grasses, euphorbia, golden feverfew, and selected annuals such as the Chinese aster *Callistephus* 'Liliput Moon' and a delectable purple larkspur, *Delphinium* 'Piccolo'. *Clematis recta* also serves as a leg warmer for the *Hydrangea aspera* 'Villosa' that reaches its fuzzy leaves to the sun getting to 9 or 10 ft. tall but losing its lower leaves. This awkwardness is easily concealed by the clematis. Both the hydrangea and the clematis get afternoon sun, which prevents the hydrangea leaves from scalding.

Clematis recta 'Purpurea' is also widely grown in the O'Byrnes' borders as a repeated element, a filler flower that doesn't get quite as tall as its green-leafed parent and will rebloom at a shorter height if hard-pruned after its first flowers have finished. Remember that this is an herbaceous perennial that can be divided in the traditional way (digging and splitting) or propagated by semihardwood cuttings, so you can make a lot of this plant for yourself.

The background needn't be subtle. In the urban garden of Linda Ernst (in northeast Portland), a garland of the yellow *Rosa* 'Mermaid' covers the top of a privacy screen helped by the dramatic double-flowered, mauve-

Clematis recta and *C.* 'Polish Spirit' serve as backgrounds and leg warmers at Northwest Garden Nursery in Eugene, Oregon.

Clematis recta provides filler for alstroemeria at Northwest Garden Nursery.

aging-to-blue *Clematis* 'Vyvyan Pennel'. Blooming with them, but shorter, is the large-flowered hybrid *C.* 'Sano-no-murasaki' in a darker, richer purple. This trio stops the eye from looking beyond the fence until the daylilies in the foreground are ready to announce summer's arrival.

CLEMATIS UNDERFOOT

One of the most unexpected things you can do with large-flowered hybrid clematis is use them short—anything below waist high or even less than knee high. This is really the best way to look the up-turned, large-flowered hybrids right in the face. They will want to climb, but new vertical shoots are easy to snip off, making a bushier plant captured in the clutches of gravity. A brief list of good large-flowered hybrid clematis to use for ground cover would include but not be limited to *Clematis* 'Will Goodwin' (pale blue), *C.* 'Marie Boisselot' (white), *C.* 'Margaret Hunt' (pink), *C.* 'Doctor Ruppel' (hot pink bar with pale out-line), *C.* 'Madame Grangé' (burgundy), and *C.* 'The Vagabond' (dark burgundy-purple to purple). The excellent, interchangeable shorter cul-tivars *C.* 'Sano-no-murasaki' and *C.* 'Burma Star', each velvety purple, are also ideal for this purpose. Notice I didn't mention any double-flowered forms—their flowers would be easily spoiled by such treatment because the vine would have trouble holding these heavier flowers above the foliage and off the ground.

The Clematis Viticella Group, which we think of as so very vertical, can easily be used in low postures to accent stairs or tumble down a bank over the top of a more year-round ground cover, such as the spreading forms of hypericum (St. John's wort) and the genista brooms. In the fall, when the clematis has gone dormant, it can be cut off at 8–10 in. tall and the withered top growth removed. The new growth of the St. John's wort—or vinca major or pachysandra or whatever—will cover the short

Clematis 'H. F. Young' winds around the base of a tree at Penshurst Place in Kent, England.

Clematis 'Venosa Violacea' will run along the ground as well as grow skyward. In the author's garden.

clematis remains easily and there will be no bare earth, ever. Try to choose a clematis that won't look too bad blooming with the evergreen ground cover you're using, because even though it might not be your primary plan, the plants may occasionally bloom together, especially if you don't really want them to. The viticellas are also good at covering tree stumps and other unsightly garden blemishes that are not necessarily tall.

Nonvining clematis are excellent as edgings, defining borders and spilling over them. *Clematis integrifolia* itself forms a long row beneath my front porch along a concrete walk, its nodding blue bells watching my feet pass several times a day. It reblooms, which is a good characteristic for edging to have. Watch for new selections of integrifolia that are short and bushy to serve this purpose.

In Jeff Clark's Vancouver, Washington, garden, he has chosen the robust nonclimber *Clematis* 'Mrs. Robert Brydon', with its tiny but multitudinous ice blue flowers, to serve two functions. Although he uses this clematis to cover a 4-ft.-deep by 8-ft.-long boundary between roses and lawn, the crown of *C.* 'Mrs. Robert Brydon' takes up a surprisingly small

Clematis 'Rooguchi' forms a blue pool on the brick terrace in Jeff Clark's Vancouver, Washington, garden.

amount of space. The clematis blooms throughout the height of the summer, a cool pool in front of the brighter roses behind it. However, in the spring this area has bulbs to start the floral show rolling before the roses commence. As the bulb foliage ripens and then declines, the new clematis leaves, large and coarse in the case of *C*. 'Mrs. Robert Brydon', easily cover that from which we would avert our eyes. Gardeners in small spaces sometimes grow bulbs only as annuals, discarding them after they've bloomed because these gardeners haven't figured out a good way to cover the tracks of their daffodils, tulips, and hyacinths. Nonvining clematis are brilliant in this function.

Elsewhere in Jeff's garden, the popular Japanese cultivar *Clematis* 'Rooguchi' marks the edge of a shade garden and a brick terrace. It can be a lanky plant, but early pinching of growing tips will make it thicker and produce many more flowers. Like a lava flow, it streams onto the brick. With a plant this commanding nearby, Jeff had no choice but to paint his Adirondack chairs blue. *Clematis* 'Rooguchi' also serves as the main blue element in a blue-and-yellow color scheme including

Phygelius aequalis 'Yellow Trumpet', a golden grass, and a gold-leafed Japanese maple. Beyond all this in the deeper shade are a burly blue hosta and a lovely urn of bubbling water. If Jeff's composition were in my garden, I'd spend all my time in the chair admiring it and I would never get any work done.

What I see in these examples is that clematis used for ground covering and edging should be used in bold sweeps, creating minivistas where the ingenuity of using clematis in this way will not be lost on the casual observer.

FABULOUS FOCAL POINTS

What better way to mark a path's turning point or the entry from one garden room into another than with clematis? How better to accent garden art or draw attention to a handsome trellis than with clematis? An elegant large-flowered hybrid, well grown and in full bloom, will steal the show from anything else nearby—animate or inanimate—drawing the eye in, perhaps just the way we want, to highlight an area or feature. Clematis can turn even the simplest garden accessory into an accent of great wit and charm. A simple melodic color composition can become a great symphony.

To start with the magnificent, let's pay another visit to the garden of Lonesomeville in southeast Portland, Oregon. The gardeners in this well-designed mélange of pass-along plants—Danny Hills and Wayne Hughes—have skirted a Victorian-era house with structures of their own design including towering birdhouses, fences, pillars, wattle flower-border edging, and several particularly graceful arbors. The garden is further detailed by found objects, and a ribbon of garden lights made of mosaicked glass brandy snifters guides an evening stroll through the garden's main features. *Clematis* 'H. F. Young' was chosen to bedeck the arbor that signals the entry from the sunny front garden to the eastern garden's shady sitting area, hinting at more sun and fun beyond. Looking through the portal in either direction, we view tall birdhouses, and the clematis looks equally lush from either side of the arbor.

In the picture, notice the wise use of a few brick pavers to reinforce the grass pathway, which gets a lot of use by both humans and dogs.

Clematis 'H. F. Young' is a showstopper in an arbor at the garden called Lonesomeville in Portland, Oregon.

Clematis 'H. F. Young' was specifically chosen for its color and its ability to provide a big floral show during late May and early June when the garden is teeming with visitors and events. It is deadheaded after this first wave of bloom is through—the spent sepals turn the pathway the most amazing shade of blue—and there is another, more modest bloom later in the summer. Originally, as the picture illustrates, there were two plants of *C.* 'H. F. Young' decorating this arch, one on either side of the walkway. After enjoying their progress over the arch for several years, Danny decided he wanted to see more of the built structure, so the plant on the house side was moved to another part of the garden.

In Lonesomeville the *Clematis montana* var. *rubens* on the front porch and *C.* 'H. F. Young' are the only clematis performing arias. The other clematis in the garden (such as *C.* 'Jackmanii Superba' and *C.* 'Ernest Markham') form ensembles with climbing and rambling roses that all have room on the one-acre site to attain their full size. The clematis in the garden are not rare or unusual, but because of their effective placement passersby stop to ask which clematis and rose are which. Plants in this garden are selected for impact and companionability.

In much smaller gardens placement is just as important. On the east side of my back garden a 4-ft.-wide, 7-ft.-tall screen of metal fencing cloth with wood framing blocks the direct view of the raised vegetable and cutting-garden beds beyond. The screen is planted with tall climbers (a rose, a honeysuckle, and *Clematis* 'Lasurstern'), but detail in the ground-to-waist-high basal planting encourages visitors to stop and appreciate the small things before rushing to the garden's next enticement. At this stopping place I have indulged in one of my favorite color combinations, blue with chartreuse. Included in the planting is *C.* 'Fujimusume', arguably the best of the midblues and not aggressively tall; *Baptisia australis,* or false indigo, gives the composition a different texture in blue; *Sambucus racemosa* 'Sutherland Gold' is kept vigorously pruned to ensure plenty of vividly loud new foliage; and spires of *Digitalis lutea* add yet another texture, since the flowering stems are soft and pleasing to stroke. Seedlings from other parts of the garden, such as feverfew and columbine, are allowed into this little vignette as long as they harmonize.

Clematis 'Fujimusume' stops traffic along a path in the author's garden.

Connie Anderson (in northeast Portland) also has a small city garden, but by a combination of well-placed shrubs and a moveable feast of favorite containerized plants, Connie is able keep her garden fascinating and open to new possibilities for plant partnership. She loves ginkgo trees (*Ginkgo biloba*), although a small garden can handle only one or two in the ground. By housing unusual ginkgo forms in pots, Connie is able to put off the inevitable decision—which ones will be planted and which given away. At the end of the back deck, a forsythia in the ground anchors the back corner of the garden, providing a benign host for the double large-flowered *Clematis* 'Vyvyan Pennell'. Never one to miss an opportunity to show off good plants together, Connie moves one of her potted ginkgos into the arms of the clematis, with *Parahebe perfoliata* and *Corydalis lutea* at their feet. Connie has thus created a focal scene easily visible from the house and readily changeable to accommodate what is best in a given season.

A favorite garden to visit to see many, many healthy clematis grown every-which-a-way is Kinzy Faire in Estacada, Oregon. Penny Vogel is the plantswoman here, and several seasons ago, after being tipped off to a great clematis deal offered at a chain store, Penny launched into her "clematis year," when loads of new vines were added to the garden all at once. Luckily, the bargain price on clematis was followed by the discovery of inexpensive metal-tubing arches at a craft store, so her gardening partner Millie Kiggins, who builds the birdhouses and wooden structures found throughout the garden, didn't have to drive herself frantic creating vertical supports for the sudden influx of clematis.

Kinzy Faire is a garden originally founded on Penny's first love, roses, and the original farmyard garden is filled with those that have proven themselves to be fragrant, free blooming, and healthy. Perennials and woody shrubs have been added to encompass outbuildings and the remains of an apple orchard. A wide mixed-shrub border marks the far southeast boundary of the garden proper, and two dogs, Dolly and Bear, are assigned to keep the deer out or at least on the move. The garden surrounds Millie's house and, just a few years ago, Penny encircled her own house, across the driveway from the original area of the garden, with a deep border of perennials and shrubs; a shady walk for woodland plants, hostas, and hardy fuchsias; and a serene grove of 'Jacquemontii' birches (*Betula utilis* var. *jacquemontii*) underplanted with blue-flowering perennials, many having white variegation to echo the stark white trunks of the birches. This is my new favorite spot in this garden and the place where you are most likely to get Penny to actually sit down and talk about her garden.

This sweeping new garden is punctuated by the arches placed at every junction with pathways and revealing focal points. The metal-tubing arches are not exceptionally sturdy, so Penny often places on them clematis that must be hard-pruned so the winter-decayed stems and foliage will not act as sails in her windy garden. Blasting easterly gusts could easily torque the arches out of whack, knocking them all over the place, but they offer no wind resistance when stripped bare for the winter. In sheltered parts of the garden, clematis requiring less pruning are kept at 4 ft. tall through the winter.

Clematis-lined paths and mysterious arches lead to a delightful country view at Kinzy Faire, in Estacada, Oregon.

There are now many ways to enter and exit the older part of the garden at Kinzy Faire, but this wasn't always the case. An opening in a split-rail fence and a welcoming sign still mark the original entrance for visitors. The left side of that fence has a Millie-built bird townhouse to mark its end at an old apple tree. Since Penny has discovered clematis, no fence goes unclothed, and an athletic plant such as *Clematis* 'Polish Spirit' easily vaults the fence, ascends the birdhouse, and leaps into the apple tree, blooming the whole way from late July to mid-September. A coordinating hardy fuchsia has been planted in the shade between the fence and the tree, and volunteer annual larkspur are allowed to stay if they blend favorably with the purple harmony.

Elsewhere in the old garden, Millie's birdhouses are set on 4 × 4 posts, some of which are wrapped with chicken wire so clematis can form floral pillars, making it seem as though the clematis are strong

Clematis 'Polish Spirit' is a super vine, able to "leap tall buildings." At Kinzy Faire, Estacada, Oregon.

enough to support Millie's original creations. Now that the garden has matured, some of the clematis are in partial shade, but they have had a chance to adapt to this slowly and the partial shade enhances those plants with subtle colors.

It is a joy to note that the town of Estacada is proud enough of this garden to honor it with a mural. Their downtown area is known for its many murals representing historical events and points of local interest. Old softy that I am, I cannot visit the mural for Kinzy Faire without getting a little choked up. Great gardens, and the appreciation of them in their communities, have that effect on me.

SELECTIONS FOR THE SEASONS

There is another way to look at the gardens we've just visited and how they use clematis and that is to focus on the seasons. We can look at what is blooming when; how the clematis involved are used; and predict what will come next, or what came before, the scenes used as examples. What good is having a riveting clematis focal point if it is not seen in a flattering context because the clematis blooms too early or late to give the best effect? What happens in these gardens earlier and later than the scenes we've discussed thus far?

In Jeff Clark's garden the clematis show really begins in June when the pergola along his driveway starts to bloom with a succession of small-flowered clematis, including viticella and texensis forms. Even earlier, the garage that serves as the structural background for his rose and *Clematis* 'Mrs. Robert Brydon' scenario is partially covered by the abundant blooms of *C. montana* var. *rubens.* Don't be surprised to see this clematis producing a second, more modest display of flowers to cap the garage when *C.* 'Mrs. Robert Brydon' gets going in early August. Enamored of the integrifolia forms, Jeff uses them throughout his garden to fill spaces other plants don't like. He grows *C.* 'Arabella' right into *C. integrifolia* and together they can cover a large patch of ground, with out-of-bloom shrubs behind them in case they want to lean on something. Since both have a long period of bloom, these clematis will solve the problem of bare earth for about four weeks. Both *C.* 'Arabella' and *C. integrifolia* can be coaxed into rebloom by removing spent flowers and fertilizing.

Bruce and Jerry's garden is large enough that they occasionally forget where they have put a clematis, making the spring bloom of some vines an even bigger treat. Fortunately, they are good record keepers and can always look up the cultivar names in their site log. Certain key clematis are employed in the garden to fill certain spaces, though, such as the placement of *Clematis* ×*durandii* to grow over a stump in the midlevel lawn. This reliable clematis provides "stump dressing" at the same time *C.* ×*jouiniana* 'Praecox' is in bloom across the same lawn. Earlier in the season, *C. montana* var. *wilsonii,* the latest of the Montanae to bloom, climbs the native *Acer macrophyllum* (big-leafed maple) at the garden's edge, helping to integrate the garden proper with the untamed areas beyond. Linking the early and late seasons, *C.* 'Polish Spirit' has one of the black iron enclosures that keep it vertical, so this clematis provides a handsome background for Bruce's seed-grown delphiniums. Bruce and Jerry have planted them in mixed drifts for a luxurious tapestry effect and all the delphinium colors look splendid in front of the clematis.

Do not think that Bruce and Jerry's wrought-iron folly lies idle until the sweet autumn clematis display. The lovely, blue, large-flowered hybrid *Clematis* 'Ascotiensis' blooms in June, followed by a huge specimen of *Dicentra scandens,* the climbing bleeding heart with yellow flowers resembling its cousin *Corydalis lutea.* In August the large-flowered *Clematis* 'Madame Baron-Veillard' decorates the black structure in swathes of rose-pink.

In Connie Anderson's smaller garden, *Clematis* 'Polish Spirit' also has a role to play. The focus in Connie's garden shifts to the shadier north side of her house as summer heats up, and *C.* 'Polish Spirit' provides the summer color there after a few *C. alpina* and *C. macropetala* forms have finished having their say. A sitting area on this side of the house gets the best view of the clematis, but *C.* 'Polish Spirit' is large enough to wander down a short fence, providing a backdrop for summer perennials along a narrow driveway border.

City gardens often call upon clematis to hide the unsightly during the time of year when people are outside most often. At Lonesomeville the Montanae Group member *Clematis spoonerii* sparkles in a young hemlock (*Tsuga canadensis*). This clematis has white flowers that are enhanced by the partially shaded setting. By using both the tree and the clematis, unsightly neighborhood vistas are effectively blocked from view. Later in the summer after the main spring clematis show is over, the pink *C.* 'Comtesse de Bouchaud' blooms in the back garden through roses along the top of a low, stacked-stone wall and over an arbor made from the fallen limbs of a black walnut tree that grows on the west boundary of the garden.

In the Mike Snyder garden, clematis are expected to provide their biggest show with his roses, but in some cases clematis are asked to provide color atop out-of-bloom rhododendrons and to revitalize the back wall of the house where Mike's Lady Banks rose (*Rosa banksia* 'Lutea') rests after her tremendously energetic early spring extravaganza. Any clematis growing there must be a comfortable companion for the not-reliably-tender summer vine (you can't count on it to die in a mild winter), *Eccremocarpus scaber*.

The O'Byrne garden, Northwest Garden Nursery, is usually considered at its height of loveliness in midsummer when cleverly used clematis seem to be everywhere you look, but their show starts much earlier than that. Near the front road a buffer of bamboo is separated from the main garden by a 6-ft. board fence that hosts numerous May-blooming large-flowered hybrids. These provide interest to an area that will be shaded once the deciduous trees and shrubs nearby are in full leaf, but the spring effect is most important here. An irrigation tank in the middle of the garden is screened from view by a curved fence that, starting in June, is a stage for numerous vines, including clematis. The one vine that makes visitors ooh and aah in appreciation is the small-flowered *Clematis* 'Betty Corning', which is a cross of *C. crispa* with *C. viticella*. The open bell-shaped flowers are a soft mauve-lavender-blue with the characteristic white *C. crispa* bar in the middle of each of the four sepals. The 2-in.-wide flowers are produced in a continuous mass from June well into August. The plant is 8–10 ft. wide and as tall, but the 6-ft. high fence allows the vine to fold back down onto itself, completely obscuring its foliage. Individual blossoms of *C.* 'Betty Corning' have a slight fragrance that is magnified by the tumult of flowers the vine produces.

At Kinzy Faire clematis don't just occupy built structures and arbors. In midspring, the popular pink-barred, large-flowered hybrid *Clematis* 'Nelly Moser' faces off across the path from a shrieking pink rhododendron. The shady placement allows the flowers of both plants to stay sharp and unfading, hooting and hollering back and forth for several weeks instead of just a few days.

In a sunnier area of the old farmyard garden, Millie's house, surrounded by garden, has a great view of *Clematis* 'Paul Farges' (pronounced slurred with a French accent, "farzhj," and sort of rhymes with "large") when it blooms mid-June through July. The small flowers are in long-stalked clusters, each floret having four to six sepals that are creamy white in full sun. The anthers are soft yellow, giving the massed flowers a lit-from-within effect. *Clematis* 'Paul Farges' is a big plant, blooming on new wood as it grows (around 20 ft. in a year). The show of late-summer seed heads is magnificent. Penny has "Paul" wandering over dwarf conifers and out-of-bloom viburnums who are unbothered by the seasonal weight and may, in fact, appreciate the shade during the hottest summer weather. This clematis is hard-pruned every winter or in the late fall. This big vine solves the problem of an out-of-bloom area of the garden with a lot less maintenance than a mass of summer-blooming perennials would need.

Thus all the gardens in this chapter, from the largest, Kinzy Faire, to the smallest, Connie Anderson's, are relying on a colorful cast of clematis characters to provide interest throughout the growing season. Although they are grown primarily because they are lovely, these clematis all have a job to do, from accenting a beloved containerized *Ginkgo biloba* to covering big structures and mature shrubs with flowers and scent during a garden's season of maximum beauty. Each has a role to play, and each clematis is a star.

IN SUMMATION

You will have noticed that throughout this book I have lapsed occasionally into referring to clematis, and other plants, by using personal pronouns. I do not believe plants are human, but they do seem to be entities with distinct personalities. Other gardeners have stated—better than I—that gardening is a reflection of human life and plants resemble the people in our lives. For gardeners, some plants are friends who stick by you and never let you down. Some plants are con men, all flash and no substance, and they leave you feeling you've been sold a bill of goods without actually getting the goods. Some plants are feminine, some masculine. There are plants you hear a lot about before you meet, like being set up on a blind date by well-meaning friends—the date works out or it doesn't. And it is hard not to personalize plants when so many cultivars are, for better or worse, named after people.

For me, clematis are not *like* family, they *are* family. In this vast, broad genus of plants, there is a disposition in each species and cultivar. The fascination of clematis is their comedy, drama, and whole gamut of evoked emotions in between. Clematis can be quarrelsome (*Clematis* 'Barbara Dibley'), elusive (*C. texensis*), eccentric (*C.* 'Multi Blue'), mellow (*C.* 'Niobe'), lumbering (*C. montana* var. *wilsonii*), statuesque (*C.* 'Gipsy Queen'), clever (*C.* ×*durandii*), breathtaking (*C.* 'Fujimusume'), exuberant (*C.* 'Helios'), charming (*C. crispa*), tawdry (*C.* 'John Warren'), pliant (*C.* 'Brunette'), moody (*C.* 'Sunset'), precocious (*C. macropetala* 'Mountaindale'), egocentric (*C. armandii*), and sly (*C.* 'Romantika'). Some clematis are like my dad—they really know how to tell a good joke (*C.* 'Perle d'Azur' blooms amid a hardy banana in Lucy Hardiman's garden, foregoing its pretense of refinement and taste).

And some are merely beautiful (*Clematis* 'Venosa Violacea').

Weaving the forms and colors of clematis throughout your other garden plants will show you how versatile this genus truly is. Creating a clematis garden will make you wonder how gardens can possibly be successful without growing many, many of them. My hope is that now you will go forward seeking clematis that are new to you for your garden, including the justifiably beloved antiques and the best modern cultivars. My hope is that you will be emboldened to use clematis in new ways, plant them confidently, ignore the setbacks, applaud their successes.

My hope is that you will now create a clematis garden that is innovative, that will challenge you, and that you love.

MY TEN FAVORITE CLEMATIS

Clematis 'Ai-Nor': The most striking pink, large-flowered hybrid yet introduced comes to us from the Ukraine. Watch for this one. The color is nearly peach when it opens and after two or three days it becomes a clean, true pink with no lavender shading. Wish I had it.

Clematis 'Allanah': From New Zealand, this is a great, red, large-flowered hybrid with not a ton of flowers, but twice blooming, and the plant responds well to midsummer pruning. The gappy flower form is engaging and the color is bright.

Clematis crispa: These remarkable small flowers are chunky bells that have tightly recurved sepals crenellated along their edges. The flowers are pale lavender or blue and the sepals have a white bar, so the flower face shows a white plus sign. The easiest of the North American species to grow.

Clematis ×durandii: An integrifolia hybrid like no other, this is the most vigorous, reliable, and bluest. Long blooming and site adaptable. I have a great sentimental attachment to my own plant, the first clematis I ever purchased from Brewster Rogerson.

Clematis 'Gipsy Queen': The grand dame of purple large-flowered hybrids. Once your plant is mature, try not pruning it some winter and watch how early it blooms and for how long. It is the color of grape jelly.

Clematis 'Louise Rowe': Not every clemateer's favorite double, but I love the ice blue color, the crispness of the sepals, and the random way the plant produces its double, semi-double, and single flowers on its own schedule.

C. macropetala 'Mountaindale': This is a new selection of a fine species, free flowering and of the clearest blue; well doubled.

Clematis texensis: This is *the* red ancestor from which all other red clematis spring. Historically valuable and utterly charming. The rarely available forms of this vine fall into two camps: either with a red exterior and a yellow interior or all red throughout. Were I a plant breeder, I would use the all-red form as a parent. When the French were developing such gorgeous red clematis as *C.* 'Ville de Lyon' and *C.* 'Madame Julia Correvon', they must have been using a very fine *C. texensis* form indeed.

Clematis 'Venosa Violacea': This has large flowers for a viticella type, white sepals with purple veining that intensifies toward the margins, making a variably intense outline of purple. There can be notable variations of color among the flowers on one plant. Reliable and beautiful. I can gaze at this for hours at a time.

Clematis 'Westerplatte': This is another great, red, large-flowered hybrid introduction from Poland where so many good reds have come from recently, but this one has a persistent velvet sheen and amazing depth of color. Not the strongest grower, but what a flower. Stunning.

ACKNOWLEDGMENTS

I need to thank many people for stirring me to action on this project. My garden buddy Mike Snyder was there at the conception of this book—as we rode around England on a tour bus in 1998, he kept saying, "You must write. You've got to write a book." Mike pre-edited tirelessly, for which I cannot thank him enough. I thank my dear friends, Brooke Hansen (who keeps me young) and Jacky Mitzel (the best friend), for their unbridled enthusiasm. I thank Dorothy and David Rodal, and Mary Hoffman, who never turned away anything I submitted to the Hardy Plant Society of Oregon *Bulletin*. They are unfailingly kind to the insecure. Dorothy was an angel to help with the eleventh hour proofreading of this book. I also thank Wendy Street and Robin Miller, for their years of mentorship and hilarity. During the sprint to the finish (how easy to pretend deadlines will never come), Sharon Kaito really kept my spirits up. Dottie Ferrell, Opal Kickbusch, Amy Burbach, and the long-suffering staff at Laurelhurst Florist put up with my odd scheduling requests, giving me the freedom to devote myself to the writing of this book.

My parents have always been my most ardent fans. Mom (Betty Crisp) and Dad (the late Glenn S. Crisp, Jr.) always said, "If you're going to write it, you'd better be proud to sign it." My late Cayo grandparents, Ray and Bernice, taught me that gardening is an integral part of living. I thank also my husband, Larry (who continues to attempt to reason with me, keeping me from throwing the computer into the street), and the Beutler family, especially my mother-in-law, Shirley, and my traveling companion and sister-in-law, Carla.

In the world of clematis I thank Maurice Horn (for his friendship and enthusiasm about our writing, together and solo), Dr. Mary Toomey (who is the soul of generosity), Victoria Matthews (our amazing clematis registrar), Mike Darcy (the encouraging public voice of Portland gardening), Diana Reeck (she knows her Ranunculaceae), the Pacific Northwest Clematis Society, and the International Clematis Society.

My life as an ornamental gardener began when I joined the Hardy Plant Society of Oregon, so I thank all of those who served on the Board of Directors and on the plant sale committee with me over the years, especially Deborah Meyers (who can manage anything and gives the best hugs). I can't leave out a nod to a special friend and Hardy Plant woman, Nancy Goldman. When she is on your side, good things happen.

Thanks to Allan Mandell, garden photographer, who is uniquely able to articulate his artistic vision, so that a camera novice like myself can occasionally accomplish something printable. Without his instruction, this book would not have been possible.

Many helpful gardeners are found throughout the world of horticulture, and I would be remiss to not acknowledge the friendship and knowledge passed on to me from Elizabeth Howley (head of the Horticulture Department, Clackamas Community College), Andy Van Hevlingen (the best herb grower anywhere), Laura Murray (who started me on daylilies), Jean E. Driver (who started me on *Narcissus*), Carol Pollard Nehring (who started me on dwarf conifers), Ann Lovejoy (who reminds us that we garden in paradise), and C. Colston Burrell (my honorary Oregonian).

To the gardeners who allowed me into their gardens and let me carefully take pictures of or describe their life's work, I say a most humble, "Thanks." I have had the privilege of watching some of these gardens evolve over many years, and it is an honor to include them here. They are (in no particular order): Bruce Wakefield and Jerry Grossnickle, Old Germantown Gardens; Ernie and Marietta O'Byrne, Northwest Garden Nursery; the Gossler family, Gossler Farms Nursery; Penny Vogel and Millie Kiggins, Kinzy Faire; Craig Quirk and Larry Neill; Jeff Clarke; Susan Saxton, Harmony Hill; Mike Snyder; Jill Schatz, Jill Schatz Plants; Diana Reeck and Bill Janssen, Collector's Nursery; Dorothy and David

Rodal, Exuberant Gardens; Connie Anderson; Joann Thomas, Catswalk; Margaret Willoughby; Danny Hills and Wayne Hughes, Lonesomeville; Brewster Rogerson; Linda Ernst; Maurice Horn and Mike Smith, Joy Creek Nursery; and the folks at Heronswood Nursery. And thanks to Jan Robertson, my westerly next-door neighbor, who at times has better views of my vines than I do, and allows me to photograph my side from her side. They have all been generous with their gardens, plants, and humor, and patient with me.

Thanks also to Neal Maillet at Timber Press, who guided *Gardening with Clematis* into being. His willingness to take a chance on a novice author has earned his place in garden heaven.

And the biggest of *all* possible thanks to Lucy Hardiman, who graciously inhabits and transcends all of these groups. She is the sister, the co-conspirator, the sounding board, the fashion consultant; gardener *extraordinaire*, visionary, unrepentant bleeding-heart liberal, and advocate of free speech. She knows, more than anyone, what a miracle this book is.

APPENDIX 1

THE CARE AND FEEDING OF CLEMATIS: PLANTING, WATERING, FERTILIZING, COMMON PESTS AND DISEASES

SOILS

It is generally assumed that clematis need soil with a neutral pH or slightly higher and that all of North America has acidic soil. Clematis are actually quite forgiving about most soil conditions, and large portions of North America, especially the Midwest, have perfect clematis soil. Indeed, these are the areas where some of the most interesting North American native clematis are found (*Clematis texensis, C. fremontii, C. addisonii*). Soil pH should always be tested in new gardens and adjusted to 6.5 to 6.8 to accommodate the greatest diversity of garden plants. Clematis will operate well within this range, with the exception of those species coming from habitats with a more basic pH. Collectors grow these in containers so the soil environment can be completely controlled (see chapter nine).

Clematis prefer free-draining soil that is rich in organic material. The only clematis that is both readily available to gardeners and tolerant of having occasionally wet roots is *Clematis crispa.* It hails from the American Southeast and has the common name marsh clematis. Other species and their near hybrids and the large-flowered hybrids prefer heavy sand (called builder's sand or road grit), poultry grit, or small-diameter gravel mixed into the soil to promote drainage in areas with heavy clay content. This is especially true for *C. texensis* and its hybrids as well as the other members of the Viorna Group of the genus.

WATER AND FERTILIZING

Although they require good drainage, clematis need a lot of water to bloom prolifically and consistently. This is especially true of plants grown in containers placed in full sun. Water-stressed plants are more susceptible to pests such as aphids and spider mites and to fungal diseases such as powdery mildew. Plants that are about to bloom are the most in need of even soil moisture. If spiking high temperatures are expected when your plants are about to bloom, monitor their water carefully. In times of hot weather, it is better to overwater than to be stingy, hoping that your plants will "toughen up." They won't. Clematis that are too dry are more likely to show sunburn on their leaves, with drooping buds or misshapen flowers and sudden influxes of opportunistic pests.

Clematis are heavy feeders and like to be given mild fertilizers often. I use a rose and flower food with a 4–6–2 formula, sprinkled over the ground around (but not on) the crown of the plant once a month from March through September, *unless the plant is full of buds and about to bloom.* The feeding is continued once bloom has ceased. If you find you need or want to prune a clematis during the growing season, treat it to a diluted dose of fertilizer immediately afterward.

I know gardeners who have had great success using slow-release pellets such as Osmocote's flowering-plant formula. A twice-yearly application of alfalfa pellets (such as are fed to rabbits and are available at feed stores) given in April and July is also a successful regimen for clematis and roses both. Be sure to purchase alfalfa pellets that have no additives.

Clematis complain when iron and magnesium levels get too low. Chlorosis (low-iron disease) is displayed when clematis leaves retain green veins but otherwise have yellow coloring. Several companies make trace-mineral fertilizer supplements containing iron that will relieve this in just one or two doses. Magnesium shortage is shown by a general yellowing of the entire leaf including the veins, especially the newest growth. Epsom salts (magnesium sulfate) are the best cure for this deficiency. Epsom salts can be purchased in five-pound boxes in most garden centers, with a formula on the box for making a liquid drench for flowering plants. Tomato fertilizers occasionally contain magnesium sulfate, and those that do can be used as an excellent general purpose clematis fertilizer throughout the growing season. Both these mineral deficiencies tend to show up in early spring or late summer when the plant is in active growth and just starting to form buds.

Because clematis grown in containers are watered more often than clematis planted in the ground, the fertilizer you give them will be washed away rapidly. Many gardeners who use a blossom-booster type of fertilizer to keep pots of annual plants looking colorful have good luck giving clematis a diluted form of the same fertilizer (half-strength is enough). This should be given every two weeks throughout the growing season, except when your plant is about to bloom.

Whether in the ground or in a decorative pot, a clematis should not be fertilized when it is about to bloom (the buds are turning the color the flower is going to be and the sepal tips are starting to separate). The plant is already beginning to do what you want it to do, so adding more fertilizer stresses the plant and will often shorten the bloom time by causing all the buds to open at once. A bloom period that should last four to six weeks will be over in two weeks if you give the clematis too much food when the buds are showing. The exception to this warning is if the plant is starting to show a magnesium deficiency as it forms buds. A mild drink of Epsom salts will not harm developing flowers.

PLANTING

Generally speaking, clematis like to be planted into an 18-in.-by-18-in. hole that has had compost and a handful of bone meal or other slow-release fertilizer added at the bottom. Fill the hole halfway with water and let it drain. If the drainage is slow, add some poultry grit or gravel to the bottom of the hole and mix gravel into the soil you will use to refill it. The clematis should be placed so it is 3–4 in. deeper in the hole than it was in the pot, so you are burying several inches of stem. Remove any leaves that will be buried. This is done so new roots and shoots can emerge from the underground stems should anything unfortunate happen to the top growth. Pack the new soil around the root ball and up to the surrounding soil level, then water the plant again. If you have planted your new clematis in spring or summer, give it a mild (half-strength) drink of fertilizer when all the soil is in place.

The same steps should be followed if you are planting a clematis into a decorative pot. Make sure the pot is big enough to accommodate 18 in. of depth. Clematis can become stressed by too much root competition from other plants in a container, so choose companions that have shallow roots. Annual flowering plants are great for this purpose because many have surface root systems that stay in the top 3–4 in. of soil (see chapter nine).

No matter how careful you are some roots will be adversely disturbed when a clematis is transplanted from a nursery pot, whether it is into the ground or into your large container. For this reason, up to one-third of the top growth should be removed from your new clematis at planting time. If the plant is about to bloom, let it bloom where it is before transplanting so you can cut off the required amount without feeling as if you're missing out on flowers. We all know that sometimes the plants we buy are not true to name, so let your clematis bloom if it has buds, then deadhead and transplant. Early pruning of a newly transplanted clematis will give you a bushier plant with more sideshoots that will produce more flowers.

DISEASES AND PESTS

Clematis wilt disease is probably the scariest malady that can befall your vine. However, getting clematis wilt is not your plant's way of disrespecting you, and you shouldn't take this setback personally, however temporarily heartbroken you may be. This fungus typically attacks early-season large-flowered hybrids, but a handful of other species, such as *Clematis armandii,* can also be affected. The nasty pathogen in question is *Phoma clematidina.* A great deal of research has been done, and is being done, on clematis and this disease, but definitive answers remain elusive. The disease enters the vascular system of the vine, clogging the fluid-carrying tubes, and all growth above the clog wilts as if it needs water (which, technically, it does). This often happens just as the plant is about to flower—first the flower buds go limp, then the rest of the new growth.

When I see a clematis in my garden that appears to have come down with wilt disease, I begin an investigation. Starting at the end of the affected vine, I start removing the branch two nodes at a time, looking to see if there have been any breaks or other visible damage to the length of vine I'm removing. If I find a snapped vine with broken bark, I know that the plant was damaged (by wind, pets, deer, or me being an oaf with the clippers) and that it does not have wilt disease. I simply cut off all the wilted material above the break and fertilize the plant.

If I find no evidence of foul play and the entire plant is limp, only then do I blame *Phoma clematidina*. Wilt disease does not affect the crown or roots of the plant, so all top growth should be removed. Composting will not destroy this fungus, and the leaves and stems you have removed should be burned or bagged with your garbage. Water and fertilize your plant, even if you have only 6-in. stumps left. Chances are, the crown of the clematis will produce new shoots within forty-five days.

Why does your plant of *Clematis* 'Will Goodwin' (for instance) get wilt and your neighbor's never does? I can't answer that and I don't think anyone else can either. But that's not to say I don't have a theory. There is a great deal of variation in how clematis cuttings are taken and handled from nursery to nursery. A nursery may be pushing plants onto the market too quickly, without waiting for sufficient root formation to support the top growth encouraged with strong fertilizers and growth hormones, and growers may be taking cuttings from weakened stock plants. Many large-flowered hybrid clematis may get wilt once or twice and then seem to outgrow it. Mary Toomey has taken to calling *Phoma clematidina* "juvenile wilt disease" because she has noticed the problem primarily on young plants. Experience with clematis leads me to agree with her. Typically, only one or two plants in my garden get the disease per year, and it is nearly always a new plant.

When I notice that one of my plants consistently sickens at bloom time, I have a "three strikes" policy. The root ball is dug and destroyed (why would you ever give away a plant you knew to be sick?). A clematis that is not susceptible to wilt can be planted in place of the weakling. Remember, the small-flowered species and their hybrids seem to be immune to this disease. Disinfect any tools and gloves you use in handling a diseased plant.

The other common fungal disease of clematis in North America is powdery mildew, characterized by patches of white to gray powder (spores) on the stems, leaves, and flowers. Lower leaves on the plant may yellow. In my garden it seems that the dark purple clematis are most often the victim and the mildew develops during warm, dry weather following a brief summer rain (or from overhead watering where plants are too thickly planted and air circulation is poor). Most organic or nonorganic fungicides are preventative, not curative, but if you have one clematis, such as *Clematis* 'Romantika', that tends to get mildew, it isn't so hard to remember to spray it. To control this disease in my garden I hard-prune the affected plant, then water and fertilize. The plant will probably recover quickly with clean new growth and flower within thirty to forty-five days. This treatment has been successful with *C.* 'Viola', *C.* 'Romantika', and *C.* 'The Vagabond'.

Slugs and snails love tender new clematis growth, eating irregular holes in buds and leaves and peeling the outer bark from young stems to the point where the plant will collapse, leading you to believe it has wilt disease. Slugs cause me to reach new heights of vicious behavior, and I kill them with whatever means are at hand. The new organic slug baits are very effective. Earwigs cause flower and foliage damage. Aphids can cause distorted leaves and buds, but clematis are much less affected by aphids than some other garden plants are. Notched leaves are an indication of root weevil damage, and root weevils can be controlled by the use of beneficial nematodes. Clematis that are constantly in need of water and never quite get enough can become infested by spider mites who love nothing so much as a stressed-out, weakened plant. An infestation is characterized by a yellow stippled effect on otherwise green leaves and fine webbing appearing at the leaf nodes. The only good organic cure is to start watering your plants more consistently and to make repeated efforts to wash away the webbing with a strong stream of water. Chemical controls for spider mite are extremely toxic, and from time to time products to control this pest are not available to home gardeners. Clematis can also be attacked by Japanese beetles, leaf miners, cutworms, and whitefly.

Deer like clematis and they really love roses. The country gardeners I know who grow a lot of roses and clematis together have dogs that chase the deer. Moles do not eat clematis roots, but their digging can create air pockets around roots that cause the plant to dry out, and mole tunnels offer access to gophers and other creatures that will eat clematis roots.

APPENDIX 2

THE COMMON CLEMATIS GROUPS

Because of the size and variety of the genus *Clematis,* with an estimated 300 species and an ever-increasing armada of named cultivars, dividing the genus into smaller groups helps the gardener come to terms with the choices available.

LARGE-FLOWERED HYBRIDS

Large-flowered hybrids are divided into two groups, early-flowering and late-flowering. While this seems simple enough on the face of it, early and late are relative terms. The earliness or lateness is certainly climate dependent, and we further manipulate these terms based on when and how hard we prune our vines.

Speaking in a purely general way, early large-flowered hybrids are those first to bloom, in May and early June. Milder climates will occasionally see the first large-flowered hybrids appear in late April. A half-dozen examples of this earliest group are: *Clematis* 'Kakio', *C.* 'Dawn', *C.* 'Daniel Deronda', *C.* 'W. E. Gladstone', *C.* 'Duchess of Edinburgh', and *C.* 'Miss Bateman'. Notice I have included the double-flowered *C.* 'Duchess of Edinburgh' in the list; all the large-flowered doubles are considered early.

The late large-flowered hybrids are said to bloom for the first time in a growing season from mid-June through August. Many of these can be compelled to bloom earlier than expected by simply failing to prune them at the usual time (winter to early spring). A half-dozen examples of this group are: *Clematis* 'Gipsy Queen', *C.* 'Madame Baron-Veillard', *C.* 'Lady Betty Balfour', *C.* 'Viola', *C.* 'Romantika', and *C.* 'Comtesse de Bouchaud'.

SMALL-FLOWERED GROUPS

The groups for the small-flowered forms are often named for one species within the group that is thought to be the characteristic type within that group. This species may be the dominant genetic contributor to a group of hybrids. Thus we say the Texensis Group, or the Viticella Group, or the Integrifolia Group, because these species tend to impart their respective hybrids with a set of unique traits; most notable are growth habit and flower color and form.

When I discuss these groups, I consult *The International Clematis Register and Checklist,* which is, on the whole, an invaluable document. Clematis cognoscenti do disagree with the list on minor points, and I do too. Before *The Register*'s publication, large-flowered hybrids were written with their cultivar names in single quotes. The fact that the name was not preceded by a species name was our clue that a large-flowered hybrid was being discussed. Thus we could know from a plant tag that *Clematis* 'Will Goodwin' is a large-flowered clematis and *C. viticella* 'Royal Velours' is a small-flowered type. Now all cultivars are identified by their cultivar names alone. The *C. viticella* or *C. texensis* or *C. alpina* prefix to a small-flowered cultivar name has been dropped, thus removing a clue to the plant's possible flower form, bloom time, mature size, and pruning care. I consider this omission very unfortunate for those gardeners new to clematis. I hope American clematis producers will be painfully slow to make this transition on their labels.

The good news is that *The Register* has divided the small-flowered forms into simpler groups than have been suggested before in other publications. Here I will discuss those groups (as suggested by *The Register*) that we gardeners are most likely to encounter frequently and their basic cultivation needs.

Armandii Group: This group is named for *Clematis armandii,* one of the few evergreen clematis available in the United States. The cultivars in this group have white or pink flowers that appear in early spring. The leaves are long, dark green, and shiny. The vines are quite vigorous and need frequent pruning unless they are given ample space. The Armandii Group is hardy only to USDA Zone 7, and if grown in that zone should be given a protected site. These plants are particularly troubled by cold, dry winter wind, which turns their foliage black. Late freezes in March will damage or destroy the flower buds. As with many late-winter-flowering woody vines, the fragrance is heavenly.

Atragene Group: These plants are known collectively as the atragenes (pronounced at-RAH-jen-ees), although there is no such thing as "Clematis atragene." The dominant species in this group are *Clematis alpina* and *C. macropetala,* but other commonly encountered species are *C. chiisanensis, C. koreana, C. fauriei,* and *C. sibirica.* There are numerous named cultivars. As a group, the atragenes are quite cold hardy. The flowers are small and bell-shaped with four tepals, although *C. macropetala* has many petaloid stamens, giving it and its hybrids a distinctly double, more fluffy appearance than the other species in the Atragene Group. The color range for this group is quite broad, including white, pink, lavender, purple, burgundy, blue, and, in the case of *C. chiisanensis* and its hybrids, yellow. The atragenes vary in their vigor and require winter dormancy to mature the vines and enable their early flowering (March and April). Plants that have outgrown their allotted space or have become snarled are best pruned right after the end of their spring display. If just deadheaded, hybrids *C. chiisanensis* 'Lemon Bells' and *C.* 'Brunette' will bloom all summer. This group of clematis will do well in climates with cold winters, since many of the common cultivars have come to us from breeders in Canada and Sweden.

Heracleifolia Group: Named for *Clematis heracleifolia,* this group is composed of herbaceous species that do not generally climb and will form a woody base as they mature. Thus they turn themselves into the clematis versions of a woody deciduous shrub. All have tubular flowers to about an inch long. The cultivars of *C. heracleifolia* and the species itself have a spicy fragrance, most notable at the end of a hot afternoon. The common colors available are pale-to-dark blue and purple. The leaves of this group are large and coarse. The Heracleifolia Group is hardy to USDA Zone 4.

Integrifolia Group: This nonclimbing group (although many forms are great leaners) is named for that exemplary plant, *Clematis integrifolia.* Sometimes called "subshrubs," the species and its cultivars die back in the winter, regenerating themselves with new shoots from the roots or ground-level old wood. *Clematis integrifolia* is native to northern Europe, thus an excellent candidate for Canadian and prairie gardens. The bell-shaped flowers have four sepals, with the species having blue flowers. Pink and white variants have been used to create hybrids such as *C. integrifolia* 'Rosea' and *C. integrifolia* 'Hakuree'. Typical height is 18–24 in., but cultivars including crosses with *C.* 'Jackmanii' and *C. viticella* have produced the tall leaners (such as *C.* ×*durandii* and *C.* 'Alionushka'), which may be given support or allowed to find their own way through shrubs. The white forms are often fragrant. The period of bloom is quite long, especially if the plants are deadheaded and well fertilized.

Montana Group: *Clematis montana* carries the flag for this group of big, heavy, spring-blooming vines. Most of the species and cultivars in this group are scented, with some lively debate occurring over whether *C. montana* var. *wilsonii* actually smells of chocolate. With the exception of the correct form of *C. chrysocoma* (which gets only to 10 ft. tall and does not cling well), the Montana Group contains large plants, growing to 20–30 ft. or more. Colors are limited to shades of pink and white (with four to six sepals), and there are double forms (*C. montana* var. *rubens* 'Broughton Star', *C. montana* var. *rubens* 'Marjorie', and *C. montana* 'Jenny Keay'). The flowers are open and flat, resembling Japanese anemones. Montanas are thought to be hardy only to USDA Zone 6; some winter dieback may be welcome to help keep these vines under control. Pruning is best done directly after their spring flowering period. Some forms will randomly rebloom in late summer.

Tangutica Group: Characterized by *Clematis tangutica,* the species and cultivars in this group are summer- and fall-flowering, with lantern-shaped blossoms in yellow, cream, or white, occasionally touched with cinnamon or purple. The stamens can be dark (reddish brown) or yellow. These are vigorous vines, growing 12–20 ft. in a season, and it is recommended that they be hard-pruned during dormancy. They like heat. This group blooms on its new wood. The seed heads are particularly fine, and when in flower the new blossoms nestle among the shimmering seed heads left from previous flowers. Certain species and cultivars of this group have the brightest yellow color of any clematis.

Texensis Group: *Clematis texensis* does in fact come from Texas, and it is the only clematis species that is red. Every red cultivar grown—large- or small-flowered—has this clematis as an ancestor. It's true. *Clematis* 'Ville de Lyon', *C.* 'Allanah', *C.* 'Niobe', *C.* 'Kermesina',

C. 'Abundance'—all them are red because of *C. texensis.* This species also has a distinctive flower shape, either chubby or elongated but always constricted where the pointed sepals separate; they flair open to reveal an interior either red or yellow. The look is reminiscent of lily-flowered tulips. The shape and color can be found in all the near progeny of *C. texensis* included in this group, including *C.* 'Princess Diana', *C.* 'Gravetye Beauty', and *C.* 'Étoile Rose'. This group needs a lot of sun and plenty of water accompanied by sharp drainage. The texensis cultivars establish more quickly when given plenty of gravel or coarse sand in their planting holes and as mulch. They all bloom on new growth and so require hard pruning while dormant.

Viorna Group: This group is named for *Clematis viorna* and contains many North American native species. In fact, there are few cultivars in this group because they tend to get moved to the group of the more dominant parent. *Clematis viorna* is a lightweight climber, producing slender vines that flower in midsummer for a period of six weeks. The flowers are mahogany-colored bells lined with cream, and the four sepals have pronounced ridges. All the species in this group have a similar flower shape, although some are fuzzy (*C. fusca*), some are curly-edged (*C. crispa*), and some are purple (*C. pitcherii*). All have a long period of bloom, and all should be hard-pruned when dormant. Although technically of this group, *C. texensis* cultivars have been given their own group (see above).

Viticella Group: Named for *Clematis viticella* from southern Europe, this is a remarkably hardy group of cultivars that make prolific annual growth and flower on their new wood. The Viticella Group seems to be happy wherever it is grown, as long as there is some period of winter dormancy. *Clematis viticella* has purple, pagoda roof-shaped flowers of great charm. The French clematis breeders in the 1890s made some lovely crosses with it and *C. texensis.* Most viticella forms tend to be purple (*C.* 'Étoile Violette'), red (*C.* 'Carmencita'), white (*C.* 'Alba Luxurians'), or some variation of white with a red or purple outline on the sepals (*C.* 'Minuet'). The flower shape can be like that of *C. viticella* itself or up-facing or flat and open like a smaller version of a large-flowered hybrid. The viticella cultivars are quite free flowering, often obscuring their foliage at peak bloom time.

BIBLIOGRAPHY

Armitage, Allan M. 1997. *Herbaceous Perennial Plants: A Treatise on Their Identification, Culture and Garden Attributes.* 2nd ed. Champaign, Illinois: Stipes Publishing L.L.C.

Bath, Trevor, and Joy Jones. 1994. *The Gardener's Guide to Growing Clematis.* Portland, Oregon: Timber Press.

Beales, Peter. 1992. *Roses.* New York: Henry Holt and Company.

Davies, Dilys. 1992. *Alliums, the Ornamental Onions.* Portland, Oregon: Timber Press.

Evison, Raymond. 1992. *Making the Most of Clematis.* 2nd ed. Wisbech, Cambridgeshire: Burall Floraprint.

Evison, Raymond. 1998. *The Gardener's Guide to Growing Clematis.* Portland, Oregon: Timber Press.

Fisk, Jim. 1962. *Success with Clematis.* London: Thomas Nelson & Sons.

Fisk, Jim. 1994. *Clematis, the Queen of the Climbers.* London: Cassell Publishers.

Fretwell, Barry. 1989. *Clematis.* Deer Park, Wisconsin: Capability's Books.

Fretwell, Barry. 1994. *Clematis as Companion Plants.* London: Cassell Publishers.

Gooch, Ruth. 1996. *Clematis, the Complete Guide.* Ramsbury, Marlborough, Wiltshire: The Crowood Press.

Grey-Wilson, Christopher. 2000. *Clematis: The Genus: A Comprehensive Guide for Gardeners, Horticulturists and Botanists.* Portland, Oregon: Timber Press.

Hill, Susan, and Susan Narizny, comps. 2000. *Pacific Northwest Plant Locator, 2000–2001.* 2nd ed. Portland, Oregon: Black-Eyed Susans Press.

Howells, John. 1994. *Growing Clematis.* London: Ward Lock.

Johnson, Magnus. 2001. *The Genus Clematis.* Södertalje, Sweden: Magnus Johnsons Plantskola AB.

Kuriyama, Satomi, and Yoshiaki Aihara. 2003. *Photographs of Clematis Flowers.* Japan: Hekitensha.

Lewis, Peter, and Margaret Lynch. 1998. *Campanulas, A Gardener's Guide.* Portland, Oregon: Timber Press.

Lloyd, Christopher. 1989. *Clematis.* Deer Park, Wisconsin: Capability's Books.

Matthews, Victoria. 2002. *The International Clematis Register and Checklist 2002.* London: The Royal Horticultural Society.

Mikolajski, Andrew. 1997. *The New Plant Library Clematis.* London: Anness Publishing.

Murray, Ian. 1992. *Practical Clematis Growing.* Ramsbury, Marlborough, Wiltshire: The Crowood Press.

Phillips, Roger, and Martyn Rix. 2001. *Annuals and Biennials*. Buffalo, New York: Firefly Books.

Toomey, Mary. 1999. *Clematis, a Care Manual*. London: Octopus Publishing Group.

Toomey, Mary, and Everett Leeds. 2001. *An Illustrated Encyclopedia of Clematis*. Portland, Oregon: Timber Press.

Whitehead, Stanley. 1959. *Garden Clematis*. London: The Book Clubs.

Yeo, Peter. 1992. *Hardy Geraniums*. Portland, Oregon: Timber Press.

$\mathcal{C}$ONVERSION TABLES

INCHES	CM		FEET	M
1/10	0.3		1	0.3
1/6	0.4		2	0.6
1/4	0.6		3	0.9
1/3	0.8		4	1.2
1/2	1.3		5	1.5
3/4	1.9		6	1.8
1	2.5		7	2.1
2	5.1		8	2.4
3	7.6		9	2.7
4	10.0		10	3.0
5	13.0		20	6.0
6	15.0		30	9.0
7	18.0		40	12.0
8	20.0		50	15.0
9	23.0		60	18.0
10	25.0		70	21.0
20	51.0		80	24.0
30	76.0		90	27.0
40	100.0		100	30.0
50	130.0			
60	150.0			
70	180.0			
80	200.0			
90	230.0			
100	250.0			

$\mathscr{I}$NDEX